International Perspectives of Crime Prevention 6

Contributions from the 7th Annual International Forum 2013
within the German Congress on Crime Prevention

Eds.

Marc Coester and Erich Marks

with contributions from:
Cecilia Andersson, Nils Christie, Marc Coester, Caroline L. Davey, Noël Klima, Erich Marks, Christian Pfeiffer, Wiebke Steffen, Jan van Dijk, Belinda Wijckmans, Andrew B. Wootton

Forum Verlag Godesberg GmbH 2014

Bibliographic information published by the Deutsche Nationalbibliothek

The Deutsche Nationalbibliothek lists this publication in the Deutsche Nationalbibliografie; detailed bibliographic data are available in the Internet at http://dnb.d-nb.de .

© Forum Verlag Godesberg GmbH,
Mönchengladbach.
All rights reserved.
Mönchengladbach 2014

Produced by: Books on Demand GmbH, Norderstedt
Printed in Germany

Print layout: Kathrin Geiß

Cover design: Konstantin Megas, Mönchengladbach

978-3-942865-29-6 (print)
978-3-942865-30-2 (ebook)

Content

Introduction

The German Congress on Crime Prevention is an annual event that takes place since 1995 in different German cities and targets all areas of crime prevention: Administration, the health system, youth welfare, the judiciary, churches, local authorities, the media, politics, the police, crime prevention committees, projects, schools, organizations, associations and science. The desired effect is to present and strengthen crime prevention within a broad societal framework. Thus it contributes to crime reduction as well as to the prevention and the reduced risk of becoming a victim as well as fear of crime. The main objectives of the congress are:

1. Presenting and exchanging current and basic questions of crime prevention and its effectiveness.
2. Bringing together partners within the field of crime prevention.
3. Functioning as a forum for the practice, and fostering the exchange of experiences.
4. Helping to get contacts at an international level and to exchange information.
5. Discussing implementation strategies.
6. Developing and disseminating recommendations for practice, politics, administration and research.

Since its foundation the German Congress on Crime Prevention has been opened to an international audience with a growing number of non-German speaking participants joining. Because prevention is more than a national concern and should be focused internationally this step seemed crucial. Bringing together not only German scientists and practitioners but also international experts in crime prevention and therefore developing a transnational forum to foster the exchange of knowledge and experience constitutes the main focus of this approach. To give the international guests a discussion forum, the Annual International Forum within the German Congress on Crime Prevention was established in 2007. For non-German guests this event offers lectures in English language as well as other activities within the German Congress on Crime Prevention that are translated simultaneously. International guests are able to play an active role by presenting poster or displaying information within the exhibition.

Over the next few years we intend to develop this concept further. It is our wish to build an international forum for crime prevention that ensures a competent exchange of ideas, theories and applied approaches.

This sixth edition of "International Perspectives of Crime Prevention" includes the outcomes of the 7th Annual International Forum which took place within the 18th German Congress on Crime Prevention on the 22th and 23th of April 2013 in Bielefeld and gathered together more than 3000 people from the field of crime prevention in Germany and worldwide.

All articles in this book reflect worldwide views on crime prevention as well as the current status, discussion and research in crime prevention from different countries.

We hope to find a broad audience, interested in the upcoming events of the Annual International Forum as well as the German Congress on Crime Prevention. For more information please visit our website at http://www.gcocp.org.

Marc Coester and Erich Marks

Lectures and Documents from the 7th Annual International Forum

Erich Marks

The 18th German Congress on Crime Prevention

"The 18th, no less!"

Ladies and Gentlemen, welcome to the 18th German Congress on Crime Prevention. Europe's biggest annual crime prevention congress is being held in Bielefeld this year and I'd like to assure those of you who are joining us via live video link that, despite the conspiracy reports that would have us believe otherwise,[1] Bielefeld really does exist. In fact there's a standing joke among the 2,000 plus crime prevention experts assembled here today: "If we never meet again in this world, we'll meet again in Bielefeld."

As in previous years, I'd like to give a particularly warm welcome to our many guests of honour, among them crime prevention practitioners and researchers, high-ranking representatives from government and civil society, members of the media, and visitors from overseas. It delights me to see a further increase in attendance by legislative, executive, judicative and civil society decision-makers.

Please allow me to name just a few names from our large group of special guests, our prominent participants from Germany and further afield, members of parliament, holders of public office, heads of authorities, presidents, directors, chairpersons and high-ranking representatives of numerous organisations and institutions:

Cecilia *Andersson*, Safer Cities Programme, UN-HABITAT Kenya
Heike *Bartesch*, Director, German Federal Ministry for Families, Senior Citizens, Women and Youth (BMFSFJ)
Prof. Dr. Andreas *Beelmann*, Head of the Department for Research Synthesis, Intervention and Evaluation at the University of Jena
Michael *Bischoff*, Departmental Head, Office of the Public Prosecutor in the State of North Rhine-Westphalia
Dr. Wilfried *Blume-Beyerle*, City of Munich Administration
Matthi *Bolte* MdL, Member for Bündnis 90/Die Grünen in the North Rhine-Westphalia State Parliament
Prof. Dr. Nils *Christie*, University of Oslo, Norway
Pit *Clausen*, Lord Mayor of Bielefeld
Prof. Jochen *Dieckmann*, Chair of the North Rhine-Westphalia Crime Prevention Council
Thomas *Dittmann*, Ministerial Director, German Federal Ministry of Justice (BMJ)
Günther *Ebenschweiger*, President of the Austrian Centre for Crime Prevention

---

[1]   See: http://en.wikipedia.org/wiki/Bielefeld_Conspiracy

Hans *Feuß* MdL, Member of the SPD in the North Rhine-Westphalia State Parliament

Wolfgang *Gatzke*, Director of the North Rhine-Westphalia Police Force

Angelika *Gemkow*, North Rhine-Westphalia Disabilities Commissioner

Dr. Katharina *Giere*, Bielefeld Police President

Jens *Gnisa*, Director, Bielefeld District Court

Prof. Dr. Christian *Grafl*, University of Vienna and Representative of the German Congress on Crime Prevention in Austria

Prof. Dr. Wolf *Hamann*, Baden-Württemberg Police President, Chair of the German Police Crime Prevention Programme (ProPK)

Prof. Dr. Sangkyou *Han*, Kangwon National University, South Korea

Dagmar *Hanses* MdL, Bündnis 90/Die Grünen Speaker, North Rhine-Westphalia Parliamentary Legal Committee

Frank *Herrmann* MdL (Piraten), Piraten Party Speaker, North Rhine-Westphalia Parliamentary Committee on Home Affairs

Frank *Hofmann* MdB (SPD), Deputy Chair North Rhine-Westphalia Parliamentary Committee on Home Affairs

Inge *Howe* MdL (SPD), Deputy Chair North Rhine-Westphalia Parliamentary Petitions Committee

Prof. Dr. Theresia *Höynck*, Chair of the German Juvenile Court Association (DVJJ)

Ralf *Jäger*, North Rhine-Westphalia Minister for Municipal and Home Affairs

Elizabeth *Johnston*, Secretary General of the European Forum for Urban Security (EFUS), Paris

Prof. Dr. Hans-Jürgen *Kerner*, Chair of the German Foundation for Crime Prevention (DVS)

Ralph *Klom*, Attorney General Bielefeld

Regina *Kopp-Herr* MdL, SPD Member of Parliament of the State of North Rhine-Westphalia

Kirstin *Korte* MdL, CDU Member of Parliament of the State of North Rhine-Westphalia

Prof. Dr. Michael *Kubink*, Director North Rhine-Westphalia Crime Prevention Council

Thomas *Kutschaty*, North Rhine-Westphalia Minister of Justice

Thomas *Lenz*, Mecklenburg West-Pomerania State Secretary for Home Affairs and Sport

Marc *Lürbke* MdL (FDP), Parliamentary Speaker for the North Rhine-Westphalia Sports Committee

Gisela *Mayer*, Chair Aktionsbündnis Amoklauf Winnenden

Roswitha *Müller-Piepenkötter*, National Chair Weisser Ring

Jürgen *Mutz*, Chair of the Board of Trustees of the German Foundation for Crime Prevention (DVS)

Ralf *Nettelstroth* MdL, CDU Member of the North Rhine-Westphalia State Parliament

Prof. Gerd *Neubeck*, Head of Group Security at Deutsche Bahn and Chair of the Executive Board of the German Forum for Crime Prevention (DFK)

Richard *Oetker*, Chair of the Weisser Ring Foundation

Daniel Hark-Mo *Park*, Delegation Head, Korean Institute of Criminology

Prof. Dr. Christian *Pfeiffer*, Director, Criminological Research Institute of Lower Saxony (KFN)

Norbert *Pieper*, Senior Expert, Deutsche Post AG

Boris *Pistorius*, Lower Saxony Minister for Home Affairs and Sport, Chair of the Standing Conference of the Ministers and Senators of the Interior of the Federal Länder (IMK)

Prof. Dr. Elisabeth *Pott*, Director, Federal Centre for Health Education (BzgA)

Peter *Reckling*, National Director, Federal Association for Social Work, Penal Law and Criminal Policy (DBH)

Sebastian *Rode*, Professional Footballer and Ambassador of the Hesse Crime Prevention Council

Dr. Martin *Schairer*, Chair of the German-European Forum for Urban Security (DEFUS)

Wilhelm *Schmidt*, President of the German Association for Public and Private Welfare (DV)

Jürgen *Schubert*, Vice President Federal German Police

Günter *Schwieren*, President, Bielefeld District Court

Prof. Dr. *Hans-Dieter Schwind*, Council President, German Foundation for Crime Prevention (DVS)

Dr. Tina *Silbernagl*, Deutsche Gesellschaft für internationale Zusammenarbeit (GIZ)

Dr. Wiebke *Steffen*, German Congress on Crime Prevention (DPT)

Klaus *Stüllenberg*, Chair, Foundation for Crime Prevention

Willem *van der Brugge*, Secretary General of the CEP, Utrecht

Prof. Dr. Dr. Jan *van Dijk*, University of Tilburg

Bernd *Wesemeyer*, Vice President, Detmold District Administration

Hartfrid *Wolff* MdB, Chair of the FDP Parliamentary Group's Working Group on Home Affairs and Law

Jörg *Ziercke*, President of the Federal German Policy (BKA), Deputy National Chair, Weisser Ring

I would also like to welcome and thank all those involved in organising and managing this 18th German Crime Prevention Congress, be they speakers, organisers, moderators or the numerous accredited journalists.

(1) The Congress at a Glance

The 18th German Crime Prevention Congress comprises four main parts and several sub-parts which, as usual, are described on the Congress website and in the Congress catalogue together with several abstracts:

1. Plenary sessions

   - Opening session

   - Evening reception hosted by Congress Patron Hannelore Kraft, Minister President of the State of North Rhine-Westphalia

   - Closing session

2. Presentations

   - Focus topics and other crime prevention issues

   - Project spots

   - International forum

   - Presentation on Demand (PoD)

3. Exhibition

   - Information stands

   - Infomobile

   - Special exhibitions

   - Posters

4. Workshop

   - Side events

   - Stage

   - Film forum

   - Crime prevention in action

Focus topic: More prevention, fewer victims

The Congress Patron, Minister President Hannelore Kraft, fittingly summed things up in her welcome address when she said: "Preventing crime from happening is the best form of victim protection. It thus plays an important role in securing social cohesion."

The scope of the highly impressive presentations on this focus topic is deliberately broad, ranging from the personal experience of a kidnapping victim (Richard *Oetker*), current trends in victimology (Prof. Dr. Hans-Jürgen *Kerner*) and victim research (Prof. Dr. Jan *van Dijk*), and victim support strategies in schools (Dr. Christian *Böhm*) to the pending launch of a national hotline in Germany (Dr. Gesa *Schirmacher*) and EU-level victim support systems/services (Dr. Helgard *van Hüllen*). Right-wing issues are addressed by Prof. Dr. Bernd-Dieter *Meier* (Wiedergutmachungsstrafe – ein notwendiges Element des Sanktionssystems (Make-Good Punishments: A Necessary Component of the Sanctioning System)), by Dr. Wolfram *Schädler* („Nicht noch einmal? Der Schutz von Opfern vor dem Täter durch den Strafprozess – höchstens

Zufall" (Not again? Safeguarding Victims from Perpetrators during Criminal Proceedings: Coincidental at most)) and Prof. Dr. Michael *Walter* und Claudia *Gelber* (Wege zu einer opferbezogenen Vollzugsgestaltung (Towards Victim-Focused Prisons)). Approaches for restorative justice are well-represented, with presentations by Professor Dr. Nils *Christie* (Restoring Societies. Norway after the atrocities.), Dr. Michael *Kilchling* (Neue Impulse in Deutschland und Europa (New Ideas in Germany and Other European Countries), Dr. Beate *Ehret* (Friedenszirkel. Eine nachhaltige Methode der außergerichtlichen Konfliktschlichtung im Rahmen der Restorative Justice (Peace Circle. A sustainable methodology for out-of-court conflict resolution by means of restorative justice)) and a workshop on the topic of Restorative Circles – Konflikte austragen und in soziale Impulse verwandeln (Restorative Circles: Transforming Conflict into Social Stimulation). Other parts of the Congress such as the exhibition, the educational theatre performances, the films and the poster session, also take up the focal topic of Congress. Building on the parallel justice[2] approach developed by Susan **Herman** in the U.S., Professor Dr. Christian **Pfeiffer** closed the Congress with a presentation in which he justified The Need for Greater Legal and Social Support for Victims of Crime (*Warum brauchen wir eine Stärkung des Opfers in Recht und Gesellschaft?*).

When looked at overall, it is hoped that the Congress will contribute to long-overdue intensification of victim research and victim support research, and supply new impetus for the focal topic of 'more prevention, fewer victims'. Finally, with the new focus on parallel justice, it is hoped that equally as much attention will be given to the increasing interests, needs and wants of the victims of crime as to the penal needs of the state and of civil society, and also to the provision of targeted crime prevention offerings in the tertiary sector.

Centre for the Prevention of Youth Crime marks 15th anniversary

Since its launch in 1997, the Centre for the Prevention of Youth Crime (DJI) has informed practitioners, policy-makers, the media and the research community about models and strategies for the prevention of juvenile crime. "The crime prevention approaches used in child and youth welfare, in schools, and by the police and the justice sector are compared for their prerequisites and conditions for success, their target groups and objectives and – where possible – evaluated for their achievements. The aim is to further the specialist debate and improve specialist practice. The DJI sees childhood and juvenile delinquency as an educational responsibility, not only towards children and youths, but towards other responsible institutions such as schools, the police and the justice sector.[3]

---

[2]   Susan Herman, Parallel Justice for Victims of Crime, New York 2012; see also www.paralleljustice.org

[3]   http://www.dji.de/cgi-bin/projekte/output.php?projekt=150 (viewed 4 October 2013)

At a special event held on the occasion of the 18th German Congress on Crime Prevention, the DJI in its capacity as a Congress partner presented the seventh sub-topic in a kind of status report following 15 years of research work: Dr. Christian *Lüders*: Prävention von Delinquenz im Kindes- und Jugendalter – über die Bedeutung der pädagogischen Orientierung (Preventing Delinquency in Childhood and Youth: The Role of Education); *Bernd Holthusen* and Dr. Sabrina *Hoops*: Die Kinder- und Jugendhilfe – zentraler Akteur und Kooperationspartner in der Prävention von Delinquenz (Child and Youth Welfare: Key Actors and Cooperation Partners in Deliquency Prevention); Professor Dr. Thomas *Feltes*: Polizei und junge Menschen – mehr präventive Repression? (The Police and Young People: More Prevention Repression?), Professor. Dr. Theresia *Höynck*: Jugendkriminalrecht – die Umsetzung des Erziehungsgedankens als zentrale Herausforderung (Juvenile Crime: The Challenge in Fostering Education as the Answer), Professor Dr. Wolfgang *Melzer*: Kriminalitätsprävention an Schulen – zwischen Einzelprojekten und Schulentwicklung (Crime Prevention in Schools: Island Projects and School Development); Professor Dr. Karin *Böllert*, Jörg *Freese* and Regina *Kraushaar*: Podiums Discussion: The Role of Youth Policy in Preventing Juvenile Crime (Was kann Jugendpolitik für die Kriminalitätsprävention im Kindes- und Jugendalter leisten?), Dr. Michael *Brünger*: Kinder- und Jugendpsychiatrie – Perspektiven für den Ausbau der Kooperation (Child and Youth Psychiatry: Perspectives for Greater Cooperation).

Congress Report and the Bielefeld Declaration

Since the 12th German Congress on Crime Prevention in Wiesbaden back in 2007, criminologist Dr. Wiebke *Steffen* has written an annual Congress Report on the respective focal topics addressed at each subsequent congress. These reports provide the speakers, the participants and the interested specialist public with the basic facts and figures on the various topics covered and provide the basis for the annual crime prevention policy declaration made jointly by the Congress, its hosts and permanent event partners.

This year's report by Dr. Steffen, the seventh in succession,[4] bears the title Opferzuwendung in Gesellschaft, Wissenschaft, Gesetzgebung und Prävention: Stand, Probleme, Perspektiven (Victim orientation in society, research, criminal justice and crime prevention: Status, problems and perspectives). By way of advance information for the Congress speakers and participants, the report gives answers to the following questions: Do we have the right penal and social laws in place to do justice to both victims and perpetrators? Is the victim of a crime always helpless and without rights? Looking back, how have legal and social support for victims changed in the past twenty years? Are we really aware of victims' needs and wants? Can crime prosecution really take account of them?

---

[4]   All Congress reports are available for download on the Congress website: www.praeventionstag.de

At the end of the 18th Congress, the Congress hosts and their permanent event partners will publish their joint Bielefeld Declaration based on the findings of the report.

Congress partners

Ever since the first congress back in 1995, it has been acknowledged that the annual congress is the product of excellent cooperation between many people and organisations. I should thus like to take this opportunity to thank the Congress partners, funders and sponsors, and their respective teams, for their help and support.

The 18th German Congress on Crime Prevention is funded by the German Federal Ministry for Families, Senior Citizens, Women and Youth (BMFSFJ) and the German Federal Ministry of Justice (BMJ). The Congress also has many partners:

Hosting partners

- The State of North Rhine-Westphalia
- Bielefeld City Council
- The Crime Prevention Council of the State of North Rhine-Westphalia

Permanent Congress Partners

- Association for Social Work, Criminal Law and Criminal Policy (DBH)
- Federal/Länder Police Crime Prevention Programme (ProPK)
- German Forum for Crime Prevention (DFK)
- WEISSER RING e.V.

Main sponsor

- Deutsche Bahn AG

Cooperation partners and sponsors

- Federal Centre for Health Education
- German-European Forum for Urban Security (DEFUS)
- Deutsche Gesellschaft für internationale Zusammenarbeit (GIZ)
- Deutsche Post DHL
- Deutsche Sportjugend (DSJ)
- German Juvenile Court Association (DVJJ)
- German Family Courts Congress (DFGT)
- German Youth Institute (DJI)
- European Forum for Urban Security (EFUS)
- International Centre for the Prevention of Crime (ICPC)
- Korean Institute for Criminology (KIC)

- Criminological Research Institute of Lower Saxony
- Austrian Crime Prevention Congress
- proval
- Foundation for Crime Prevention
- Independent Commissioner for Child Sexual Abuse
- UNHABITAT
- WHO Crime Prevention Alliance

Media partner

- Neue Westfälische (NW) (Regional daily newspaper)

Further information and contact details for all Congress partners can be found on page nine of the Congress Catalogue and on the Congress website.

Annual International Forum 2013

The 18th German Congress on Crime Prevention and the associated 7th Annual International Forum for Crime Prevention (AIF) attracted some 71 overseas experts from 23 countries.[5]

Presentations in English:

- Prof. Dr. Dr. Jan *van Dijk*, Tilburg University, Netherlands: Situational crime prevention works; or why burglary rates dropped less steeply in Germany than in The Netherlands
- Prof. Dr. Nils *Christie*, University of Oslo, Norway: Restoring Societies. Norway after the atrocities
- Dr. Erik *Wennerström*, Swedish Council for Crime Prevention: The development of the Swedish model of Crime Prevention in the last two decades and its future challenges
- Elizabeth *Johnston*, European Forum for Urban Security (EFUS), Paris: Security, Democracy and Cities – A new manifesto of European cities on urban security
- Terence *Smith*, Deutsche Gesellschaft für Internationale Zusammenarbeit (GIZ), Südafrika: GIZ's systemic approaches to violence prevention
- Dr. Caroline. L. *Davey* & Andrew B. *Wootton*, Design Against Crime Solution Centre, UK: The Crime Prevention Maturity Model: Embedding security within urban design & planning
- Dr. Eugene *Lee*, National Youth Policy Institute & Dr. Ok-Kyung *Yoon*, Kyonggi

---

[5]   Argentina, Austria, Belgium, Cameroon, Czech Republic, El Salvador, France, Kenya, Luxembourg, Nepal, Netherlands, Nigeria, Norway, Poland, Portugal, South Korea, Saudi Arabia, Sweden, Switzerland, South Africa, Ukraine, United Kingdom, Zambia

University, South Korea: A Study on Comprehensive Plan to Protect Children and Youths from Sexual Violence and Support Victims

- Belinda *Wijckmans*, European Crime Prevention Network (EUCPN), Brussels; European Crime Prevention Network (EUCPN): Crime prevention activities on EU, national and local level

Presentations in German with international reference:

- Julia *Mölck*, Municipality of Alkmaar, Netherlands: Approaches to Crime Prevention

- Professor Dr. Thomas *Görgen*, Benjamin *Kraus* and Anabel *Taefi*, Federal German Policy Academy, Munster: Juvenile Delinquency and Crime Prevention in Europe: As Seen by Youths and Practitioners

- Philip *Willekens*, Belgian Ministry for the Interior, Brussels: From Top-Down to Bottom-Up: Integral and Integrated Municipal Crime Prevention

- Gregor *Burkhart*, European Monitoring Centre for Drugs and Drug Addiction (EMCDDA), Portugal: American Crime Prevention Programmes in Europe

- Dr. Helgard *van Hüllen*, WEISSER RING e. V., Mainz: Victim Support Europe – Timely Help at International Level

- Sebastian *Sperber*, Europäisches Forum für Urbane Sicherheit (EFUS), Paris: European Forum for Urban Security, Paris: EU Street Violence: Youth Gang Violence Database

- Prof. Dr. Dr. Grygorii *Moshak*, Nationa Meeresuniversität in Odessa, Ukraine: Ukrainian Militia Systems and the EM 2012

- Prof. Dr. Dr. Christiane *Spiel*, University of Vienna, Austria: Violence Prevention in Austria – National Strategy Development, Implementation and Evaluation

- Dr. Michael *Kilchling*, Max Planck Institute for Foreign and International Criminal Law; Chair of the European Forum for Restorative Justice, Freiburg

- Maarten *van de Donk*, VVD Party Chair on Rotterdam City Council, Netherlands: Municipal Juvenile Crime Prevention Policy – Implementing Communities that Care (CTCs) in the Netherlands

(2) About the Congress

German Congress on Crime Prevention on the Internet

Information about the Congress is available on the following websites and via two iPhone Apps:

German Congress on Crime Prevention	www.praeventionstag.de
Annual International Forum (English)	www.gcocp.org
DPT University/Academy	www.dpt-uni.de
Crime Prevention Search Portal	www.dpt-map.de
Daily Crime Prevention News	www.praeventionstag.de/news
Facebook	www.facebook.com/praeventionstag
Twitter	https://twitter.com/praeventionstag
Wikipedia	http://de.wikipedia.org/wiki/Deutscher_Präventionstag

DPT App in the App Store for iPhone and iPad
Can be used to search the DPT archives on all presentations, speakers and exhibiting organisations from previous congresses

TPN App in the App Store for iPhone and iPad (daily crime prevention news)
Can be used to receive daily crime prevention news while 'on the road', including via push messaging

DPT Institute for Applied Crime Prevention Research

Scientific-empirical research has played an increasingly important role in (crime) prevention projects and programmes in the past twenty years. In that time, the German Congress on Crime Prevention has become one of the key forums for discourse between practitioners and researchers working in the broader field of crime prevention. To foster this trend in a systematic way, DPT launched the DPT Institute for Applied Crime Prevention Research (dpt-i) in 2013. Crime prevention research is seen as a multi-disciplinary approach which takes in the findings, methodologies and standards of a range of scientific disciplines and fields. The integrated basic sciences and the increasingly specialised and differentiated disciplines and fields include sociology, psychology, education, biology, medicine, political science, law, economics, ecology, criminology and victimology. These very varied and specific research fields come together in the process of profile-building in cross-discipline crime prevention research with a view to its specific research subject matter.

In line with the philosophy of the international Society for Prevention Research (SPR),[6] the dpt-i sees prevention science as the scientific investigation of:

---

[6] According to the SPR mission statement: "The Society for Prevention Research is an organization dedicated to advancing scientific investigation on the etiology and prevention of social, physical and mental health, and academic problems and on the translation of that information to promote health and well being.

- The social distribution and frequency of preventable events and situations such as crime, violence, addiction, physical and mental illness, insecurity, etc.
- The causes of and conditions which foster these events and situations
- The development, management and monitoring of effective intervention measures to prevent these events and situations
- The provision of support to enable broad implementation of approved intervention measures in 'real world' conditions

Prevention research aims to achieve its goals via integrated, multi-disciplinary cooperation and partnerships with prevention practitioners and the makers of prevention policy. The dpt-i sees its role as an active promoter of partnerships between the worlds of research, practice and policy-making. The DPT Institute for Applied Prevention Research sees its general responsibility primarily in:

- Conducting its own research projects whose findings will flow into prevention practice
- Cooperation with other research institutes to implement practice-related research projects
- Intensifying dialogue between science and research, governments and administrations, associations and civil society on the findings of prevention research with to provide a greater prevention knowledge base
- Advising the German Congress on Crime Prevention and its partner organisations on the findings and current trends in prevention research

(3) Current Crime Prevention Issues and Strategies

The past decade has seen a largely positive trend in crime prevention, both nationally and internationally. At every level, from urban to global, numerous projects, programmes, strategies and recommendations have been drafted, approved and adopted. But despite all of this, there remain a number of issues which must still be addressed regarding communication, networking and cooperation.

1. Inter-disciplinary cooperation

- In practice, crime prevention is still not adequately integrated into cross-disciplinary prevention networks
- Crime prevention research is not adequately integrated into (modern) multi-disciplinary prevention research which includes criminology, health research, public health, victimology, sociology, education, psychology, economics, and law.

The multi-disciplinary membership of SPR is international and includes scientists, practitioners, advocates, administrators, and policy makers who value the conduct and dissemination of prevention science worldwide." www.preventionresearch.org/about-spr/mission-statement/, viewed January 25 2013

- Current prevention policy is characterised by the lack of (and where it exists the poor degree of) coordination of programmes and projects at national, Länder (state), regional and municipal level.

Inter-disciplinary cooperation in prevention practice, prevention policy-making and prevention research remains under-developed. Thus, shared attention and multi-disciplinary cooperation efforts across the various disciplines in and levels of crime prevention must improve significantly in the coming years.

2. Knowledge management

- Many standards, memoranda and findings in (crime) prevention[7] are not sufficiently well distributed and are rarely known to the responsible decision-makers
- Available prevention knowledge (data) remains inadequate when it comes to prevention planning and activities
- At all levels, existing programmes, instruments, standards and guidelines/directives are not utilised to the degree they could and should be used

Awareness and use of available prevention knowledge leaves a lot to be desired. The findings of and experience gained in prevention practice and prevention research must be better communicated and made available to all free-of-charge in barrier-free online formats.

3. Moving from 'either or' to 'both'

- Society still seems to be afflicted by a kind of 'morbus punitivum'
- Safety and crime prevention are still not adequately debated as an holistic topic
- In some cases, victim support and resocialisation are still seen/presented as a contradiction in terms
- The debate on and implementation of mediation models, victim-perpetrator compensation and restorative justice remain lacking

Leaving the trodden path of 'more of the same' and of 'combating' crime to embrace socially cohesive crime prevention is seen to have great potential at individual, social and policy level.[8] The aim should thus be to place greater focus on parallel criminal justice law which takes in the increasingly recognised and acknowledged interests, needs and wants of the victims of crime to the same extent as it does the criminal jus-

---

[7] For example: Those of the UNODC (United Nations Office on Drugs and Crime), EFUS (European Forum for Urban Security), ICPC (International Centre for the Prevention of Crime), VPA (Violence Prevention Alliance der WHO), Beccaria-Standards (Lower Saxony Crime Prevention Council), UNHABITAT, EU-CPN (European Crime Prevention Network), SPR (Society for Prevention Research), etc.

[8] See also Ronald Dworkin, Gerechtigkeit für Igel, Berlin 2012, and www.justiceforhedgehogs.net; Ronald Dworkin is one of the leading contemporary law theorists and holder, among other things, of the Bielefeld Science Award. In his latest work, he attempts to build a philosophical-historical theory which describes what constitutes success in life and explains the behavioural changes needed to life that kind of lifestyle.

tice needs of the state and society, as well as the resocialisation of those who commit punishable crimes.

4. New risks, new crimes

- Crime prevention continues to focus on juvenile and violent crime, and what are known as mass/common offences despite a significant increase in areas such as online and industrial crime which cause tremendous damage

- While business continuity management plays an increasingly important role in industry, the contribution crime prevention makes in achieving some form of 'social continuity management' remains comparatively low.

- The field of crime prevention has yet to adequately recognise the UN's eight Millennium Development Goals,[9] which closely correspond to new types of crime and risk.

- We may be living in the Anthropocene[10] age, but a caring and sustainable prevention mindset has yet to fully evolve.

The global problems currently faced call for a new, fundamental focus on prevention. New goals, priorities and strategies for (crime) prevention must be integrated into existing approaches. New risks and types of crime, and more structural forms of crime, must be debated earlier and perceived as far more serious than they have been to date.

5. Knowledge base

- Crime prevention '*projectitis*' appears to be widespread in Germany: targeted selection and adaptation of evidence-based prevention programmes plays only a subordinate role in prevention practice

- Available knowledge on impact-focused prevention programmes remains poorly communicated, debated and utilised

- International databases for best-practice projects and evidence-based programmes are little known and have not been adequately utilised to date.

At all levels, those responsible should lend greater support to the call for evidence-based strategies in crime prevention. When in doubt, it would make sense to adapt and align a tried, tested and evaluated programme, rather than developing something from scratch. Existing databases that give insights into evaluated prevention strate-

---

[9] (1) Eradikate Extreme Poverty and Hunger (2) Achieve Universal Primary Education (3) Promote Gender Equality and Empower Women (4) Reduce Child Mortality (5) Improve Maternal Health (6) Combat HIV/ AIDS, Malaria and Other Diseases (7) Ensure Environmental Sustainability (8) Global Partnership for Development; see: http://www.un-kampagne.de/index.php?id=1

[10] See Christina Schwägerl's presentation at the 16th German Congress on Crime Prevention: http://www. praeventionstag.de/nano.cms/dokumentation/details/1687

gies must be better disseminated and better utilised.[11]

6. Sustainability and resources

- The positive cost-benefit analyses and available knowledge about 'return on investment' options in crime prevention are not adequately utilised and often appear to be less compatible with (short-term) parliamentary legislature periods.

- Apart from the availability of good managers, many places lack the financial and staffing resources needed for effective crime prevention

- Few evaluations are performed in the broad field of (crime) prevention

Numerous data analyses and research findings[12] highlight the need to provide adequate resources and to redirect finances if crime prevention is to be made effective and pay over time.[13]

Finally, I should like to thank our speakers for the tremendous work that went into their impressive presentations, and for travelling some very long distances. I appreciate your willingness to share your knowledge and experience with us and with our broader audience via the Congress website. My thanks go to all who have actively participated in and supported the Congress. I'm sure we will all benefit from this interesting and informative event.

---

[11] A number of (inter)national databases can be accessed online: www.colorado.edu/cspv/blueprints (Center for the Study and Prevention of Violence der University of Colorado Boulder); www.campbellcollaboration.org (Campbell Collaboration, Oslo); www.preventviolence.info(WHO Violence Prevention Alliance); www.gruene-liste-praevention.de (Lower Saxony State Prevention Council); www.eucpn.org (European Crime Prevention Network)

[12] See also DPT reports by W. Steffen since 2007 at www.praeventionstag.de and I. Waller: Mehr Recht und Ordnung! – oder doch lieber weniger Kriminalität? (More Law and Order? Or Simply Less Crime?) (2011)

[13] See also R. Wilkinson & K. Pickett: The Spirit Level: Why Equality is Better for Everyone (2009) and www.equalitytrust.org,uk

Jan Van Dijk

Understanding the international falls in crime; or why burglary rates dropped less steeply in Germany than in The Netherlands[1]

Introduction

In 1905 a young Dutch sociologist, Willem Bonger, defended his PhD thesis on the economic conditions of crime at the University of Amsterdam. He was shortly thereafter appointed as the first professor of criminology in The Netherlands. His thesis was translated into English and other languages and has become a classic in sociological criminology. In Bonger's view criminologists should study not the personal pathologies of offenders but the societal causes of crime. He studied the macro determinants of crime by analyzing inter-country differences and trends in official criminal statistics. His work stands in the 19 century epidemiological tradition of Quetelet, Guerry, Von Mayr and Lacassagne. Bonger's criminology was strongly policy-oriented. Criminology should, in his words "before anything else show mankind the way how crime can be effectively combated and, most of all, prevented" (Bonger, 1932). He used to underline his preference for policy-oriented criminology with a quote from the French, positivist philosopher Auguste Comte: "*Savoir pour prevoir et prevoir pour prevenir.* Loosely translated as "Knowledge with the aim of prediction and prediction with the aim of preventing". In other words, Bonger preached and practiced evidence-based crime prevention *avant la lettre.*

In his PhD thesis Bonger asserts that "the economic conditions of the common people exert a preponderant, even decisive impact on levels of crime" (Bonger, 1905). He would stay faithful to this Marxist view of the root causes of crime throughout his professional life. Since he liked to express his convictions in strong, sometimes polemical statements, he might, had he lived in our days, have paraphrased the famous dictum of Bill Clinton in his electoral debate with Bush sr.: *It's the economy, stupid* !

As key evidence for the predominant links between economic conditions and levels of crime Bonger submitted the correlation between changes in the price of a loaf of bread and in the numbers of people arrested for theft in the German state of Bavaria during the 19th century. When the bread prices went up, so did the numbers of people arrested. People were in Bonger's view driven to crime by extreme poverty. Figure 1 shows these statistics, collected and analyzed by the German criminologist Von Mayr.

---

[1]   This lecture presented at the Deutscher Preventionstag 2013 is largely based on my unpublished acceptance speech of the Stockholm Award 2012.

Figure 1 Parallelism between bread prices and arrested
offenders in Bavaria (1835-1861)

source: W. Bonger (1905), *Criminalité et conditions economiques*, diss.
University of Amsterdam

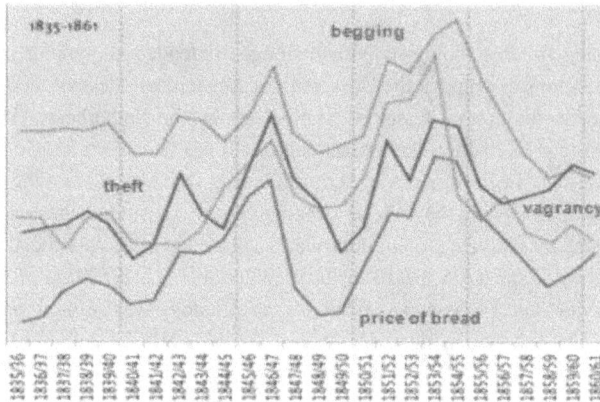

The remarkably strong correlations between the price of bread and the numbers of persons arrested for theft, begging and vagrancy suggest indeed a causal link between economic conditions and levels of crime. Bonger has referred to this analysis in many subsequent publications. It also received, together with the notorious cranial measurements of Cesare Lombroso, a prominent place in the opening chapter of a Dutch textbook on criminology (Van Dijk, Junger & Sagel-Grande, 2011/7th edition). During classes, students sometimes raise their hands and say: the parallelism is very impressive indeed but what happened after 1860? Does Von Mayrs law still hold? Did crime continue to track bread prices ever since? A pertinent question, indeed.

As convinced Marxist and social democrat, Willem Bonger held the firm belief that most forms of crime would automatically disappear as soon as a more just and egalitarian society was established. In one of his latest publications, just before the outbreak of World War II, he compared the numbers of persons convicted for various types of crime per 100.000 inhabitants of twenty European nations (Bonger, 1937). He proudly noted that the Netherlands showed a relatively low rate. Even lower rates were shown by Sweden, Denmark and England/Wales. For Bonger the favorable ranking of these nations confirmed once more the link between economic conditions and crime. Relatively affluent and egalitarian societies such as The Netherlands, the Scandinavian countries and England/Wales would in Bonger's view of necessity enjoy relatively low levels of crime as a kind of bonus for their welfare policies.

The question that comes up is whether developments after World War II have born out Bonger's criminological optimism. Are economic conditions and levels of crime still as closely linked as they apparently were in 19th century Bavaria? In other words, does the criminology of Bonger still provide a useful theoretical frame to understand, predict and prevent the crime problems of today? Or, to be more to the point: are trends in the level of crime of countries still tracking variations in "bread prices"? And specifically are the affluent, egalitarian Dutch still enjoying a relatively low level of crime?

When reflecting on these pertinent issues, the first consideration that comes to mind is that today's criminologists no longer, as in Bonger's time, use numbers of arrested or convicted persons as a measure of the extent of crime. Criminology has lost its methodological naivity. No serious criminologist beliefs in administrative statistics as reliable indicators of the levels of crime. Crime is nowadays preferably measured with sample surveys among the population with questions about victimization experiences or about self-reported offending. Unfortunately, these new, survey-based measures have only become widely available over the past two, or at most three, decades. To determine trends in crime since the end of WWII, there is no other option than to use the numbers of crimes recorded by the police as our default measure of crime.

Figure 2 shows the numbers of crimes recorded by the police per 100.000 inhabitants since 1950 in Sweden, Germany, The Netherland and Ireland.

Figure 2 Trends in police recorded crimes
source: Jan Van Dijk, Marianne Junger & Irene Sagel-Grande (2011), *Actuele Criminologie*, 7th edition, Den Haag: SDU

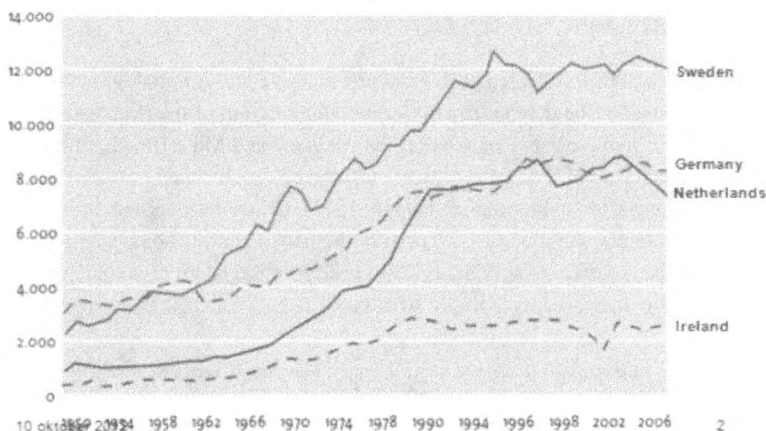

The first feature that catches the eye is that recorded crime has boomed in all four countries, most notably in Sweden. Between 1960 and 1990 levels of crime tripled or quadrupled. Analyses of police figures of recorded crime of the USA, France and most other Western nations show similarly steep upward trends over the same period (Gurr, 1977; Van Dijk, 1992).

Between 1960 and 1990 all Western countries experienced unprecedented booms in crime. During these three decades, known in France as the *Trente Glorieuses* (the Glorious Thirty), GDP per capita boomed. In addition, in most Western nations, and most notably so in Sweden, Germany, the United Kingdom and The Netherlands, welfare states, as imagined by social democrats like Bonger, were actually put in place. During these years most Western nations not only became more affluent, but wealth was also distributed more equally across the population. During the Glorious Decades the Gini coefficients- the most commonly used measure of economic equality- dropped considerably across the Western world (Wilterdink, 1995)[2].

The upward trends in volume crime between 1960 and 1990 in most Western nations cannot be easily reconciled with conventional criminological thinking about the root causes of crime in the tradition of Bonger. Post war trend data on crime fly squarely in the face of the Bongerian notion that crime is driven by poverty and economic inequality. Lagrange (2003) demonstrated for France, that wealth and levels of crime were not inversely related during this period in his country. Norstroem (1988) described Scandinavian crime booms as a side effect of economic prosperity. Using British indicators, criminologist Gloria Laycock made the same point in her inaugural lecture as director of the Jill Dando Institute of Crime Science in London (Laycock, 2001). The bulk of the British population was in many respects much better off in 1990 than probably ever before[3].

To make sense of the prolonged post war crime booms some criminologists started to take a fresh look at the determinants of crime, thinking out of the (Marxist) box. In 1975 British criminologists Ron Clarke, Pat Mayhew and Mike Hough, at the time in-house researchers of the Home Office, published a report called *Crime as Opportunity* (Mayhew, Clarke, Sturman, & Hough, 1975). Crime, they argued, is driven by the extent of viable opportunities of crime in the here and now. Some years later, in 1979, American criminologist Marcus Felson ascribed the boom in volume crime in the USA to the increased availability of suitable targets for theft (such as cars and

---

[2]   According to the literature, income inequalities in Europe have always been significantly lower than in the USA and have declined significantly between 1955 and 1980 in tandem with economic growth (Wilterdink, 1995).

[3]   "Recorded crime in this country has reached epidemic proportions. (...) The rise was not caused by an increase in poverty – we are, by any measure, better off now than we have ever been. Nor was it caused by a lack of education; even the worst educated members of our population spend more time in formal education than did the average child of the early 20th century. Nor is there any evidence that 'parenting' has been in catastrophic decline throughout the period, or that the population has grown proportionately".

durable consumer goods) and a dispersal of activities away from family and home, eroding natural guardianship. In this equally seminal publication the term *routine activity theory* was first coined.

In a similar vein I myself surprised the audience of my inaugural lecture at Leiden University with the assertion that high levels of volume crime were the price to be paid for living in an affluent and modern society. A high level of crime such as that of The Netherlands, I commented tongue in cheek, should not necessarily be seen as a bad sign (Van Dijk, 1990). Some years later British economist Simon Field explained at a conference of the Council of Europe in Strasbourg that in the long run thefts and burglaries are linked to the stock of criminal opportunities, represented in his model by the sum of real consumers expenditures in the recent four years (Field, 1994). In other words, also economists now agreed: the more consumer goods- the more cheap bread around- the more crime. Criminal opportunity theory had arrived as an alternative theoretical frame.

The empirical evidence presented by Felson for the causal relationships between routine activities and crime was largely based on an analysis of data from the National Crime Victimization Surveys of the USA. This analysis confirmed the weakening of informal social control exercised by American families. My own ideas about how criminal opportunities shape the nature of crime were likewise grounded in analyses of results of victimization surveys, in this case the first rounds of the Dutch victimization surveys (Van Dijk & Steinmetz, 1980). Our analyses showed that numbers of vehicle theft were related to ownership and that criminal victimization at individual and macro level was related to the amount of time spent by citizens outside their homes. In the UK, the authors of *Opportunity of Crime*, just mentioned, would later become the main protagonists of the British Crime Survey. Results from the BCS would be used in numerous articles testing hypotheses derived from what had by then become known as situational crime prevention theory. The links between the launch of victimization surveys in the 1970s and 80s and the elaboration of various versions of criminal opportunity theory around that time are not coincidental. The same circle of criminologists was involved. And from a theoretical perspective these links seem almost self evident. The data on arrested and convicted persons used by criminologists of the generation of Bonger were by definition offender-oriented. In most European countries criminal statistics could be disaggregated according to offender characteristics such as age, gender, religion, profession or alcoholism (Bonger, 1937). Results of victimization surveys are by definition victim-centered. They give no information on the motivation of the offenders but a wealth of information on vulnerabilities of victims. Analyses of the new crime data show which groups of the population are most at risk to be criminally victimized, for example yuppies leaving their houses replete of consumer goods unattended most of the time. Victimization surveys have taught criminologists to look at the other side of crime. That's how the empirical reality of criminal opportunity theory came into their sight.

In order to analyze empirically possible relationships between characteristics of national populations and levels of victimization by crime, comparable, cross-country data on victimization are needed. The international criminal statistics examined by Bonger must be superseded by results of victimization surveys. In 1987 Pat Mayhew, Martin Killias and myself launched the International Crime Victims Survey (ICVS), a standardized victimization survey modeled after the Dutch, British and Swiss national surveys (Van Dijk, Mayhew & Killias, 1990). The survey went into the field for the first time in 1989 in thirteen nations[4]. The surveys have since, with some adjustments, been carried out in 80 or more countries in five subsequent sweeps, with intervals of four or five years.

The ICVS provides comparable data not just on victimization rates but also on reporting of crime to the police by victims, satisfaction of victims with their treatment by the police, the reception of specialized victim support, fear of crime and opinions on police performance and on sentencing. In this paper, however, I will focus on the primary aim of the ICVS, the collection of comparable data on victimization by crime across countries. Initially, the survey results were mainly used to simply compare levels of victimization. Figure 3 gives an overview of the ranking of nations in terms of overall levels of criminal victimization around 2002.

Figure 3 World ranking on ICVS victimization rates
source: Jan Van Dijk (2008), *The World of Crime*, Thousand Oaks: SAGE

Fifteen Countries With the Highest Rates								
1	Colombia	48.7	6	Peru	41.0	11	Tunisia*	35.9
2	Zimbabwe	46.8	7	Mongolia	40.6	12	Namibia	35.1
3	Costa Rica	43.5	8	Bolivia	38.9	13	Paraguay	34.5
4	Swaziland	43.4	9	Mozambique	37.7	14	Zambia	34.4
5	Cambodia	41.3	10	Tanzania*	37.6	15	Slovak Republic	32.4
Fifteen Countries With Medium-High Rates								
16	United Kingdom	32.0	30	Ireland	25.7	39	Norway	21.5
19	Argentina	31.2	31	New Zealand	25.9	46	China*	21.6
21	India	29.7	34	South Africa	25.7	51	Switzerland	20.1
26	Lesotho	27.3	37	United States	23.3	53	Canada	19.1
28	Netherlands	27.0	38	Russian Federation	23.1	56	Brazil	18.4
Fifteen Countries With the Lowest Rates								
58	Turkey	17.9	63	Italy	16.6	68	Japan	10.8
59	France	17.8	64	Spain	13.7	69	Portugal	9.7
60	Austria	17.2	65	Greece	13.5	70	Philippines	9.1
61	Australia	16.9	66	Croatia	12.9	71	Hong Kong, China	7.8
62	Korea, Rep.	16.7	67	Hungary	12.6	72	Azerbaijan	7.7

Source: ICVS, 1992, 1996–2005. Latest survey available.
*Countries with data from ICVS, 1992.

---

[4]   To reduce costs, sample sizes were kept at a modest 2.000 per country, just enough to allow a comparison of the level of the main types of volume crime. Data were collected with the efficient means of computer-assisted telephone interviewing.

As can be seen in figure 3, the United Kingdom stands at the 16th place and The Netherlands at the 28th place in this league table of conventional crime. Sweden, not included here, stands at 26th with a victimization rate of 22,6% in 2005. These three countries are clearly no longer at the bottom of the rank, as they were in Bonger's table of arrested offenders per 100.000 inhabitants dating from the 1930s. The medium high levels of crime of the United Kingdom, Sweden and The Netherlands seem more in line with criminal opportunity theory than with Marxist determinism. In comparatively affluent countries with their abundance of durable consumer goods, levels of crime tend to be comparatively high, regardless of whether they are egalitarian or not.

The conduct of the ICVS in 80 nations including all main Western countries allows for cross sectional analyses of relationships between characteristics of nations and national levels of various types of crime. Analyses of the ICVS datasets have consistently refuted the notion that levels of crime are systematically lower in more affluent nations[5].

The ICVS has, as said, been repeated five times, namely in 1992, 1996, 2000, 2005 and, in a more limited number of countries, in 2010. The availability of these trend data allows analyses of relationships between changes in characteristics of countries over time and changes in the levels of victimization. In the next section I will present the trends in crime between 1987 and 2005/2010 according to the ICVS and some results of time series analyses.

Crime trends and some time series analyses

As said, the ICVS was carried out in 1989 for the first time and repeated four times till 2005 in a large group of countries. For Johannesburg, Buenos Aires, Australia, Canada and eleven European countries data are available from four or five sweeps of the survey. See figure 4 for results.

---

[5]   esults have been presented in a series of research reports with extensive documentation on the survey's methodology (Van Dijk, Van Kesteren & Smit, 2008; Van Dijk, 2012). A summing up of key findings and analytical results is provided in Van Dijk (2008).

**Figure 4 Trends in total crime experienced by national or city populations per
year during 1988-2004 (ICVS 1989-2005); source Van Dijk, 2008**

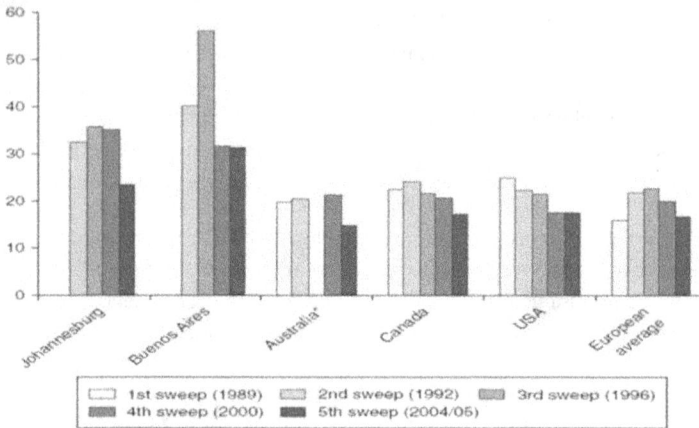

The results depicted in figure 4 show that levels of conventional crime have in Europe and most other parts of the world continued to rise between the first and the third sweep of, that is up to the mid 1990s. Thereafter crime has fallen significantly everywhere. The results in figure 8 also show that in 1988 levels of crime in the USA were still somewhat above the mean of other Western nations. The level of crime in the USA subsequently started to fall between 1988 and 1992. During these years crime was, as said, still increasing in the other Western countries. From 1992 onward the level of crime in the USA has therefore no longer been above the level in Europe or Australia. Since the third sweep in the mid 1990s crime has dropped significantly nearly everywhere in the participating nations. The steep falls in crime appear not to be a unique American phenomenon as suggested by Blumstein and Wallman (2006). Far from it. The falls are near universal in the industrialized world, including some middle income nations.

The full multi- year ICVS datasets were reanalysed by a team of British criminologists. Graham Farrell, Andromachi Tseloni and associates conducted a multilevel analysis of the trends in incidence victimization rates of 26 nations which participated in the ICVS three times or more (Tseloni et al, 2010). Their results confirm the international nature of the crime falls. Of special interest is their analysis of the *timing* of the falls of rates of victimization by various types of crime. Their results on the sequencing of the falls of various types of crime is depicted in figure 5.

Figure 5 Victimization incidence trends of five types of crime (ICVS 1989-2005); source: Tseloni et al, 2010

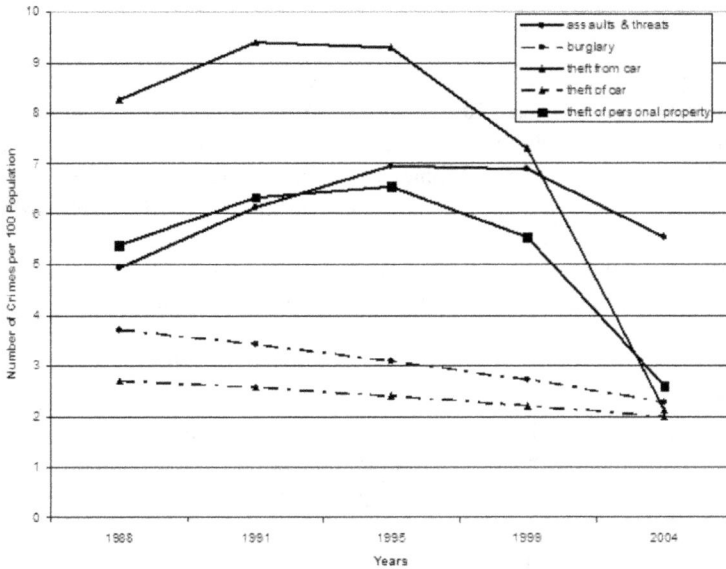

Figure 5 shows that burglary and car theft, represented by the dotted lines at the lower end, fell steadily from the late 1980s onwards. Next it were thefts from cars and other thefts from people which began to fall in the mid-1990s. And, finally, assaults started declining around the turn of the century. This sequencing was, once again, fairly universal across individual nations. We will revert to the uniform sequencing of the falls of different types of crime in the concluding section.

Now that the international nature of the falls in crime has been established, the key question to be answered, is how these fortunate changes in the seemingly entrenched problems of crime can be explained. Which macro factors may have caused the universal falls in crime during the final years of the 20th century? Let´s first examine whether the recent falls could perhaps be seen as a vindication of Bonger´s economic determinism. Has post war prosperity and reduced inequality finally, with a delay of four decades, delivered the expected bonus of lower crime rates? This interpretation seems farfetched. Especially so, since economic growth over the past twenty years has been much more modest than between 1960 and 1990 and economic inequalities have in fact deepened. This has especially been the case in the USA and the UK , where Gini coefficients have gone up. Levels of crime dropped precisely at the time when the good economic times were over. Between 2008 and 2013 the Western world even experienced an economic recession. The falls of crime, however, seem to have continued unabatedly (FBI, 2012)[6]. There has up to 2013 not been any sign of a recession-induced surge in total crime. The crime cycle and the business cycle are totally out of sync. Whatever factors may have caused the international falls in crime, it cannot have been "just the economy".

Many other explanations for the crime decline have been advanced by American scholars (Blumstein and Wallman, 2001; 2006). The USA falls have been explained as resulting from respectively massive incarceration, the ending of the crack cocaine epidemic, the use of computerized crime data (Compstat) and zero tolerance policing. Economist Levitt added an imaginative hypothesis to the list of post hoc explanations: violent crime was reduced by the legalisation of abortion in 1976, reducing the cohort of unwanted young males (Levitt, 2006). As demonstrated above, the falls in volume crime are a global phenomenon for which a global explanation must be sought (Van Dijk, 2006; 2010). The American factors simply do not fit the bill. In most European nations, Canada and Australia prisoners rates have remained modest compared to those in the USA, there never was a crack cocain epidemic, Compstat was never practiced and zero tolerance policing remained a slogan of some politicians at best. And yet in all these countries with their highly varying criminal policies, crime started to fall around the same time and with the same magnitude as in the USA. All explanations mentioned in the American literature on the crime drop may have some validity for the USA but can be duly eliminated from the list of possible explanations of the international drops This argument was earlier convincingly made by Zimring (2006) regarding Canada. The question to be answered is not why crime has fallen in the context of the criminal policies of a particular country at a given time but why different types of crime have fallen, regardless of national contexts, at around roughly the same time and with the same sequencing nearly everywhere in the developed world.

Let's now turn to criminal opportunity theory for a possible explanation of the falls in crime and examine whether ICVS data can be used to test relevant hypotheses. As I have suggested elsewhere, rates of victimization are determined by interactions between the rational choices of offenders and victims on a market of crime (Van Dijk, 1994). As long as the benefits of crime outweigh the costs of offending, the pool of offenders keeps expanding and crime rates will continue to go up. Resulting rises in the losses of crime incurred by victims, will trigger more investments in self- protection by potential victims. When the proportion of well-protected potential victims expand, criminal opportunities will be reduced. When the scale of such *responsive securitisation* reaches a critical level, potential new offenders will be discouraged from entering the criminal market. The pools of offenders will shrink and crime rates will start to fall. The key dynamics of the post war crime waves are represented in figure 6.

---

[6]   There was no change in the level of crime according to the BCS in 2011 compared to 2010 (Home Office, 2012). Results of the annual Dutch national surveys show a continued downward trend in both property and violent crime in recent years up and including 2011 (Ministerie van Veiligheid en Justitie, 2012).

Figure 6 Understanding the crime epidemics in the west: criminal opportunity and responsive securitization; source: Van Dijk, 2008

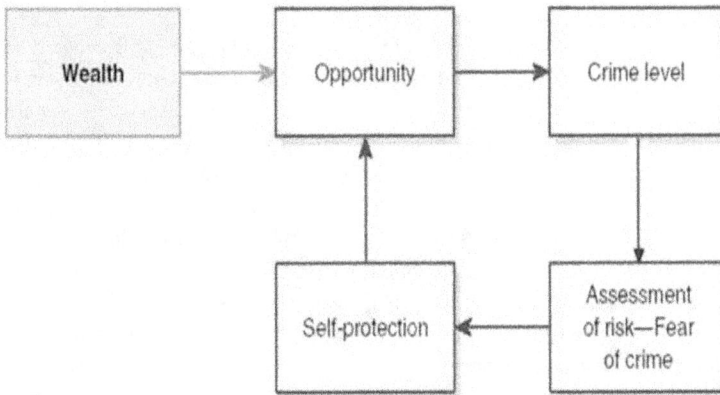

The theoretical perspective of *responsive securitization* is obviously informed by criminal opportunity theory (Felson & Clarke, 1998). It is also informed by the economical notion of markets of crime whereon offenders and victims interact (Becker, 1986; Cook, 1986). Especially in Europe, the new theoretical perspective was geared towards practical applications to reduce criminal opportunities through situational crime prevention. In the Netherlands criminal opportunity theory was adopted by the government as the policy theory underpinning its national crime prevention policies launched in 1985 (Ministry of Justice, 1985).

If levels of crime have, as supposed by Felson, been driven up by expanding pools of suitable targets of crime, improved security reducing these pools will eventually drive crime rates down. From this perspective criminal opportunity theory is intrinsically optimistic about long term trends in crime. It has always held the promise of drops in crime when criminal opportunities are contracted by forms of responsive securitization.

But if this is the case, have any protagonists of criminal opportunity theory then predicted this reversal of fortunes before it had actually started to take place? The answer to this sceptical question can be positive. Following the logic of situational prevention theory I myself predicted in 1994 in the Festschrift for Wouter Buikhuisen, my predecessor at Leiden University, that opportunistic criminality in the 21st century would, and I quote *"no longer be a mass phenomenon due to more and better situational prevention"* (Van Dijk, 1994). On similar grounds British criminologist Ken Pease predicted in 1997 falls in amateur thefts. He predicted a bifurcation of future offending into either clever e-fraud or predatory violent street crime (Pease, 1997). Responsive securitization, then, is not a post hoc explanation of observed falls in crime. That potential victims would take action to reduce their risks, follows logically from criminal opportunity theory and the international falls in crime have on this theoretical basis been duly predicted years before their onset.

In a keynote at the European Society of Criminology conference in Bologna in 2007, Ron Clarke addressed the key issue whether situational crime prevention can reduce the overall crime rate, considering that at the micro level displacement is always possible (Clarke, 2007). His first argument is that investments in self protection have since the 1970s grown phenomenally, impacting on almost every aspect of society. A prime example are the huge increases in private security guards and alarm centers. In 'Western' countries private security guards now outnumber police officers (Van Steden and Sarre, 2007)[7]. If public policing is widely supposed to impact on levels of crime to at least some extent, it would, according to Clarke, be strange if private security with its exclusive focus on crime prevention, would not. But responsive securitization is not limited to human surveillance by the private security industry. A wide range of different measures to prevent crime have become mainstreamed into modern society. Harnessing new technology, security provisions have been built into homes, cars, stores and parking lots, public transport and public/ social housing, schools and hospitals, offices and other work places, entertainment venues and sports stadiums, airports and seaports, and to warehouses and transportation terminals (Clarke and Newman, 2008).

The universality and pervasiveness across 'Western' countries of the security response, and thereby its potential impact on trends in crime, seem difficult to dispute. The ICVS database shows upward trends in home security across the world with very few exceptions (Van Dijk et al, 2008). Trends in home security show much greater communality than the criminal policies pursued by governments. The security response also fully meets the requirement of synchronized timing across countries. The lasting rise in private security started in the seventies in the USA and somewhat later everywhere in Europe (Cullingham et al, 1991). It is likely to have reached critical mass around 1985 in the USA and around 1990 in Europe, just in time to have had an impact of the subsequent falls in crime. The pervasiveness and timing of the boom in private security make it a promising contender as explanatory factor of the international falls in crime at the end of the 20th century. We will now examine whether empirical data including from the ICVS can be used to put the security hypothesis to the test. We will first look at the type of crime which, as we have seen, started to fall first, namely car theft. What has been the role of improved security in the falls in car thefts?

---

[7] Worldwide more people are employed as security guards (348 per 100.000) than as police officers (310 per 100.000) (Van Dijk, 2008). According to the latest figures collated by Jaap de Waard, the number of private security employees in Western Europe has over the past ten years increased further by 90% (De Waard, Berghuis, 2010).

Security and the falls in car thefts

Vehicle crimes provide an important testing ground for the hypothesis of responsive securitization. Car thefts used to make up ten percent or more of the total costs of volume crime in Western nations (Mayhew, 2003). Levels of car theft have gone up universally in Western nations from 1960 onwards in tandem with rates of car ownership. Considering the costs of car thefts, responsive securitization among owners stands to reason. Although car ownership levels are stable or still rising, thefts of cars have gone down considerably since the 1990s in all Western nations, sometimes by more than 50% (Van Dijk, Van Kesteren & Smit, 2008).

In Germany rates of car theft had already fallen by almost 50% in 1961. The story about the German falls in car theft has been documented by Pat Mayhew and Mike Hough in the Home Office publication Crime as Opportunity, just mentioned (Mayhew et al, 1975). In 1960 the federal government passed legislation which made high quality steering column locks mandatory in all cars. Car thefts dropped already the same year. In this case responsive securitization was promoted by legislative measures. In the USA and Britain similar legislation was passed ten years later but limited to the fitting of steering column locks in newly sold cars. As was to be expected, the impact of these regulations was less immediate than in Germany (Webb, 1994). In Britain it took almost ten years before over 80% of cars were fitted with steering column locks. It was indeed around that time that rates of car theft per 100 owners started to stabilize. In the USA the impact of the new regulation manifested itself sooner, probably because of a faster renewal of the vehicle population. The critical penetration rate of 80% was reached earlier than in the UK and car thefts rates started to fall accordingly. Studies into the impact of state- of- the- art security measures against car theft have since been conducted in many countries, often using data from victimization surveys. Electronic immobilizers became the new preferred security measure to prevent theft of cars. In Australia, the USA, Europe and Canada the falls in car theft have tracked increases in the penetration rate of new anti- car theft security (Mayhew, 1992; Farrell, Tseloni & Tilley, 2011; Fujita & Maxfield, 2012). Electronic immobilizers were made mandatory in 1998 for all newly sold cars within the European Union. Within ten years after the regulation took effect, it had reduced car thefts by 70% in The Netherland and by 80% in Britain (Van Ours & Vollaard, 2012).

Traditionally a large part of car thefts are committed by juveniles for temporary transportation, known in Britain as joyriding. A smaller part is committed by professional thieves for resale or sale of car parts. If the recent falls have indeed been caused by improved security, this effect is likely to have been stronger on theft for temporary transportation by opportunistic juveniles than on theft by experienced professionals. In the ICVS victims of car theft are asked whether the stolen car was ever recovered. To test the hypothesis that drops in thefts in car theft have been most pronounced among the category of theft for temporary transportation, we have looked at trends over time in recovered and non recovered car thefts in thirteen Western nations. Figure 7 shows results.

Figure 7 Trends in one-year victimization by joyriding and car theft (ICVS 1989-2005); source: van Dijk, 2008

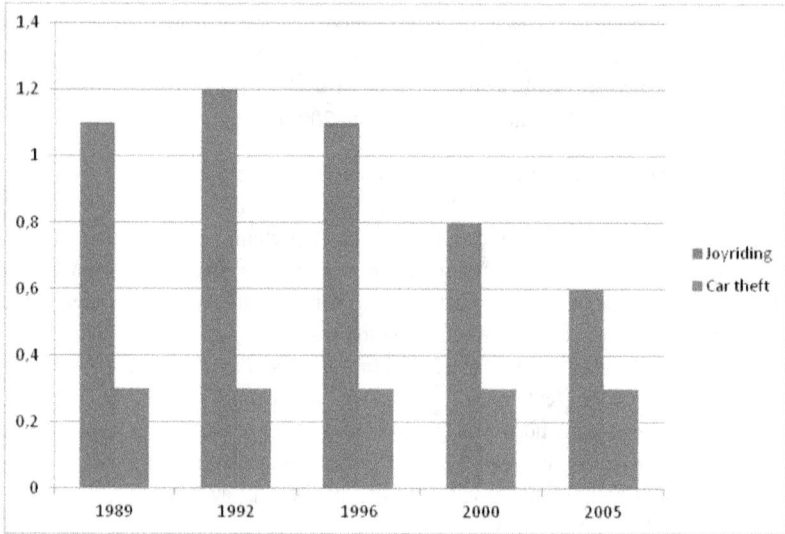

The trends in figure 7 confirm the hypothesis. In the thirteen Western countries together rates of joyriding dropped by 50 % (from 1,4 % in 1988 to 0,6 in 2005) while rates of car theft remained stable at a one year victimization rate of 0,4%[8].

Security and trends in household burglary

As discussed, the second main type of crime which started to fall across Western nations is household burglary. As car theft, household burglary makes up a considerable part of the total costs of crime. For many victims the experience to see once house burgled is also highly traumatic. Responsive securitization is to be expected. Over the years several forms of household security have been introduced such as high security locks and bolts, burglar alarms, outdoor lightning etcetera. Analyses of results of national victimization surveys in The Netherlands and Britain have shown that individual houses equipped with such security have a reduced risk to be burgled. For example in the Netherlands houses without any special security run an 8 times higher risk to be burgled than houses with a comprehensive package of security measures in place (Van Dijk, Junger & Sagel-Grande, 2011).

---

[8]   From 2010 onwards total numbers of car thefts are rising again in Germany and The Netherlands. This new upward trend seems to be caused by the improved capacity of professional car thieves to circumvent electronic security measures.

In the ICVS respondents are asked about the installment of basic security measures such as a burglar alarm. Using data from 114 regions in Europe and North America, collected in the first two sweeps of the ICVS, we analyzed the relationships between regional levels of affluence, degree of urbanization, burglary victimization rates, fear of burglary and the use of burglar alarms with the help of path analysis (Van Dijk, 1995). Figure 8 shows the results in the form of a model explaining a fair amount of the variation in levels of burglary victimization and burglar alarm ownership.

Figure 8 main drivers of the use of burglar alarms; a secondary analysis of the (ICVS 1989-2005); source: van Dijk, 1994

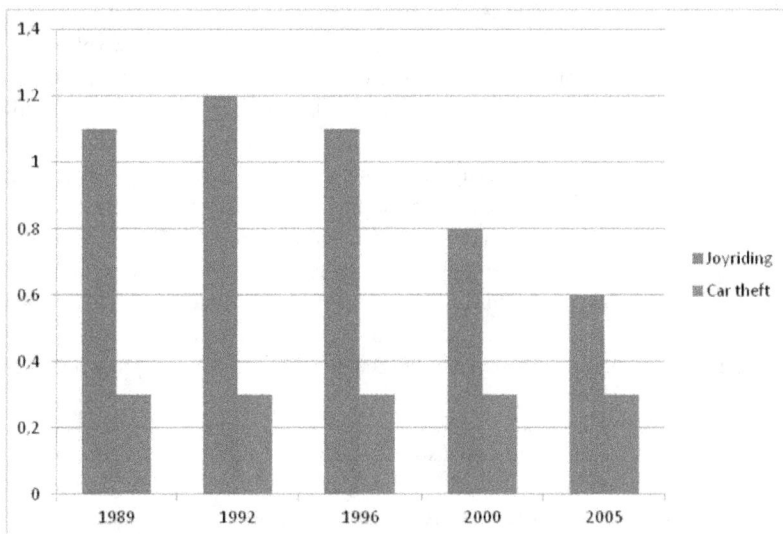

The model shows strong links between the level of burglary in regions and fear of burglary and between such fears and the purchasing of burglar alarms. This causal path reflects the first stages of responsive securitization regarding household burglary. The model also shows that people living in relatively wealthy regions are more likely to invest in burglar alarms, regardless of their situation in other respects. This results demonstrates that well off households can more easily afford investments in such devices. Finally the model shows that people in wealthy and urbanized regions more often live in detached houses and experience more burglaries. Obviously responsive securitization takes place in a multi-factorial setting.

In wealthier regions more people live in detached houses which offer ample opportunities for burglars. In such regions rates of victimization by burglary are higher. The negative experiences of victims generate increased awareness of risks to be burgled and this promotes investments in self- protection, including in expensive measures that normally only very rich people can afford. The model, first presented at a conference of the Council of Europe on Crime and the Economy, covers all stages of responsive securitization except the final and crucial one. The statistical model shows that responsive securitization as such takes place but it falls short of showing that ensuing reduced opportunities of burglary actually result in lower rates of burglary victimization. For a test of the final step in the model longitudinal data are needed. In 1995 the ICVS had only been repeated once and no longitudinal data were yet available.

In The Netherlands the installment of basic household security measures has been actively promoted by the central government since the mid 1980s (Ministry of Justice, 1985). In 1999 basic household security was incorporated in the Building Regulations and since then such security is mandatory for all newly built houses. Ben Vollaard of Tilburg University has analyzed results of the Dutch national victimization surveys to determine the impact of the new building regulations upon burglary victimization rates. He compared burglary victimization rates of owners of newly built houses with those of older houses. His analysis shows that risks to be burgled of newly built houses were reduced by 50%, controlling for the impact of external factors (Vollaard & Van Ours, 2010). Supplementary analyses found no evidence of displacement to houses in other neighborhoods or cities or to other types of theft. According to the authors the new building regulations had been responsible for almost a fifth of the total drop in burglaries in The Netherlands in recent years. The one off costs of the security measures were found to be a fraction of the benefits in terms of losses prevented over the years.

The litmus test of the impact of responsive securitization on burglary rates is whether national trends in rates of victimization by burglary can be predicted by the penetration rate of elementary security measures. In other words are countries with a higher penetration of household security rewarded by lower burglary rates in the years ahead. The repeats of the ICVS in 2005 and 2010 allow us to explore this issue empirically. In 2005 and 2010 the ICVS was repeated in just eight Western nations, Canada, Denmark, England/Wales, Estonia, Germany, The Netherlands, Sweden and Switzerland (Van Dijk, 2012). Fortunately these eight nations, however similar in many other respect, show considerable variation in the penetration of household security in 2005. The data therefore allow us to put responsive securitization to an empirical test by examining the possible link between security penetration at time 1 (2005) and the changes in burglary victimization between time 1 and time 2 (2010). The next figure shows results.

Figure 9 Levels of home security and burglary victimization in ten Western nations (ICVS 2005 and 2010); source: van Dijk, 2012

	High-grade door locks, 2004 (%)	Burglar alarm, 2004 (%)	Burglary rate, 2004 (%)	Burglary rate, 2010 (%)	Change burglary rate (%-point)
England and Wales	60	41	3.5	1.5	- 2.0
Netherlands	78	15	1.3	0.8	- 0.5
Canada	48	28	2,0	1.3	- 0.7
Germany	63	14	0.9	1.2	+0.3
Sweden	46	16	0.7	1.0	+0.3
Estonia	40	7	2.5	3.0	+0.5
Switzerland	29	5	1.1	1.9	+0.8
Denmark	32	9	2.7	3.6	+0.9

In this table we can see that trends in burglary victimization between 2005 and 2010 have been divergent. In England/Wales, The Netherlands and Canada rates have fallen, in Germany and Sweden rates remained stable and in Estonia, Denmark and Switzerland they went up. The results are graphically depicted in the next figure.

Figure 10 Levels of household security in 2004 and (sum of high grade locks and alarms) and changes in burglary rates between 2004 and 2010

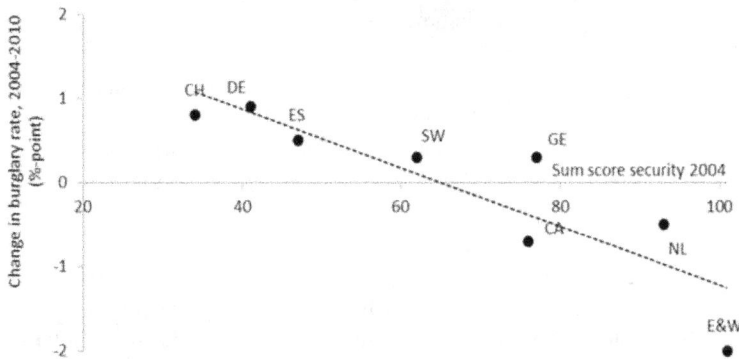

This figure depicts the statistical significant relationship between the levels of security in 2004 and the changes in burglary victimization between 2004 and 2010. During this period rates of burglary victimization went down in countries with the highest penetration of home security and went up in countries with the lowest penetration. In

2010 the burglary victimization rates in Denmark was 3.6%. In Estonia it was 3.3% and in Switzerland 1.9%. These rates are twice as high as in The Netherlands and Sweden, countries similar in many other respects, including open borders with Central and Eastern European countries. The results suggest that the active promotion of household security in Britain and The Netherlands has indeed paid off and that Denmark, Estonia and Switzerland and to a lesser extent Germany are paying the price for their government's policies of *laisser faire* on the security market. The European experience with burglary rates over the past ten years underlines the wisdom of the universal saying that opportunity makes the thief, pointedly expressed in the Spanish version " Open doors make thieves even of holy men"[9].

In conclusion

We have presented evidence from the ICVS and other sources supporting the hypothesis that falls in car theft and household burglary have at least in part been security-driven. As discussed many other types of crime , including violent crime, have also fallen. Farrell, Tseloni, Tilley & Mailley (2011) have suggested that these falls might not be unrelated to the preceding falls in other types of crime. Falls in car theft might have had a knock on effect on other types of crime. As mentioned above many thefts of cars are committed by juveniles, in fact the typical starting age for this type of criminality is 14 or younger. According to the authors young boys are typically initiated into a life of delinquency by participating in acts of joyriding with peers. Car theft is so to speak their *debut crime*. The first successful acts of car theft act as *stepping stone* to their involvement in subsequent, more serious types of crime. This stepping stone hypothesis could readily be extended to burglaries in the neighborhood, also mainly committed by young teenagers. Improved security may have reduced opportunities for easy crimes such as car theft and burglaries and this may have blocked access to the first stages of a criminal career for new cohorts of would be delinquents. Others have observed that the early introduction of steering column locks in Germany, mentioned above, may have had a lasting impact on levels of car theft in the country by preventing the emergence of a subculture of joyriding among juveniles (Clarke & Harris, 1992). From this perspective, the fact that the post war crime boom seems to has been less severe than those in the UK and The Netherlands may have been the unintended side effects of the early adoption of car security legislation. In a more general sense improved car and home security may have blocked the emergence of new delinquent subcultures in vulnerable neighborhoods across the Western world around 2000.

---

[9]   The original title of the lecture was Closing the Doors, a reference to a now largely forgotten book by Ron Clarke, called Suicide: Closing the Exits. In this book, and in a follow up article from Clarke and Pat Mayhew, empirical evidence was presented showing that changes in the composition of household gas in Britain and The Netherlands in the mid1980s had caused abrupt falls in the numbers of people committing suicide by gas without major displacement to suicides by other means (Clarke & Mayhew, 1989). If highly motivated acts such as suicide can be reduced by simple situational measures, why, the authors argued, not various acts of opportunistic thieving such as joyriding or burglaries in the neighborhood? Why not indeed?

As discussed earlier, the international falls in crime started with car theft. Then burglaries went down as well, followed by thefts from car and other types of personal theft. Finally, crimes of violence started to fall belatedly too. This uniform sequencing of the crime falls according to ICVS results is in line with the stepping stone hypothesis. In many other respects too criminal acts seem to feed on other criminal acts. Victims of bicycle thefts are known to be more prone than others to become bicycle thieves themselves (Van Dijk, 1986). They are also more prone to buy stolen bicycles, thereby driving up demand. If levels of bicycle theft are somewhat reduced by improved security, chain effects will act as negative multipliers and the market of bicycle theft may fall into a deep recession. Responsive securitization is as yet more an hypothesis than a proven theory. The falls in crime may have had many other causes besides improved security. But it certainly seems an hypothesis suggesting interesting new directions in criminological research (Van Dijk & Tseloni, 2010). It may even prove to be nothing less than a new agenda for comparative international criminology.

In the introduction I have referred to Bonger's thesis of 1905 about the close links between economic conditions and recorded crime. Official crime statistics are no longer taken at face value as measures of crime. And although economic conditions surely impact on levels of crime, the relationship is far from straightforward. Crime seems to pursue to some extent its own cyclical course, largely independent from the business cycle.

The availability of data on crime collected by survey research among the population has opened new theoretical perspectives, focusing on the roles of victims rather than solely on those of offenders. These new data have also opened new avenues for international comparative research on the societal causes of crime. Both methodologically and theoretically criminology has made great strides. Some fundamentals of the discipline have remained the same, though. As in the days of Bonger theoretical ideas about the societal determinants of crime are tested by analyzing international criminal statistics. Also, this new epidemiological criminology is, just like the work of Bonger, no purely academic exercise. The comparative analysis of trends in security and trends in burglary rates has obvious policy implications. In this political context I want to stress that situational crime prevention is not just a matter of individual or collective efficiency. It is also a matter of social justice.

Results of the ICVS show that across twelve Western nations the lowest income groups have stepped up their household security to a lesser extent than the middle and upper classes. They simply cannot afford to protect their houses as well as the others. As was to be expected, the survey shows that the lowest two quartiles have benefited less from the falls in burglary victimization than the rest of the population (Van Dijk, 2008) (see figure 11 for results).

Figure 11 Trends in the use of burglar alarms (left side) and trends in burglary victimization since 1992 (rights side) by income quartiles in twelve Western nations, including the USA (ICVS 1989-2005); source: van Dijk, 2008

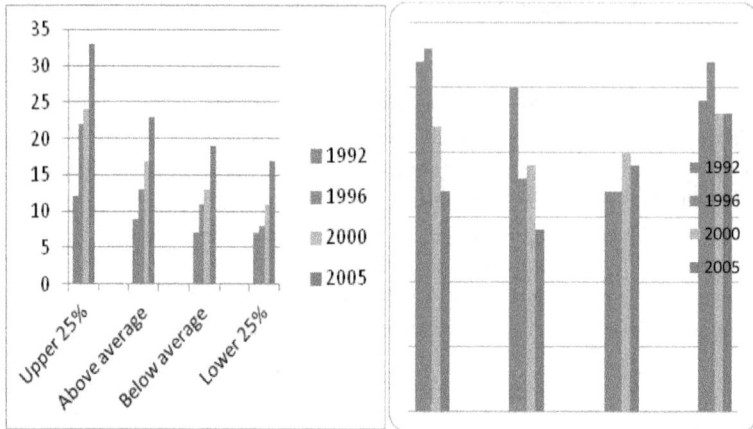

When left to market forces alone, responsive securitization is bound to increase the security gap between the haves and have nots. Our hypothesis is that in countries where the government has actively intervened in the home security market, such as the UK and The Netherlands the security gap will have been grown less sharply than in for example the USA. Regrettably in several countries, including The Netherlands, the UK and Belgium, the government has in recent years stepped down its efforts to promote household security.

A topical issue these days is the theft of cars by highly professional groups that can circumvent electronic security measures. In Germany the numbers of car thefts seem to edge upwards again. There is solid research evidence at the individual and collective level that the technique of parts marking can effectively curb professional car theft against relatively small costs (Van Dijk, 2014). Proposals for the introduction of an EU Directive on parts marking have been shelved due to opposition from the (German) car industry[10]. In recent years the first steps of young people of what might develop into a criminal career are typically made on the internet. Once again, these petty e- offences such as hacking, harassment and stalking are met with a laisser faire attitude by governments. The may later prove to have been the stepping stones to an online crime boom.

---

[10]   BMW has published on the internet the results of a small comparative study on the rates of car theft among cars with and cars without parts marking. In Taiwan parts marking was made mandatory in 2006 for all cars and motorcycles resulting in an immediate drop in thefts of around 70-80 percent (Van Dijk, 2014/ forthcoming)

The ultimate aim of our criminological work is to gain knowledge about crime with the aim of designing interventions which can help to reduce the costs and suffering of fellow human beings, be they victims or offenders. *Savoir pour prevoir, prevoir pour prevenir.* Or, in modern jargon: evidence-based crime prevention. Proud to stand in that century-old , Bongerian tradition, though with a twist.

Literature

Blumstein, A., and Wallman, J. (2000). *The Crime Drop in America.* New York: Cambridge University Press.

Blumstein, A. *and* Wallman, J. *(*2006*).* *The Crime Drop in America* (revised edn). Cambridge*:* Cambridge University Press.

Bonger, W.A. (1905), Criminalite et conditions economiques, In English (1916). *Criminality and Economic Conditions,* Boston: Little/Brown; also published in English by the Political Economy Club, 1916, Vancouver, B.C., Canada

Bonger, W.A. (1932), *Inleiding tot de Criminologie,* Haarlem: Erven Bohn

Bonger, W.A. (1937), Over criminele statistiek. Een bijdrage tot haar geschiedenis en haar theorie. In *Tijdschrift voor stafrecht,* Vol 48.

Clarke, V.C. (2007). Can Situational *Crime Prevention Reduce the Crime Rate ?,* presentation at the ESC Conference in Bologna, 27 September, 2007.

Clarke, R.V. & D. Lester (1989), *Suicide: Closing the Exits.* New York: Springer Verlag

Clarke, R.V. & P. Mayhew (1989), Crime as Opportunity; a note on domestic gas suicide in Britain and The Netherlands, *British Journal of Criminology,* Vol 29, No. 1, pp. 35-46

Clarke, R.V.C. & P.M. Harris (1992), Auto theft and its prevention. In M.Tonry (ed). *Crime and Justice; a review of Research,* Vol.16.Chigago: Uni. Of Chicago Press

Clarke, R.V. and Newman, G. (2006). *Outsmarting the Terrorists,* Westport: Praeger

Cohen, L. E., and Felson, M. (1979). Social change and crime rate trends: A routine activity approach. *American Sociological Review,* 44, 588-608.

Cunningham, W., Strauchs, J., van Meter, C. (1991). *The Hallcrest Report II: Private Security Trends, 1970-2000.* Stoneham, MA: Butterworths-Heinemann.

Dijk, J. J. M. van (1986). Responding to crime: Reflections on the reactions of victims and non-victims to the increase in petty crime. In), *From crime policy to victim policy,* Fattah, E. (ed.), 156-166. London: MacMillan.

Van Dijk, J. J. M. (1994a). Opportunities for crime: A test of the rational-interactionist model. In *Crime and Economy. Reports presented to the 11th Criminological colloquium (1994).* Criminological Research, Vol. XXXII. Council of Europe Publishing. 1995.

Dijk J. J. M. van (1994b). Understanding crime rates: On the interactions between the rational choices of victims and offenders. *British Journal of Criminology,*

34,. 105-121.

Dijk, J.J.M. van (1991). *Crime as Flipside; a theoretical and empirical exploration of the relationships between affluence and crime*, Arnhem: Gouda Quint (Inaugural lecture University of Leiden; in Dutch).

Dijk, J.J.M. van (1994). Professionalizing crime: reflections on the impact of new technologies on crime and crime prevention in the year 2000 and beyond, In J.Junger-Tas and I. Sagel-Grande (Eds), *Criminology in the 21th Century*, Leuven: Garant.

Dijk, J.J.M. van (2008). The world of crime: *Breaking the silence on problems of security, justice and development across the world*. Thousand Oaks: Sage.

Dijk J.J.M. van *(2006)* What Goes Up, Comes Down: Explaining the Falling Crime Rates. Criminology in Europe. *Newsletter of the European Society of Criminology, 5, 3 &* 17-18.

Dijk, J.J.M. van (2010). Why are crime rates falling? *ESC Criminology in Europe: Newsletter of the European Society of Criminology,* 9, 5-13.

Dijk, J.J.M. van (2012), The International Crime Victims Survey; latest results and outlook, In *Newsletter European Society of Criminology*, December 2012.

Dijk, J.J.M van (2014), *Autodiefstal en de security wedloop*, Schade Almanak, 2014

Dijk, J.J.M. van and C. H.D. Steinmetz (1980). *The RDC Victim Surveys, 1974-1979*, The Hague: Ministry of Justice.

Dijk, J. J. M. van , Mayhew, P., and Killias, M. (1990). *Experiences of crime across the world. Key Findings from the 1989 International Crime Survey.* Deventer: Kluwer Law and Taxation Publishers

Dijk, J.J.M. van, Kesteren, J.N. van, and Smit, P. (2008). *Criminal Victimization in International Perspective, Key findings from the 2004-2005 ICVS and EU ICS*. Den Haag: Boom Legal Publishers. (Onderzoek en Beleid, WODC, 257).

Dijk, J.J.M. van, A. Tseloni & G. Farrell (Eds) (2012),*The International Drop in Crime; New Directions in Research*, London: Palgrave/MacMillan

FBI, *Preliminary crime stats for the first half of 2011*, online: www.fbi.gov/news/ stories/2011/december/crime-stats

Farrell, G., Tilley, N., Tseloni, A. and Mailley, J. (2008). The Crime Drop and the Security Hypothesis. *British Society of Criminology Newsletter*, 62, 17-21.

Farrell, G., Tilley, N., Tseloni, A. and Mailley J. (2010). Explaining and sustaining the crime drop: Clarifying the role of opportunity-related theories. *Crime Prevention and Community Safety*, 12, 24-44.

Farrell, G., Tseloni, A., Tilley, N. and Mailley, J. (2011a). The Crime Drop and the Security Hypothesis. *Journal of Research in Crime and Delinquency*, 48, 147-175.

Farrell, G., A. Tseloni and Tilley, N. (2011b). The effectiveness of vehicle security devices and their role in the crime drop. *Criminology and Criminal Justice*, 11, 21-35.

Felson, M. (1998). *Crime and Everyday Life, Second Edition* . California: Pine ForgePress.

Felson, M. (2002). *Crime and Everyday Life* , 3rd edn. Thousand Oaks, CA: Sage.

Felson, M. and Clarke, R. V. (1998). *Opportunity Makes the Thief. Police Research Series, Paper 98*. Policing and Reducing Crime Unit, Research, Development and Statistics Directorate. London: Home Office. [www.homeoffice. gov.uk/rds/prgpdfs/fprs98.pdf]

Field, S. (1999). *Trends in Crime Revisited*, Home Office Research Study, 195, London: Home Office.

Fujita, S. & M. Maxfield (2012), Security and the Drop in Car Theft in the United States, in J. Van Dijk, A. Tseloni & G. Farrell (Eds), *The International Falls in Crime*, PalgraveMacMillan

Gurr, T. R.(1977). Crime Trends in Modern Democracies Since 1945. *Annales Internationales de Criminologie*, 16, 41-85.

Home Office (2012), Crime in England and Wales: Quarterly Update to September 2011

Home Office Statistical Bulletin 01/12, Published 19 January 2012

Killias M. & B. Lanfranconi (2012), The crime drop discourse – or the illusion of uniform continental trends: Switzerland as a contrasting case. In: Dijk, J.J.M. van, A. Tseloni & G. Farrell (Eds) (2012) (forthcoming), *The International Drop in Crime; New Directions in Research*, London: Palgrave/ MacMillan

Lagrange, H. (2003). Crime and Socio-Economic Context. *Revue française de sociologie*, 44, Supplement: An Annual English Selection (2003), 29-48

Laycock, G. (2001). Scientists or Politicians - Who has the Answer to Crime. *Scottish Law Gazette*: University College London (Inaugural lecture).

Levitt, S.D. (2004). Understanding Why Crime Fell in the 1990s: Four Factors that Explain the Decline and Six that Do Not, *Journal of Economic Perspectives*, 18, 163–90.

Mayhew. P., Clarke, R.V.G., Sturman, A. and Hough, M. (1975). *Crime as Opportunity*, Home Office Research and Planning Unit, London.

Mayhew, P. *(*1992*)* Steering Column Locks and Car Theft. *In: Clarke RV (ed.) Situational Crime Prevention: Successful Case Studies*. Albany, NY: Harrow and Heston*, pp* 52-65*.*

Mayhew, P. (with assistance from Glenda Adkins) (2003). Counting the Costs of. Crime in Australia. In *Crime and criminal justice*. No. 247. April 2003.

Ministerie van Veiligheid en Justitie (2012), *Integrale Veiligheidsmonitor 2011*, Maart, 2012

Ministry of Justice (1985). *Society and Crime; A policy plan for The Netherlands*, The Hague: Ministry of Justice.

Our, J.C. & B. Vollaard (2012), The engine immobilizer; a non starter for car thieves, Department of Economics, Tilburg University (unpublished)

Pease, K. (1997). 'Predicting the Future: the Roles of Routine Activity and Rational Choice
Theory'. In Newman, G., Clarke, R and Shoham, S.G. (eds.) *Rational Choice and Situational Crime Prevention: Theoretical Foundations*. Aldershot: Dartmouth.

Steden, R. van and Sarre, R. (2007). The growth of privatized policing: Some cross-national data and comparisons. *International journal of comparative and applied criminal justice*. 3,151-71.

Tseloni, A. Mailley, J. Farrell, G. and Tilley, N. (2010) The cross-national crime and repeat victimization trend for main crime categories: Multilevel modeling of the International Crime Victims Survey. *European Journal of Criminology*, 7, 375-394.

Vollaard, B. & J. Van Ours (2011), Does regulation of built-in security reduce crime? Evidence from a natural experiment, *The Economic Journal*, 121, (May), p. 485-504

Waard, de & B. Berghuis (2012), Trends in de private veiligheidszorg: de stand van zaken in 2012, *Secondant*, July 2012

Webb, B. (1994), *Steering Column Locks and Motor Vehicle Theft: Evaluations from Three Countries*, London: Home Office Police Research Group

Wilterdink, N. (1995), ,Increasing Income Inequality and Wealth Concentration in the Prosperous Societies of the West', in: *Studies in International Comparative Development*, 30, 3, 3-23.

Zimring, F..(2006). *The Great American Crime Decline*. Oxford: Oxford University Press.

Nils Christie

Restoration after Atrocities

Acts of horror

It was in the afternoon July 22-2011. A huge bomb exploded in a car parked just outside the ministerial centre in Oslo. The centre is a tall building, with the prime ministers offices at the top. The building and the surrounding looked as war had hit. Eight people were immediately killed; more were in hospital, badly hurt. The offender, in his car filled to the brim with explosives, had been delayed in the traffic and the explosion occurred an hour after ordinary office hours. If in time hundreds would have been killed.

The first attempts to explain the atrocities followed immediately: May be some Muslim revenge for our participation in the wars in Afghanistan and Libya? Or for our reprinting of those caricatures of Mohammed? If so, bad times ahead for our immigrant population.

But then, as the night drew on, other alarming news dripped in: There were shootings at a summer-camp for politically active youth from the Labour Party. It took place on a tiny island in an inland lake an hours drive from Oslo. A tall man walking back and forth, systematically killing everyone he could find – some as young as fourteen. Without mercy, just killing any youth he saw. He saw many. 69 were murdered there. All in all, he killed 77 persons.

The horror, despair, and sorrow that spread in the country need an artist's hand to describe. I refrain, but point to one piece of news that brought some sort of relief during the long night. The offender was not an immigrant. He was a tall, blond man, clearly a Norwegian. And soon it became clear; this was the same man that some hours before had exploded the Governmental Centre.

Restoration, first chapter

Are thoughts of restoration possible after such occurrences?

Those killed will never be back, – except in dreams and memories. And for those close to the killed ones, their opinion might be that the killer ought to burn in Hell, forever.

What is then left – to restore?

The social system is left.

Roses, not hatred

In the case of July 22, some elements in what can be seen as a restorative process started immediately. Soon after the bomb exploded, the Prime minister was on radio and television. His statements were those of sorrow and despair, solidarity with the victims, but also, central to his speech that night and the days and nights that followed; we will not meet these acts with vengeance and terror, but by preserving our ideals for a democratic society.

On the third day after the atrocities, a memorial meeting was held outside the City Hall of Oslo. The town has 600 000 inhabitants. Estimates suggested that 150 000 of us were there. The Crown prince spoke, the prime minister spoke, survivors spoke. I did not hear one sentence about revenge from any of them. Instead, as formulated by one of the survivors: Let us answer with roses, not with vengeance. Or, from another of the young survivors: If one man can expose so much hatred, imagine then how much love we can express together. The Mayor of Oslo put it like this in an interview: Together we will punish the killer. Our punishment will be more openness, more tolerance, more democracy. Some weeks after the massacre we had a municipal election in the country. The Mayor was re-elected with an extraordinary large margin.

Only roses, in words and reality. Nearly everyone had flowers in hand and left them later at several memorial points in town. A procession from the City Hall to the central church was planned, but cancelled. There were too many people, everywhere. Similar memorial ceremonies took place all over the country in the days that followed. Import tax on roses was temporarily removed to get sufficient supplies into the country. The public transportation system in Oslo had to be redirected not to destroy the monuments of flowers in the centre of town.

In a way, we came closer to each other these days. The politicians were an important part of this, and also driving forces. Our prime minister, Jens Stoltenberg, was quite extraordinary in his ability to bring words to feelings. Here was nothing of the political rhetoric of George Bush after September 11th or David Cameron after the youth riots in British towns. The political leaders of Norway agreed not to attack each other for a period, even though an election was close. The situation was too grave for party quibbling. The atmosphere during these last days of July reminded me of the days when the German occupation of Norway came to an end in 1945. An enormous feeling of community, a united nation. For a period.

Terrible days, but also with some hope. In an article with Hedda Giertsen two days after the atrocities, we used the title; "A better Norway is growing out of this" (Information, Copenhagen July 25, 2011). So it felt. The horror drove us to the streets, and there pulled us together.

What were we gathering around? First of all, the victims. Innocent youngsters had been together on that island to gain knowledge on how to preserve and improve our country. They were killed, without mercy. And then the system itself. We were all threatened. Basic values and perceptions of us as a nation had been under attack. The killer had challenged elements in our central value-system. International comparative studies show Norwegians to be at the very top in trusting each other and close to the bottom in killing each other. And then these atrocities!

Restoring a country

Norway was in these first weeks to some extent converted to one big arena of restoration. Usually, we think of restoration as a process going on between a limited number of participants; the victim, the offender, the mediator, – that is the prototype. But to us, in the days following July 22, the whole nation got involved. The shock and sorrow was so great that new forms had to be created. Emotions were displayed, values clarified, norms strengthened. To a large extent, the surviving youths from the island were the driving force in all this. No experts in between. Experts did not appear before the court-case was prepared. Roses, rather than hatred were these first days a gift to us all, directly from the surviving youths.

But it was a penal court

The court proceedings lasted ten weeks. It was a penal court. No other solution would have been possible. Even as an ardent believer in restorative justice – or in an alternative board for handling of conflicts, as I like to call these arrangements – I have to admit that I do not think it would have been a feasible alternative to handle a case like this outside the structure of the penal law. But much of what occurred in this court had strong similarities with what often happens in boards for alternative handlings of conflict. Much that went on in this court-caser ought to be crystalized, memorized, and used as models for how penal courts ought to operate in other, more usual cases. Elements of restorative justice ought to penetrate penal courts, not the other way around.

First and foremost, the atrocities of July 22 were not a case between a wrongdoer and a limited number of people. A whole nation was involved. It was a case of one person against most of society. We could not all be there. A suitable forum had to be found.

And that forum had to be an open forum. We all had the right to know. Most meetings of restorative justice take place in closed rooms without media-attention. That is most often a necessity to assure free talk in that form of handling of conflicts. A penal court has to operate according to the opposite principle in an open society. And the court (Oslo tingrett) lived up to that expectation. Before the proceedings commenced, a 29 pages document was distributed. Here the principle and plans for the proceedings were outlined. Altogether, some 2500 persons would have the right to attend the case. 700 journalists from 200 different media-companies from all over the world had asked for accreditation. The interior of the courthouse in the centre of Oslo was re-arranged. The major courtroom here could now give space to 193 persons, - it was planned for daily attendance of some 100 persons close to the deceased and 90 journalists. Others with rights to attend, and the remaining media had seven other courtrooms to their disposal in the building, and also rooms in a nearby hotel. These rooms were provided with large TV screens transmitting all that occurred in the major courtroom. In addition, 17 courts from North to South in the country were provided with the same equipment for those with the right to attend. Our National Broadcasting Company presented also most of what happened, in addition to numerous interviews and comments.

An additional reason for the impossibility of the use of alternative conflict-handling in this case, was that the culprit did not, and does not regret his acts. He stubbornly sees himself as a heroic soldier who had to do what he did. A martyr. He was engaged in a holy war. A saviour of the country and of Christianity from the invasion of Muslims, and also (what has received less attention) from cultural Marxism and feminism. He has spread a manuscript of more than 1500 pages with that message. He killed to rescue Norway. And Norway is not yet rescued, according to his standards. He fought a one-man war from the extreme right. He regrets nothing he says. Now he was demobilized. He could not be trusted outside. He was, and is, a dangerous man. In addition comes, that he probably soon would have been killed by someone if not protected by walls.

Roses in Courts

But as it all developed, vital restorative ideals were cared for during the proceedings. The court became an arena for creating a national understanding of what had happened, a very efficient arena due to the exceptionally well-organized communication system from the courtroom to the rest of the population. The victims have been met with quite exceptional attention. The most moving example: Experts in forensic medicine explained what had caused the death in each individual case. It was all described in the most minute details Connected to each case, a large picture of the killed victim was exposed. After the doctors description of why and how death had occurred, a short memory speech was held, a speech describing the person as she or he had been in their short lives. After a week with the death, the next week gave room to survivors, many with visible marks from heavy wounds.

Never, ever, in modern times have so many victims been given so much attention in a Norwegian court. In addition came that the relatives of the killed as well as all survivors who so wanted were supported with one or several lawyers, a sort of assistant attorneys. More than 170 such assistant attorneys were engaged in the case. These assistant attorneys create some principle problems of balance in court. Most often they side with the prosecutors. It adds up to 172 prosecutors against two for defence.

In court the killer was mostly met with courtesy. He did wear ordinary civil cloths. His handcuffs were removed. He showed a sort of Nazi-greetings while entering the courtroom the first few days, but abandoned the praxis until leaving the court on the very last day. The prosecutor shook hand with him and he was examined without pronounced aggression. In a one-hour monologue he was allowed to explain the political ideas behind his acts.

The atmosphere in the court has been quiet, serious, – often desperately sad. A sort of funeral, day after day. With one exception. A man cried out; „Go to hell, you killer of my brother." Then he threw one of his shoes in the direction of the killer. It was a symbolic act of denigration, – he was from Iraq. The shoe hit one of the defenders. Several in the room applauded. But a block away, I think it was the same day or the day before, some 40 000 people had assembled on a huge square facing the building of our Labour party – on the initiative on some youngsters on face-book. Together they sang „Children of the rain-bow", a song the killer had said he hated. It is a song for children of all colours.

On delivery of pain

So far, so good, also in a restorative perspective. But it is in a penal court this takes place. It is a court to decide three elements:

If he is guilty?

If guilty, is he fit for punishment?

If fit for punishment; what is the suitable amount of pain he ought to receive?

As to guilt: He admits to the killings, but does not see himself as guilty. He sees himself as a commander in a holy war. A Christian soldier in war. So, here the court had, seemingly, an easy case. Guilty.

Mad mans work?

But then comes the next question in a penal court: May be this man is not an ordinary man? May be he is insane and can't be punished? To find out, experts on insanity were brought in.

Already before the court case opened, two forensic psychiatrists had investigated the mind of the killer. They declared him insane. Schizophrenic paranoia. A simple way to make him different from most of us. The whole report was supposed to be kept secret, but extensive leaks revealed that the psychiatrists, in addition to talks and tests, to a large extent based their diagnosis on his acts – the atrocities – without considering the political framework of it all. Acting like this, and writing about it as he had, to the forensic psychiatrists it became the final proof that he was insane.

The diagnosis raised a folk-storm. The victims - survivors and persons who had lost someone through his acts – asked for a new forensic observation. Prosecution protested, but the court accepted. A new pair of observers was called in. They declared him sane.

A baroque situation. The two pairs of forensic psychiatrists have through the ten weeks of proceedings been seated side by side on first row in the courtroom, facing the offender. The one pair seeing a man they have placed outside normality and therefore bound for mental hospital, the other pair facing a person they see as peculiar, but not more than that he is fit for punishment.

But this strange situation had a good side. The disagreement between the experts allowed the judges to regain control of what happened in court by revealing contradictions. Disagreement between experts made them vulnerable for critique and opened for sharp examination. Experts lost heir glory, the court could function as a court, and the judges were not only secretaries for the experts.

The court decided that he was sane, – to the great relief to many among us. A diagnosis of insanity would have been a helpful way to externalize him, convert him to a being different from most of us. But he is a Norwegian – like me. Same social class. For a time, I lived close to his neighbourhood. Why him? Where did he find his models, – and ideas? Or more threatening; is it something in being Norwegian that made this possible? We live in a culture pre-occupied with material success. And in a country quite recently engaged in several wars. When Norwegian pilots returned from Libya after what was supposed to be the successful bombing there, our minister of defence at the time received them with thanks for their accomplishments in bombing.

The more we make the man behind July 22 an evil, a monster, or an insane, the less we are able to understand the roots we have in common with him and also what we ought to change in the country if we want it restored to standards we can accept to live with.

A diagnosis of insanity would also have created another problem: Such a diagnosis hides the normality of killing. Relatively many are able to carry out the most awful of acts against other people; from electric shocks to torture to mass-extermination. They are not mad. They are ordinary, placed in situations that make these acts possible. It is not only a question of the banality of evil, but on understanding elements of how hell can be created as a matter of routine. Again we must ask; what is it with us, and also the global political situation, that makes such behaviour possible? How can we improve on the system to make killing less attractive? The challenge is to create social circumstances that make us all able to see the human being, – also in the killer.

The sentence

The court sentenced him to 21 years in preventive detention with a minimum time of ten years, and with an additional clause that would enable the state to keep him in prison for an unlimited amount of five-year periods if he still was considered dangerous. If not seen as dangerous, he will have to be released considerably earlier, may be after some 15 to 20 years.

Many, and particularly journalists from abroad (there were several hundred of them on the case) expressed surprise by what they found to be an extremely lenient sentence. But how could it have been more severe if we want to remain true to basic legal principles?

Lady Justice is most often presented with a sword in one hand and a scale in the other. The amount of punishment has to be balanced against the amount of evil acts committed. Not too much, not too little. But what then when the evil acts becomes overwhelmingly terrible? How then to create balance?

How could the man who committed these atrocities ever pay back what he has done? Pay back in personal suffering? The man behind these killings belongs to the first division of evildoers in modern western history. Adolf Eichmann killed millions, but stood in some ways more distant from the concrete acts. Eichmann did it out of his office, an administrator of extermination. The man in Norway made and detonated the bomb himself. He then shot the teenagers on the island, moving around, slowly, systematically killing everyone he saw. He spared some small children. As he saw it, they were not dangerous. They had not yet been indoctrinated to accept Muslims to the country.

A punishment balancing the acts of the Norwegian killer is out of question. What he has done can never be paid back on him. Altogether he killed 77 persons. Should we bring him to the gallows 76 times, without hanging him, but let that happen on transport 77? A catastrophe has occurred, one that can only be met by adhering to the basic values of Norwegian society. Atrocities can never be balanced with the production of a similar amount of pain. We cannot answer atrocities with equal-to-equal. It has to be something less.

To find standards for this more limited answer, we must ask for help in old-fashioned values of forgiveness and grace. But to mobilize forgiveness and grace, one element is essential: We must come close enough to see him as more than a killer, we must be able to see him as a human being, simply as one of us.

The killer as one of us

This brings me to the core of what has been my personal as well as scientific interest throughout much of my life: The question about the conditions for, and consequences of coming close to others. So close, through life or art, that it becomes possible to recognize elements of common humanity in all sorts of people.

I believe that the more we are enabled to see each other as fellow human beings, the more we are controlled by that knowledge, and by the whole set of norms ingrained in us throughout life on how to behave towards people of all sorts, from babies to old folks. To see the other is to be captured in the web of norms that

makes us human. The closer we come to another person, the stronger stand the inhibitions against handling that person in ways seen as unacceptable within the culture where we belong. To accomplish this is to me the great challenge for most sorts of crime-preventive work.

The killer himself wanted to be seen as something extraordinary. A commander in war. He wanted to wear a policeman's uniform on his first day in court when he was formally imprisoned. That was of course not accepted. He has been active as a body builder, and has also gone through surgery to look even more the perfect man. It is not particularly easy to see him as an ordinary human being, one of us.

The end

The judge read her verdict on August 24, 2012. No appeals followed, and on September 7 the sentence was legally valid. Never has the word relief been used more often" was the headline in Aftenposten, the largest newspaper in the country. Their editorial the day after the sentence had become legally valid had the title: "Clarification and relief".

I think they captured the mood of the population. It is even confirmed by some research. For years, there have been international studies of the existence of trust in various countries. Norwegians seem to trust each other more than inhabitants in most other nations according to these studies, and even more so in the months just after the atrocities. Now we are back to normal, but still at the top[1]. I think this has to do with that we live in welfare state, we are not so many, five millions, and we have – not yet, – created large internal class differences. We are still able to see each other.

But I fear the future. Money might be a killer of social cohesion. It is far from certain that our present oil-lubricated affluence will become a blessing for Norway. We all get more affluent, but the top level to an extent that threaten our up to now relatively egalitarian society. For a conference on crime prevention, I think it is of the greatest importance to warn against a development towards life forms where we loose each other as members of the same society.

---

[1]   Dag Wollebæk, Bernard Enjolras, Kari Steen-Johnsen og Guro Ødegård: Tillit i Norge etter 22 juli. Pp. 29-58 in:Helge Skirbekk og Harald Grimen: Tillut i Norge. Res Publica 2012.

Caroline L. Davey and Andrew. B. Wootton

The Crime Prevention Capability Maturity Model

Policy makers and practitioners across Europe recognise the value of considering crime prevention within urban design, planning and development. However, standard principles and practices do not transfer easily across different contexts. The issue of transferability was explored by the EU-funded research project, Planning Urban Security (PLuS). The project resulted in the *Crime Prevention Capability Maturity Model (CPCMM)*—a means of analysing and classifying approaches to crime prevention in relation to the capabilities required for their implementation. The CPCMM model enables the degree to which crime prevention is 'professionalised' and embedded within formal urban planning and design processes to be mapped. The model supports those responsible for the urban environment in their efforts to improve security and quality of life for citizens.

1.0 The widening remit of design

Design Against Crime began as a UK initiative to improve security by embedding crime prevention within design education and practice, with the aim to make everyday products and places less vulnerable to crime. Initiated in 1999 by the UK Home Office, Design Council and Department of Trade & Industry, *Design Against Crime* demonstrates to users and to wider society the value of adopting a design-led approach to security. Good design is focused on the human user, and designers have the ability to creatively reframe problems, gain insight from user research and develop innovative solutions. Through the application of these skills to crime issues, designers can potentially improve security—without increasing fear of crime, inconveniencing the user or creating unattractive products and environments. Design solutions are made less vulnerable to crime by integrating crime prevention concepts within meaningful and effective design thinking and practice—rather than by retrofitting security devices after a problem emerges. Over the last decade, the role of design in addressing social and societal challenges has expanded (Burns *et al, 2006*). *Design Against Crime* has been positioned as part of a movement to help policy makers, practitioners and industry address complex social issues related to crime and security. Tackling crime and anti-social behaviour, reducing feelings of insecurity and improving urban wellbeing are all priorities for policy makers and citizens.

In partnership with Greater Manchester Police (GMP), the *Design Against Crime Solution Centre* was established at the University of Salford in 2003. The scope of Solution Centre projects has expanded to include: (i) supporting designers in their efforts to consider crime prevention within the design process; (ii) working with stakeholders to support the delivery of crime prevention services; and (iii) embedding crime prevention within urban planning and design.

Design and research undertaken by the Solution Centre has supported the improvement of crime prevention services delivered by GMP's Architectural Liaison Unit to planners and architects working in Greater Manchester. This paper presents the *Crime Prevention Maturity Model*, based on research conducted in several European countries as part of the *Planning Urban Security* (PLuS) project. The model has been designed to support stakeholders across Europe in embedding crime prevention within urban design and planning. It is currently being used by the State CID of Lower Saxony (*Landeskriminalamt Niedersachsen*) to improve delivery mechanisms in Germany.

2.0 Theoretical approach

Within the urban environment, crime, anti-social behaviour and insecurity are generally addressed using an approach termed *Crime Prevention Through Environmental Design* (CPTED). Formulated in the United States in the 1970s, CPTED aims to design out crime from the urban environment, and has been implemented to varying degrees across the world. In the UK, Home Office research focused on the decision-making approach of criminals, resulting in *Situational Crime Prevention* (SCP) theory being adopted in the 1980s. Both CPTED and SCP are based on scientific evidence that reducing criminal opportunities reduces crime, with 'opportunity' being recognised as a fundamental causal factor in the occurrence of crime (Felson & Clarke, 1998; Farrell, 2013).

The body of scientific evidence supporting the value of design in crime prevention has grown significantly over the last two decades. Improved security is credited with reversing the dramatic and sustained rise in crime that occurred from the 1960s to the 1990s, affecting countries across the world to a greater or less degree. Better design and security of residential dwellings has resulted in common crimes such as burglary being significantly reduced (Farrell, 2013; van Dijk *et al*, 2007; van Dijk, 2012/13).

3.0 Standard principles, policies and guidance

Applied research has established design principles for urban security relating to aspects such as 'natural surveillance', access control, sense of ownership and management and maintenance. These principles are commonly illustrated with examples of good practice from specific development projects and shared to enable their replication in other locations. However, such case study examples rarely describe the context dependent structures, processes and capabilities that are often critical to their successful implementation. There has tended to be reliance on copying endpoint solutions that work elsewhere, rather than on understanding the mechanisms and structures that have enabled them to be developed and implemented.

A review of practice in Europe shows that crime prevention is being implemented through a range of delivery mechanisms, including: accreditation schemes (UK, Netherlands; Germany); crime prevention services that check development designs when they are submitted for planning approval (UK; Netherlands; France; Austria); and a police consultancy service tailored to the needs of architects, developers and planners (Greater Manchester, UK).

Guidance is available on approaches to addressing crime issues within urban design and planning processes (e.g. UK's *Safer Places* document published by the ODPM in 2004), but its dependence upon specific national planning and development procedures make it difficult to apply across different country contexts. This seriously limits the practical transferability of crime prevention measures described by such context-dependent guidance.

In Europe, resources have been invested in the development of a European Standard in Urban Design and Planning (Technical Report CEN TR 14383-2). This EU Standard does not prescribe solutions, but outlines process-based principles for the design, planning and management of urban environments. Drawing on a traditional project management approach, it provides guidance on establishing a project team, identifying problems and developing and implementing solutions. However, the voluntary standard is not accepted across the whole of Europe, and has failed to be translated into a compulsory 'norm'. In 2007, it was formally accepted as a 'technical paper' intended to guide good practice (CEN, 2007).

4.0 Planning Urban Security in Europe

The issue of transferability to different settings was explored by the EU-funded *Planning Urban Security* (PLuS) research project, led by the State CID in Lower Saxony (*Landeskriminalamt Niedersachsen*) in Germany. PLuS set out to develop transferable measures for crime prevention by reviewing design and planning interventions addressing crime and related social issues in four European cities—Hanover (DE), Manchester (UK), Szczecin (PL) and Vienna (AT). In addition, empirical research was conducted to understand the specific context in each urban location. The findings revealed a number of issues affecting the transferability of best practice:

- Problems of crime, anti-social behaviour and insecurity varied considerably in type and intensity across the different contexts.
- The extent to which crime prevention was embedded within policing, design, planning and urban management also varied significantly.
- The PLuS research study areas displayed very different characteristics, some of which had implications for the potential effectiveness of CPTED principles. These included age of residents, housing tenure, level of place attachment and level of interaction between neighbours. Furthermore, it could not be assumed that the project areas were representative of each particular country (or even region) being studied.

The research team identified that while the project approach adopted by the European Standard (CEN, 2007) may support a team of stakeholders in tackling a pre-existing crime problem, it appeared less suited to the process of embedding crime prevention within broader urban design and planning activities. Interestingly, the idea of a 'standard' or 'norm' did not appear to fit comfortably with police forces and city authorities committed to responding to local needs and conditions.

The *Design Against Crime Solution Centre* worked with the State CID in Lower Saxony and its project partners to develop an alternative approach. This resulted in the *Crime Prevention Capability Maturity Model (CPCMM)*—a means of analysing and classifying approaches to crime prevention in relation to the capabilities required for their implementation. The model is based on knowledge from the design-led crime prevention (Davey & Wootton, 2008), design management and business process improvement literature—in particular, the Capability Maturity Model developed by Carnegie Mellon University (www.cmu.edu).

5.0 Crime Prevention Capability Maturity Model

The Crime Prevention Capability Maturity Model maps the degree to which crime prevention is embedded within professional design practice. Effective crime prevention is one aspect of the practice and management of design.

Figure 1. The Crime Prevention Capability Maturity Model

The Capability Maturity Model (CMM) concept was developed by Carnegie Mellon University as a way of mapping the execution of an organisation's management processes. The CMM approach suggests that business improvement results from incremental changes to such processes and ultimately to their optimisation. Such improvement is the result of discrete, evolutionary steps, rather than revolutionary innovations. The CMM provides a framework for categorising organisational processes according to different levels of 'maturity' and supports efforts to ensure continuous process improvement.

Within the original CMM, there are five levels of maturity for assessing an organisation's processes and evaluating its capability—from 'initial' to 'optimising' (Paulk et al, 1999). Each level comprises a set of process goals that, when satisfied, both stabilise part of the process, and increase the capability of the organisation.

As part of the PLuS project, the Solution Centre adapted the CMM concept to support the development of systems and processes that integrate crime prevention into routine urban planning and design processes. Processes relating to urban management are not currently included within the Crime Prevention Capability Maturity Model.

The Model begins by considering the response to *existing problems* related to crime, anti-social behaviour or insecurity amongst key stakeholders. A crime-related problem may act as a trigger for action, usually in the form of a one-off project. Stakeholders responsible for tackling such problems within the urban environment typically include police, local authorities, city managers, planners and architects, who will usually work in partnership to address the problem. It should be noted that the authors are applying the Capability Maturity Model to a group of organisations, rather than to a single enterprise as envisaged by Carnegie Mellon University.

The Crime Prevention Capability Maturity Model (CPCMM) enables the degree to which crime prevention is embedded within professional urban design practice to be mapped, detailing levels 1, 2, 3 and 4 as follows:

(1) **Initial** – One-off development projects focused on addressing existing crime or insecurity issues

(2) **Repeatable** – Crime prevention considered in strategic urban development plans and/or key development projects

(3) **Managed** – Crime prevention considered within planning control process for all projects (planning approval review)

(4) **Embedded** – Crime prevention integrated within design development process (design stage consultation).

CPCMM Level 1 focuses on a response to an existing problem. It can therefore be seen as reactive, and thus is termed **crime reduction**. Levels 2, 3 and 4 concentrate on measures to prevent problems from arising in the first place. Its activities are proactive, and can be termed **crime prevention.** This distinction between reactive and proactive strategies is important to make within urban security, but one that is rarely explicit. The CPCMM maps the increasing integration of crime prevention within the urban planning process, highlighting opportunities for crime prevention to impact on **planning decisions** via the planning approval process. Beyond urban planning, the upper level of the model contextualises effective crime prevention as one aspect of the professional practice and management of design.

As can be seen, movement through the CPCMM relates to a concurrent process of 'increasing **professionalisation**' running through all four levels. This relates not only to education and qualifications, but to Continuous Professional Development strategies and methods for ensuring high standards of performance. When stakeholders attempt to move to a higher level, resources will need to be invested in improving the professional competence of existing staff, recruiting new staff and purchasing additional facilities or equipment. The goal is not simply to strive to reach level 4, but to seek to attain and achieve a level of crime prevention capability that is commensurate with the operating context of the organisation— including the problems being experienced and the resources available. Increased capability brings benefits in terms of ability to prevent crime, but incurs a cost. Costs and benefits must therefore be considered and balanced when seeking improvement in capability.

6.0 Crime prevention capabilities and contexts

The Crime Prevention Capability Maturity Model outlines the characteristics of each level of capability. These have been divided into "Essential features" and "Optional features":

1. Initial – One-off development projects focused on addressing existing crime or insecurity issues. At Level 1 capability, a security issue is addressed within certain projects, and is ad hoc. Skills and knowledge are brought together on the project, but may be disbanded afterwards. Nevertheless, the opportunity exists to learn from and repeat the project in other similar contexts. Indeed in some cases a successful 'one-off' project may form the first step in a longer term, more widely applicable strategic process.

Essential features	Optional features
• Awareness of crime/security problem at senior decision-maker level (e.g. via local/regional crime data, resident surveys or previous crime prevention projects) • Team with necessary authority and commitment, and some knowledge of crime prevention • Access to appropriate guidance and good practice exemplars.	• Crime prevention promoted through high profile project with good media coverage • Crime prevention considered within selection criteria for those involved in development project (e.g. architect with previous experience).

Table 1: Initial level – Essential and optional features

Examples of Level 1 activity include a project in Szczecin (Poland) to renovate courtyard areas of a residential block that attracted crime and antisocial behaviour, leading to insecurity amongst residents. Voivodeship Police Headquarters worked with local partner organisations to renovate the courtyards and establish a maintenance programme supported by residents.

2. Repeatable – Crime prevention considered in strategic urban development plans and/or key development projects. At Level 2 capability, consideration of crime prevention is more formalised. Consequently, senior management and/or political commitment is necessary and agreed protocols for delivery processes are needed. This is an opportunity for formal crime prevention partnerships to develop, and/or an accreditation scheme for buildings that meet specific standards.

Essential features	Optional features
• Stated local political interest in preventing crime through urban development • Senior commitment from organisations involved in delivering crime prevention (e.g. police, planning authorities, other stakeholders). This may result from demonstrator project(s) to illustrate value of crime prevention • Agreed protocol(s) for routinely considering crime prevention within strategic urban development projects • Availability of designated individuals to advise and deliver on crime prevention objectives • Access to guidance and good practice materials agreed by delivery partners.	• Award or accreditation scheme for good crime prevention design projects.

Table 2: Repeatable level – Essential and optional features

Following a series of pilot projects, the federal state of Lower Saxony in Germany moved to Level 2 capability when it established the "Security Partnership in Urban Development in Lower Saxony" (*Sicherheitspartnerschaft im Städtebau in Niedersachsen*, SIPA). As part of this, a quality audit scheme for secure living (QSN) has been established (http://www.sipa-niedersachsen.de). The partnership includes police, local planning authorities, housing associations and business, and results in crime issues being raised when considering quality of life within urban planning.

3. Managed – Crime prevention considered within planning control process for all projects (planning approval review). At Level 3 capability, consideration of crime prevention is embedded within the planning control processes. To achieve this, local planning legislation may be required. Consequently, legal processes and criteria for assessment and enforcement are needed.

Essential features	Optional features
• A formal planning control process that is transparent and free from corruption • A municipal authority and planning department committed to taking a proactive approach to design-led crime prevention • Agreed protocol(s) for addressing crime prevention within the planning control process. For example, applicants might be made aware of need to meet crime prevention criteria and designs might be reviewed by crime prevention experts prior to approval for construction • Validated (effective) criteria against which to assess development projects (communicated via website, brochures and guidance material) • Sufficient design-led crime prevention experts to meet delivery deadlines of planning approval process.	• Supporting policies and planning legislation at national, regional or local government level.

Table 3: Managed level – Essential and optional features

Level 3 can be illustrated by Vienna City Council in Austria, where despite low levels of actual crime, safety and security are considered within the planning control process. Initiated by the City Council's "Women's Office" (*Frauenbüro*), women's safety and security is covered within its "gender mainstreaming" strategy, and applied to criteria for the assessment of planning applications. Plans for residential developments are reviewed by an Advisory Committee and, if judged to comply with the strategy, are eligible for a government subsidy. Consequently, safety is considered within most plans for residential developments in Vienna.

4. Embedded – Crime prevention integrated within design development process (design stage consultation). At Level 4 capability, consideration of safety and security is integrated within the professional practice of design—as one aspect of professional 'good practice'. At this level, crime prevention advice takes on a consultation role within the development process, with early-stage engagement to best suit the design and development process.

Essential features	Optional features
• Crime and security issues considered from early concept stage of design development process – Benefits of early consideration (including cost and design quality) is understood by stakeholders. The Need to consider crime/security issues is raised at initial meeting with planning authorities • Crime prevention experts capable of design consultation role, rather than just assessment role – Knowledge of development industry (e.g. architecture or planning background) and ability to communicate effectively with designers • Agreed protocol(s) for routinely considering crime prevention within all urban design projects • Access to and support for design-led crime prevention experts – Access to relevant crime statistics. Acquire and maintain necessary knowledge and skills.	• Fee paying crime prevention design consultation service within public sector. May be used to fund additional staff / resources required for increased crime prevention consultation provision • Dedicated crime incidence mapping and analysis function to support design decision-making – e.g. crime geographic mapping using Geographic Information Systems (GIS) technology.

Table 4: Embedded level – Essential and optional features

An example of practice that is moving towards the Level 4 capability is that of the Greater Manchester Police *Design for Security* consultancy service in Greater Manchester, UK. Consultants review all major building development projects submitted for planning approval. As local authorities have made it a condition for applicants to submit a *Crime Impact Statement (CIS)* with their application for planning approval, architects and developers are retaining *Design for Security* consultants at an early stage of the design process, incorporating their advice into the final design. The CIS contains contextual information about crime risk, as well as a review of the vulnerability of the proposed design. Early stage consultation benefits architects and developers by allowing advice to be easily incorporated into the design. GMP is able to charge a consultancy fee for this professional service, thereby covering the cost to the police of its delivery.

7.0 Conclusion

The Crime Prevention Capability Maturity Model was developed as a framework to help stakeholders understand and map their delivery of crime prevention. Importantly, the model covers three issues: (i) the shift in thinking and practice required to move from reactive crime reduction to proactive crime prevention; (ii) differences in scale and quality associated with alternative approaches; and (iii) the differing contextual factors and conditions underpinning any capability for successful crime prevention delivery.

A framework, not a prescription

The *Solution Centre* does not dictate any single approach or method for delivering crime prevention. In addition, as local conditions vary so much the model is not meant to suggest an automatic escalation to Level 4. The State CID in Lower Saxony has just begun a research project to help improve crime prevention and quality of life through urban design and planning (www.transit-online.info). However, German stakeholders remain sceptical about the benefits of integrating crime prevention within their planning approval process. The German process already considers quality of life for residents/users, and there are concerns that embedding crime prevention would incur additional costs and increased bureaucracy. The CPCMM provides a starting point for exploring the extent to which crime prevention is already integrated into planning, and the costs and benefits of further investment in the approach.

Learning from best practice

Methods for delivering crime prevention often arise from specific local conditions and contexts, and transference to other locations may not be possible or even desirable. For example, the Greater Manchester Police *Design for Security* service is held up as an example of best practice in the UK. However, it was developed in response to specific contextual problems and opportunities, so adoption by other countries may be limited by differing contextual factors. These might range from rules preventing the police from acting as paid consultants, through restrictions on the use of conditional planning policies, to a lack of practical skills in design-led crime prevention.

Valuing design-led crime prevention

While methods for delivering crime prevention vary across Europe, the authors nonetheless believe that there are benefits to embedding it within the early stages of the design process. When this is achieved, designers are able to understand all needs and requirements, use their creative skills to generate solutions and better integrate solutions into the design. This early stage integration is much preferable to 'retro-fitting' unsympathetic security devices after the design is complete.

Evolving practice

The process of developing a European Standard for urban design and planning has enabled experts in crime prevention from across Europe to share knowledge and develop a common terminology and approach. To better engage different stakeholder groups, the handbook *Planning Urban Design and Management for Crime Prevention* (2007) was published in English, French, Italian and Spanish. Effort continues to be invested in supporting development and implementation through European initiatives such as EU COST Action TU1203 *Crime Prevention through Urban Design & Planning*. The work of COST Action TU1203 is highlighting the benefit of conceptual models of crime prevention practice that can be applied across contexts, without the need for standardisation. This also underlines the value of design in helping stakeholders conceptualise their practice in ways that can be meaningfully shared across contexts.

Acknowledgements

The authors would like to thank: Dr Anke Schröder, Dirk Behrmann (LKA NI); Dr Melissa Marselle, Mike Hodge (Design Against Crime Solution Centre); Dr Günter Stummvoll, Dr Helmut Floegl, Alexander Neumann (Donau-Universität Krems); Dorota Silewicz, Andrzej Szraijber (Voivodeship Police Headquarters Szczecin).

References

Burns, C., Cottam, H., Vanstone, C. and Winhall, J (2006) "Transformation Design". *RED paper 02*. UK Design Council: London. Download from: http://www.designcouncil.info/mt/RED/transformationdesign/TransformationDesignFinalDraft.pdf

Davey, C.L. and Wootton, A.B. (2008) *"Design Against Crime Exchange Tool. Guidance for Designing Against Crime across Europe"*. University of Salford: Salford, UK.

Farrell, G. (2013) "Five Tests for a Theory of the Crime Drops". Paper presented at International Symposium on Environmental Criminology and Crime Analysis (ECCA), Philadelphia, US. Available from http://www.crimesciencejournal.com/content/2/1/5

Felson, M. and Clarke, R.V. (1998) "Opportunity Makes the Thief: Practical Theory for Crime Prevention", *Police Research Paper 98*. London, Home Office.

ODPM (2004) "Safer Places. The Planning System and Crime Prevention". Office of the Deputy Prime Minister. Thomas Telford Ltd: Tonbridge, UK.

Paulk, M. C.; Weber, C. V.; and Chrissis, M. B., "The Capability Maturity Model: A Summary" (1999). Institute for Software Research. Paper 2. http://repository.cmu.edu/isr/2

Politecnico di Milano (2010) Planning Urban Design and Management for Crime Prevention Handbook. Politecnico di Milano, Laboratorio Qualita Urbana e Sicurezza's SAFEPOLIS project.

van Soomeren, P. (2007) "Annex 15 – The European Standard for the Reduction of Crime and Fear of Crime by Urban Planning and Building Design: ENV 14383–2", Technical Report CEN/TR 14383–2, October 2007.

Van Dijk, J. (2012/13) "The International Crime Victims Survey. The Latest Results and Prospects", *Criminology in Europe. Newsletter of the European Society of Criminology,* Vol. 11, pp.24-33. Download from:http://escnewsletter.org/node/108.

Van Dijk, J., van Kesteren, J. and Smit, P (2007) Criminal Victimisation in International Perspective. Key findings from the 2004 – 2005 ICVS and EU ICS. WODC: Den Haag, Netherlands.

Wootton, A.B. & Davey, C.L. (2012) "Embedding Crime Prevention within Design", in Ekblom, P. (Guest Ed), "Design Against Crime. Crime Proofing Everyday Products". Crime Prevention Series, Vol. 27, Ronald.V. Clarke, (Series Editor).

Websites

Planning Urban Security: http://www.lka.niedersachsen.de/praevention/vorbeugung_themen_und_tipps/staedtebau-152.html

COST Action TU1203:

http://www.cost.eu/domains_actions/tud/Actions/TU1203

Noël Klima / Belinda Wijckmans

European Crime Prevention Network (EUCPN): Crime prevention activities at the EU, national and local level[1]

1. Introduction

In the past decennia, crime prevention became more and more relevant to public policies and to the implementation of crime strategies in the EU. This has had an effect on how crime and safety have been approached across the different EU Member States, as it is linked to the widespread acknowledgement that causes of crime go beyond the reach of the traditional criminal justice systems.[2] As defined by article 2.2 of the Council Decision 2009/902/JHA, which lies at the basis of the European Crime Prevention Network (EUCPN): *"Crime prevention covers all measures that are intended to reduce or otherwise contribute to reducing crime and citizens' feeling of insecurity, both quantitatively and qualitatively, either through directly deterring criminal activities or through policies and actions designed to reduce the potential for crime and the causes of crime. It includes work of government, competent authorities, criminal justice agencies, local authorities and the specialist associations they have set up in Europe, the private and voluntary sectors, researchers and the public, supported by the media".*[3]

According to scholars, cooperation and partnerships in crime prevention and community safety and the connection to wider social and urban policies became essential to take into account the broader context that is needed to approach crime and its causes.[4] Cooperation in crime prevention can be found at the local level, in local crime prevention projects and programmes, in city-to-city cooperation, in region-to-region networks, certainly between countries, at the European level and not least at the international level. The development of crime prevention strategies and policies varies a lot across Europe according to the different political and cultural traditions and socioeconomic conditions of the Member States.[5]

---

[1] In the framework of the project 'Towards a European Centre of Expertise on Crime Prevention' – With the financial support from the Prevention of and Fight against Crime Programme of the European Union, European Commission – Directorate-General Home Affairs. Legal notice: The contents of this publication do not necessarily reflect the official opinions of any EU Member State or any agency or institution of the European Union or European Communities.

[2] Crawford, A. (1998). Community Safety Partnerships. Criminal Justice Matters, 33: 4-5.

[3] Council Decision 2009/902/JHA of 30 November 2009 setting up a European Crime Prevention Network (EUCPN) and repealing Decision 2001/427/JHA [OJ L 321, 8.12.2009, p. 44–46]. http://eur-lex.europa.eu/LexUriServ/LexUriServ.do?uri=CELEX:32009D0902:EN:NOT

[4] Crawford, A. (2009). Crime Prevention Policies in Comparative Perspective. Cullompton: Willan Publishing; Hebberecht, P. & Baillergeau, E. (eds.) (2012). Social crime prevention in late modern Europe. A comparative perspective. Brussels: VUB Press; Hebberecht, P. & Duprez, D. (eds) (2002). The prevention and security policies in Europe. Brussels: VUB Press.

[5] For an overview of national crime prevention strategies, see http://eucpn.org/strategies/index.asp.

The EUCPN has grown within this diverse context with the aim to connect the local, national and European level, promoting crime prevention knowledge and practices among the EU Member States. In the first part of this contribution, the EU crime prevention policy context and its history will be outlined, as well as the establishment of the EUCPN as the major Network in Europe on crime prevention issues. Next, the structure of the Network will be presented by explaining how the EUCPN works internally. Also, the EUCPN's activities at the local, national and European level will be highlighted in more detail, by giving examples of initiatives and events which are regularly organized. Finally, an outlook will be given on the future of the EUCPN.

2. EU crime prevention policy history and the establishment of the EUCPN

2.1 The Single European Act (1986) and the Treaty of Amsterdam (1997)

From 1975 onwards, intergovernmental cooperation between the European Member States has been established gradually. First in the fields of police and judicial coope- ration with the TREVI Group where Ministers of Interior and Justice of the Member States came together to collaborate. The initial focus was on counter-terrorism, but it later gradually extended to other areas of crime.

The Single European Act in 1986[6] became a turning point in this process of coop- eration since its aim was to establish a single market in which the free movement of persons – as well as goods, services and capital – was ensured (Art 8a). From that time on, the Community institutions became involved in dealing with judicial cooperation both in criminal and civil matters. In the European integration process, Justice and Home affairs continued to be a matter of intergovernmental cooperation.

With the establishment of an area of freedom, security and justice under the Treaty of Amsterdam in 1997[7], the possibility to establish closer cooperation on Justice and Home affairs was further elaborated.

At the time, article 29 of the Treaty on European Union stated that "*the Union's objec- tive shall be to provide citizens with a high level of safety within an area of freedom, security and justice by developing common action among the Member States in the fields of police and judicial cooperation in criminal matters* [and this] *objective shall be achieved by preventing and combating crime [...]*"[8].

---

[6]   Single European Act [OJ L 169, Volume 30, 29.6.1987] http://eur-lex.europa.eu/JOHtml.do?uri=OJ:L:19 87:169:SOM:EN:HTML.

[7]   Treaty of Amsterdam amending the Treaty on European Union, the Treaties establishing the European Communities and certain related acts [OJ C 340, 10.11.1997, p. 1–144] http://eur-lex.europa.eu/LexUri- Serv/LexUriServ.do?uri=CELEX:11997D/TXT:EN:NOT.

[8]   Treaty on European Union (Consolidated version 1997) [OJ C 340, 10.11.1997, p. 145–172] http://eur-lex. europa.eu/LexUriServ/LexUriServ.do?uri=OJ:C:1997:340:0145:0172:EN:PDF.

Furthermore, the Treaty specified that closer police cooperation could be established directly or through the European Police Office (Europol)[9], and that judicial cooperation could go through the European Judicial Cooperation Unit (Eurojust)[10].

2.2 Council of Tampere 1999

The European Council of Tampere (October 1999) confirmed the importance of effective crime prevention policies. Crime prevention was identified as a common priority both in internal and external policies:

"The exchange of best practices should be developed, the network of competent national authorities for crime prevention and co-operation between national crime prevention organizations should be strengthened and the possibility of a Community funded programme should be explored for these purposes. The first priorities for this co-operation could be juvenile, urban and drug-related crime." [11]

In the document 'The prevention and control of organized crime: a European Union strategy for the beginning of the new millennium'[12], the European Commission identified, among others, priority areas in crime prevention at EU level such as: "preventing penetration of organized crime in the public and the legitimate private sector, strengthening the prevention of organized crime and strengthening partnerships between the criminal justice system and civil society." The idea for setting up a coordinated strategy and bringing together those involved in crime prevention was suggested in the Communication on the prevention of crime in the European Union[13].

2.3 The establishment of the European Crime Prevention Network

The outcome of the Tampere summit in 2000 resulted in the need to establish a platform for information exchange on crime prevention, particularly with regard to urban, juvenile and drug-related crime. This role was given to the European Crime Prevention Network, the establishment of which was proposed by various Member States (Belgium, the Czech Republic, Germany, Spain, France, Hungary, the Netherlands, Slovakia, Finland, Sweden and the United Kingdom) and officially confirmed short-

---

9   Europol https://www.europol.europa.eu/.

10   Eurojust http://eurojust.europa.eu/.

11   The prevention and control of organized crime: a European Union strategy for the beginning of the new millennium [OJ C 124, 3.5.2000] http://eur-lex.europa.eu/LexUriServ/LexUriServ.do?uri=CELEX:32000 F0503:EN:NOT.

12   The prevention and control of organized crime: a European Union strategy for the beginning of the new millennium [OJ C 124, 3.5.2000] http://eur-lex.europa.eu/LexUriServ/LexUriServ.do?uri=CELEX:32000 F0503:EN:NOT.

13   Communication from the Commission to the Council and the European Parliament. The prevention of crime in the European Union. Reflection on common guidelines and proposals for Community financial support [COM(2000) 786 final - Not published in the Official Journal] http://eur-lex.europa.eu/smartapi/ cgi/sga_doc?smartapi!celexplus!prod!DocNumber&lg=en&type_doc=COMfinal&an_doc=2000&nu_ doc=786.

ly afterwards by the Council Decision 2001/427/JHA.[14] From then on, the EUCPN would be responsible for promoting the exchange of information on crime prevention across the EU as a whole to fulfil three specific aims:

- Improve Member States' understanding of the crime phenomenon;
- Develop cooperation and networking among crime prevention stakeholders at all levels of government;
- Strengthen the multidisciplinary approach to crime prevention projects.

2.3.1 Council Decision 2001
Notwithstanding that crime prevention is primarily a matter of the individual Member States, the rationale for cooperation between countries was, and remains, strong. The 2001 Council Decision defined it as the mission of the EUCPN to promote crime prevention activities across the EU and to provide a means to share good practices.[15] The scope of the EUCPN activities was defined in the 2001 Council Decision as mainly, but not exclusively, focusing on volume or traditional crime.

At the same time, the European Commission was in favour of the establishment of a European forum for the prevention of organized crime to deal with various aspects of prevention with regard to economic and financial crime, lawful and unlawful dealings in goods, trafficking in human beings and corruption.[16] This led to the introduction of the Hippocrates programme[17], the EU Organized Crime Threat Assessment (OCTA)[18] and later to the AGIS programme[19].

2.3.2 Communication on Crime Prevention in the European Union 2004
A Communication published by the European Commission in 2004 on 'Crime Prevention in the European Union'[20] took stock of the EUCPN's progress and came to

---

[14] Council Decision 2001/427/JHA of 28 May 2001 setting up a European Crime Prevention Network. [OJ L 153 , 08.06.2001] http://eur-lex.europa.eu/LexUriServ/LexUriServ.do?uri=OJ:L:2001:153:0001:0003:EN:PDF.

[15] Council Decision 2001/427/JHA of 28 May 2001 setting up a European Crime Prevention Network. [OJ L 153 , 08.06.2001] http://eur-lex.europa.eu/LexUriServ/LexUriServ.do?uri=OJ:L:2001:153:0001:0003:EN :PDF.

[16] Communication from the Commission to the Council and the European Parliament. The prevention of crime in the European Union. Reflection on common guidelines and proposals for Community financial support [COM(2000) 786 final - Not published in the Official Journal] http://eur-lex.europa.eu/smartapi/cgi/sga_do c?smartapi!celexplus!prod!DocNumber&lg=en&type_doc=COMfinal&an_doc=2000&nu_doc=786.

[17] Council Decision of 28 June 2001 establishing a programme of incentives and exchanges, training and cooperation for the prevention of crime (Hippocrates) [Official Journal L 186, 07.07.2001].

[18] Organized Crime Threat Assessment (OCTA) https://www.europol.europa.eu/latest_publications/31.

[19] Council Decision 2002/630/JHA of 22 July 2002 establishing a framework programme on police and judicial cooperation in criminal matters (AGIS) [OJ L 203, 01.08.2002] http://eur-lex.europa.eu/LexUriServ/ LexUriServ.do?uri=OJ:L:2002:203:0005:0008:EN:PDF.

[20] Communication from the Commission to the Council and the European Parliament – Crime prevention in the European Union [COM(2004) 165 final, 12.03.2004] http://eur-lex.europa.eu/LexUriServ/LexUri-Serv.do?uri=CELEX:52004DC0165:EN:NOT.

broadly positive conclusions. It noted that the EUCPN had so far achieved good results considering the then existing context. In particular, it highlighted that:

"For the first time ever, Member States representatives and experts have begun meeting regularly to exchange experiences, set a common strategy and priorities for action and research on the basis of annual programs." [21]

The collection of information on crime prevention policies and good practices, conferences, expert meetings and the website of the EUCPN were considered to have been particularly useful to Member States. The Communication also noted the importance of the progress made with regard to the development of a common methodology to prepare, implement and evaluate concrete crime prevention projects.

The Communication emphasised the importance of the role of local authorities and the primary responsibility of the Member States in the field of prevention of volume crime. Nevertheless, EU-level co-operation was also seen as important to "effectively support prevention activities in the Member States, to avoid duplication of efforts and to use resources more efficiently" [22].

2.3.3 The Hague Programme 2004

In 2004, the Hague Programme on 'Strengthening Freedom, Security and Justice in the European Union'[23] reiterated the priorities for the EUCPN. The Hague Council went on to argue that the EUCPN should be professionalised and strengthened. It is noteworthy that in addition to its role in relation to EU Member States, the 2004 Hague Council highlighted the function of the EUCPN in helping the Council and Commission in developing crime prevention policies.

"The Union [...] needs an effective tool to support the efforts of Member States in preventing crime. To that end, the European Crime Prevention Network should be professionalised and strengthened. Since the scope of prevention is very wide, it is essential to focus on measures and priorities that are most beneficial to Member States. The European Crime Prevention Network should provide expertise and knowledge to the Council and the Commission in developing effective crime prevention policies."[24]

---

[21] Communication from the Commission to the Council and the European Parliament – Crime prevention in the European Union [COM(2004) 165 final, 12.03.2004] http://eur-lex.europa.eu/LexUriServ/LexUriServ.do?uri=CELEX:52004DC0165:EN:NOT.

[22] Communication from the Commission to the Council and the European Parliament – Crime prevention in the European Union [COM(2004) 165 final, 12.03.2004] http://eur-lex.europa.eu/LexUriServ/LexUriServ.do?uri=CELEX:52004DC0165:EN:NOT.

[23] The Hague Programme: strengthening freedom, security and justice in the European Union [OJ C 53/1, 03.03.2005] http://eur-lex.europa.eu/LexUriServ/LexUriServ.do?uri=OJ:C:2005:053:0001:0014:EN:PDF.

[24] Presidency Conclusions – Brussels, 4/5 November 2004. Annex 1. The Hague Programme: Strengthening Freedom, Security and Justice in the European Union. [14292/1/04, REV 1, 08.12.2004] http://www.consilium.europa.eu/uedocs/cms_data/docs/pressdata/en/ec/82534.pdf.

The Hague Programme argued that the EUCPN's remit should promote the exchange of experience and ideas between EU Member States. In general, the Hague Programme highlighted the importance of the EUCPN and its introduction of concrete action plans.

2.3.4 The Lisbon Treaty 2007

The Lisbon Treaty[25], which was signed by the Heads of State or Government in December 2007, highlighted crime prevention as integral to the EU's core aim of promoting the well-being of European citizens. According to Article 2.1/2.2:

"The Union's aim is to promote peace, its values and the well-being of its peoples. The Union shall offer its citizens an area of freedom, security and justice without internal frontiers, in which the free movement of persons is ensured in conjunction with appropriate measures with respect to external border controls, asylum, immigration and the *prevention and combating of crime.*"[26]

Reflecting this, Article 84 of the Treaty stated that the European Parliament and the Council, acting in accordance with the ordinary legislative procedure, "may establish measures to promote and support the action of Member States in the field of crime prevention, excluding any harmonisation of the laws and regulations of the Member States." Elsewhere, the treaty set out the EU's role in promoting cooperation between "all the Member States' competent authorities, including police, customs and other *specialised law enforcement services in relation to the prevention, detection and investigation of criminal offences"* (Article 87 - 1)[27].

2.3.5 Council Decision 2009

Following the European Commission's recommendations based on an external evaluation of the EUCPN[28], which was conducted in 2007-2008 under the supervision of the European Commission and which identified several opportunities for strengthening the Network, an informal and internal working group was set up to discuss the future of the Network on the following issues:

---

[25]   Treaty of Lisbon amending the Treaty on European Union and the Treaty establishing the European Community, signed at Lisbon, 13 December 2007 [OJ C 306, 17.12.2007] http://eur-lex.europa.eu/LexUriServ/LexUriServ.do?uri=CELEX:12007L/TXT:EN:NOT.

[26]   Treaty of Lisbon amending the Treaty on European Union and the Treaty establishing the European Community, signed at Lisbon, 13 December 2007 [OJ C 306, 17.12.2007] http://eur-lex.europa.eu/LexUriServ/LexUriServ.do?uri=CELEX:12007L/TXT:EN:NOT.

[27]   Treaty of Lisbon amending the Treaty on European Union and the Treaty establishing the European Community, signed at Lisbon, 13 December 2007 [OJ C 306, 17.12.2007] http://eur-lex.europa.eu/LexUriServ/LexUriServ.do?uri=CELEX:12007L/TXT:EN:NOT.

[28]   Centre for Strategy & Evaluation Services (CSES) (2009). Evaluation of the European Crime Prevention Network. Kent. http://ec.europa.eu/dgs/home-affairs/what-we-do/policies/organized-crime-and-human-trafficking/crime-prevention/docs/evaluation_of_eucpn_final_report_(cses_11_03_09).pdf.

- The role and purpose of the EUCPN and its target groups;
- The EUCPN's website and use of languages;
- The EUCPN Secretariat and financing;
- Issues relating to the Chair, National Representatives, Contact Points, and Committees.

Many proposals of this working group found their way into a new Council Decision 2009/902/JHA on 30 November 2009, repealing the establishing Council Decision 2001/427/JHA.[29] This Council Decision from 2009 still lies at the basis of the EUCPN today.

Article 2.1 of the 2009 Council Decision states:

"The Network shall contribute to developing the various aspects of crime prevention at the Union level, taking account of the European Union crime preventive strategy, and shall support crime prevention activities at the national and local level."

Although this definition was already included in Art.1 of the 2001 Council Decision, the focus was no longer put explicitly on juvenile, urban and drug-related crime after 2009.

The Network's key target groups were governments, competent authorities, criminal justice agencies, local authorities and 'specialist associations', the private and voluntary sectors, researchers and the public, supported by the media.

2.3.6 The Stockholm Programme 2010

The Stockholm Programme[30] reiterated the importance of crime prevention, for example in paragraph 4.3.2 on more effective crime prevention:

"The best way to reduce the level of crime *is to take effective measures to prevent them from ever occurring, including promoting social inclusion, by using a multidisciplinary approach which also includes taking administrative measures and promoting cooperation between administrative authorities, citizens of the Union that have similar experiences and are affected in similar ways by crime and related insecurity in their everyday lives"*.

Art. 4.3.2 argued that *"Member States have developed different methods to prevent crime and should be encouraged to share experiences and best practice.[...] in addition, the cross-border dimension underlines the importance of enhancing and develo-*

---

[29]   Council Decision 2009/902/JHA of 30 November 2009 setting up a European Crime Prevention Network (EUCPN) and repealing Decision 2001/427/JHA [OJ L 321, 08.12.2009, p. 44-46] http://eur-lex.europa. eu/LexUriServ/LexUriServ.do?uri=OJ:L:2009:321:0044:01:EN:HTML.

[30]   The Stockholm Programme — An open and secure Europe serving and protecting citizens [OJ C 115, 4.5.2010, p. 1–38] http://eur-lex.europa.eu/LexUriServ/LexUriServ.do?uri=CELEX:52010XG0504%280 1%29:EN:NOT.

ping knowledge at European level on how crime and criminality in the Member States is interconnected, to support Member States when taking individual or joint action, and to call for action by Union institutions when deemed necessary".

Against this background, the Stockholm Programme set out a very clear vision for the future of the EUCPN. The European Council invited the Commission:

"to submit a proposal building on the evaluation of the work carried out within the European Crime Prevention Network (EUCPN) with a view to setting up an Observatory for the Prevention of Crime (OPC), the tasks of which will be to collect, analyse and disseminate knowledge on crime, including organi*zed crime (including statistics) and crime prevention, to support and promote Member States and Union institutions when they take preventive measures and to exchange best practice."*

To achieve this, the Observatory should build on the work carried out within the framework of the EUCPN and the evaluation of it. It should include or replace the EUCPN, with a secretariat located within an existing Union agency and function as a separate unit. The European Council invited the Commission to submit a proposal on setting up the OPC by 2013 at the latest.

A second external evaluation undertaken at the end of 2012 concluded, however, that it is too early to establish a Crime Prevention Observatory since it does not seem to correspond to a pressing need in the short term and is currently less desirable politically or financially[31]. Hence, for the time being, the Member States have opted to continue the work with the support of the EUCPN Secretariat in its current structure (cfr. infra) and with its current level of resources and to focus instead on the improvement of the Network's functioning by implementing an approved and concrete action plan (see also: 6. Outlook, p.20).

3. Structure/Composition of the EUCPN

Today's structure of the EUCPN and its operating framework date back to 2009, formalized in the Council Decision 2009/902/JHA[32]. The EUCPN's Rules of Procedure[33], which were adopted in 2010, outline the role and responsibilities of the various actors of the Network and define the Network's working terms with regard to the decision-making processes, the formal working language and the collaboration with third parties.

---

[31] Report from the Commission to the Council, Evaluation report on the European Union Crime Prevention Network [COM(2012) 717 final, 30.11.2012] http://ec.europa.eu/dgs/home-affairs/e-library/documents/policies/organized-crime-and-human-trafficking/crime-prevention/docs/20121130_eucpn_report_en.pdf.

[32] Council Decision 2009/902/JHA of 30 November 2009 setting up a European Crime Prevention Network (EUCPN) and repealing Decision 2001/427/JHA [OJ L 321, 08.12.2009, p. 44-46] http://eur-lex.europa.eu/LexUriServ/LexUriServ.do?uri=OJ:L:2009:321:0044:01:EN:HTML.

[33] Rules of Procedure for the European Crime Prevention Network of 30.08.2010. http://eucpn.org/key-papers/index.asp.

As can be seen in figure 1 below, the EUCPN Board consists of a Chair, an Executive Committee (ExCom) and the National Representatives (NRs) from 28 Member States[34], with their Substitutes if appointed. Furthermore, the Network encompasses a permanent Secretariat and National Contact Points (CPs), who may be experts from policy, practice or academia designated by each Member State and who can support the National Representatives in collecting and exchanging national crime prevention information and expertise within the Network.

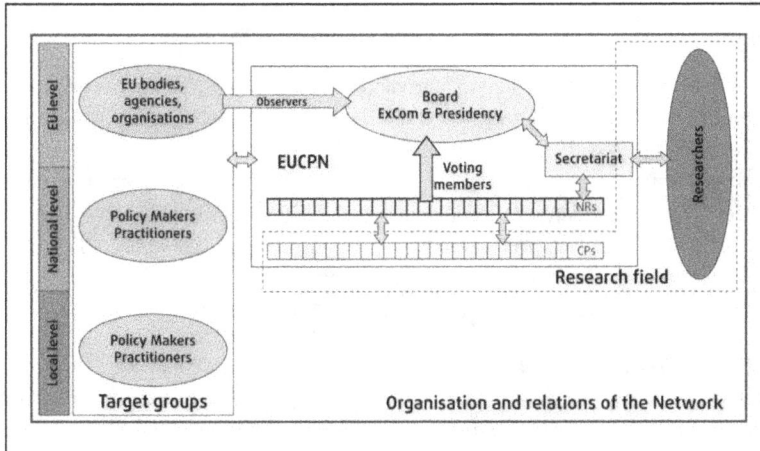

Figure 1: Organization and relations of the EUCPN | ExCom – Executive Committee
NRs – National Representatives
CPs – Contact Points

The **Board** of National Representatives comprises of the voting members of the Network. Each Member State has one vote and together the National Representatives are responsible for the approval of the Network's strategic approach, the realisation of the EUCPN Work Programme and the adoption of the Annual Report of the Network's activities.

The Board is chaired by an appointed Member from within the body of National Representatives. The **Chair** heads the Network and guarantees its working. The position of the Chair is currently rotating every six months according to the Presidency of the Council of the European Union. The Chair convenes and chairs at least one Board Meeting per semester and also chairs the Executive Committee.

Together with the Chair, the **Executive Committee** prepares the strategy and decisions of the Network for approval by the Board. The Executive Committee is composed

---

[34] On 1 July 2013, Croatia became the 28th Member State of the European Union and Member of the EUCPN.

of up to three National Representatives, selected by the Board for the term of 18 months, and three National Representatives from the current and the next two Presidencies of the Council of the European Union. In addition, a representative of the European Commission is attending the Executive Committee as an observer.

The EUCPN **Secretariat** is based in Brussels at the Belgian Federal Public Service Home Affairs and has been fully operational since 2011 with the financial support of the European Commission DG HOME's Prevention of and Fight against Crime Programme (ISEC)[35]. The Secretariat currently consists of three permanent staff members: a coordinator, a research officer and an administrative officer.

The task of the Secretariat is to provide general administrative, technical and analytical support to the Network and to represent the Network externally. It acts as a focal point for communication with the Network Members, identifies ongoing research activities in the field of crime prevention and other related information that would be of use to the Network. The Secretariat hosts and maintains the EUCPN website and is also responsible for delivering systematic output on crime prevention. Finally, through the Secretariat, the Network is closely collaborating with academic researchers and experts in the field bringing together scientific research, policymaking and (local) practice.

The **target groups** of the Network are practitioners and policymakers at both the local and national level, as well as other relevant EU and international agencies, organizations and working groups some of which are non-voting observers.

4. The working of the EUCPN

The European Crime Prevention Network contributes to developing the various aspects of crime prevention at the Union level, taking account of the European Union crime preventive strategy, and supports crime prevention activities and good practices at the national and local level. Article 4 of the Council Decision 2009/902/JHA[36] mentions the following specific tasks for the EUCPN:

- To facilitate cooperation, contacts and exchanges of information and experience between actors in the field of crime prevention;

- To collect, assess and communicate evaluated information including good practice on existing crime prevention activities;

---

[35] Council Decision 2007/125/JHA of 12 February 2007 establishing for the period 2007 to 2013, as part of General Programme on Security and Safeguarding Liberties, the Specific Programme Prevention of and Fight against Crime [OJ L 58, 24.2.2007, p. 7–12] http://eur-lex.europa.eu/LexUriServ/LexUriServ. do?uri=CELEX:32007D0125:EN:NOT.
For more information on the ISEC Programme: http://ec.europa.eu/dgs/home-affairs/financing/fundings/ security-and-safeguarding-liberties/prevention-of-and-fight-against-crime/index_en.htm.

[36] Council Decision 2009/902/JHA of 30 November 2009 setting up a European Crime Prevention Network (EUCPN) and repealing Decision 2001/427/JHA [OJ L 321, 08.12.2009, p. 44-46] http://eur-lex.europa. eu/LexUriServ/LexUriServ.do?uri=OJ:L:2009:321:0044:01:EN:HTML.

- To organize conferences, in particular an annual Best Practice Conference, and other activities, including the annual European Crime Prevention Award, designed to achieve the objectives of the Network and to share widely the results thereof;

- To provide its expertise to the Council and the Commission as required;

- To report to the Council on its activities each year through the Board and the competent working bodies. The Council shall be invited to endorse the report and forward it to the European Parliament;

- To develop and implement a work programme based on a clearly defined strategy that takes account of identifying and responding to relevant crime threats.

4.1 Multiannual Strategy 2011-2015

The EUCPN's basic goals are reaffirmed in the Multiannual Strategy which was adopted by the Board in December 2010 for the period 2011 until the end of 2015, as shown in figure 2 below. The Multiannual Strategy 2011-2015[37] sets out the long-term orientations for the Network.

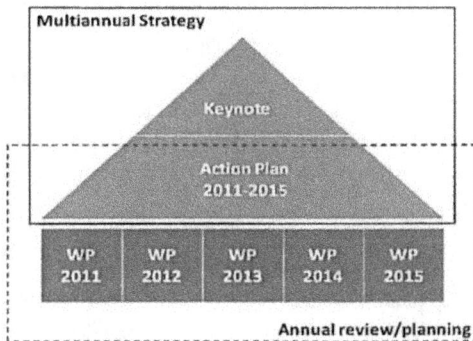

Figure 2: EUCPN's Multiannual Strategy and annual planning

The general objective stipulated in article 2.1 of the Council Decision 2009/902/JHA has been translated into the mission of the Network[38]:

"The Network contributes to the development and the promotion of a multidiscipli-nary and preventive approach to crime *and feelings of insecurity at European level. The Network therefore actively supports policymakers and practitioners of European, national and local level.*"

---

[37] The Multiannual Strategy for the European Crime Prevention Network http://eucpn.org/key-papers/index. asp is complemented by a general 'Keynote to the Multiannual Strategy for EUCPN' http://eucpn.org/key-papers/index.asp and an 'Annex 2' http://eucpn.org/key-papers/index.asp with a concrete action planning.

[38] Multiannual Strategy for the European Crime Prevention Network http://eucpn.org/key-papers/index.asp.

The goals of the Network, as defined in the Multiannual Strategy, are:

- To be a point of reference for the target groups of the Network
- To disseminate qualitative knowledge on crime prevention
- To support crime prevention activities at the national and local level
- To develop the EU policy and strategy of crime prevention and to develop various aspects of crime prevention at EU level in respect of the strategic priorities of the EU.

Concrete actions and projects to reach these goals of the Network are planned in annual Work Programmes[39] and reported in Annual Reports[40]. During the working year, new projects and initiatives can be added to the Work Programme. National Representatives report on a regular basis on the progress of these projects via the Secretariat to the Board.

Every year, both the Work Programme and the Annual Report are presented to the relevant European Union working groups, such as GENVAL[41] and COSI[42].

4.2 Funding

The EUCPN currently relies on three funding sources. The financing of projects by individual Member States, EU financial programmes managed by the European Commission (ISEC – Prevention of and Fight against Crime, Hercules, Daphne, etc.) and the EUCPN Fund, an internal fund established by voluntary contributions from Member States to support the execution of the Work Programme and the Multiannual Strategy.

5. Field of activities: local, national and European level crime prevention

As laid out in the goals summed up in the Multiannual Strategy, the Network's vision is to be a primary source of crime prevention development and good practices within the EU. The following paragraphs will go into more detail on the specific actions and tasks the Network is taking to accomplish its goals.

---

[39] EUCPN's Work Programmes can be downloaded using the following link: http://www.eucpn.org/work-prog/index.asp.

[40] EUCPN's Annual Reports can be downloaded using the following link: http://www.eucpn.org/key-papers/index.asp.

[41] Working Party on General Matters including Evaluation. GENVAL draws up some of the Community's strategies and policies aimed at coordinating measures to prevent and counter organized crime. In addition, this working party plans evaluations of the Member States' compliance with international obligations in this area.

[42] Standing Committee on Operational Cooperation on Internal Security. COSI was created to strengthen operational cooperation regarding the internal security of the EU. Thus, the key objective of the Committee, set out in the Lisbon Treaty, is to promote the coordination of operational actions between the EU Member States, including in the area of law enforcement.

5.1 EUCPN as a point of reference for crime prevention

The first goal mentioned in the Multiannual Strategy, i.e. to be a point of reference for the target groups of the Network, addresses the need of and the communication with the various target groups. To achieve this, the Network has set up a contact database comprising members of the various target groups: policy makers, academics and experts in fields related to crime prevention, as well as practitioners.

People within this database are regularly asked to share their knowledge and expertise on certain matters, they are invited to workshops, they are requested to share their opinion about the functioning of the Network, etc. Conversely, requests and questions on crime prevention by these target groups are dealt with by the Secretariat, either through own research or through facilitating contact with other experts.

The communication towards the target groups and the general public has been continually improving by the introduction of a quarterly newsletter, updating the EUCPN-website on a regular basis and disseminating the latest research results.

The EUCPN newsletter[43] is meant to be a platform for policymakers, practitioners and everyone who is interested in crime prevention. In the newsletter, a compilation of news, research, good practices and experiences on crime prevention in the Member States and in Europe are presented.

Finally, to be able to respond to the needs of the target groups, the Secretariat developed an event feedback tool which is used after every EUCPN event to measure participant satisfaction with the organization of and the communication about the event, and to make recommendations to the Board on further improvements for future events.

5.2 Disseminating qualitative knowledge on crime prevention

One way to achieve the goal of disseminating qualitative knowledge on crime prevention is through the collection and exchange of information and best practices in crime prevention. In practice this means that, first of all, the EUCPN is aiming to collect existing knowledge and information – (research) reports, policies and (local or national) prevention strategies, etc. –, combine that information and share it with the Network's target groups. Additionally, own initiatives are taken to increase the knowledge on certain themes by, for example, the organization of expert workshops or panel sessions, the development of toolboxes for local practitioners and the collection of information on national and/or local crime prevention initiatives through the Members of the Network.

The Secretariat is also publishing a six-monthly report series called 'European Crime Prevention Monitor' which combines information from administrative data on crime

---

[43] It is distributed in PDF-format and entirely downloadable on the EUCPN website. EUCPN Newsletter Series http://eucpn.org/newsletter/index.asp.

figures and trends across the European Member States, as well as large-scale survey and own collected data. The aim of these reports is to provide a substantial but targeted overview of the situation and trends on crime and crime prevention across Europe and, at the same time, gain insight into the policy measures and strategies used to prevent and to tackle crime.

The first European Crime Prevention Monitor report[44], which was published in June 2012, presents findings from different international cross-country crime statistics, surveys (such as victimization and self-reported surveys) and reports (such as e.g. Europol's OCTA). The second report[45], published in December 2012, focused on the public opinion and people's perceptions regarding the work of the police and the perceived 'success rate' of crime prevention policies at the national and the European level. The third Monitor Report, published in October 2013[46], zoomed in on the priorities of crime prevention policies of the Member States and the fourth, which is due in early 2014, will be addressing the theme of domestic violence.

Next, a toolbox and thematic paper series have been created, which are usually linked to the thematic work within each European Presidency. A toolbox consists of different parts: a theoretical part, which is in the form of a thematic paper, giving a broad theoretical background and introduction to the topic; a more practical part, like a manual or guidelines, which provide useful recommendations for local practitioners or policymakers on how to approach certain challenges of crime problems; and finally, an overview of existing good practices from the Member States.

The toolbox as a whole is aimed to provide more knowledge on a specific theme, but each chapter can also be read as an individual, stand-alone part which gives people the opportunity to pick the information they need.

In 2012, three thematic papers and two toolboxes were published. The thematic papers were written either by the EUCPN Secretariat or by external academic experts. The toolboxes were composed by the EUCPN Secretariat but in close collaboration with the Network Members, with experts in the field as well as with the Presidency under which they were created. The first paper was on 'Sport, science and art in the prevention of youth crime'[47], the second, on the prevention of youth crime through local cooperation involving the police[48], was written in the framework of the first

---

[44] European Crime Prevention Monitor 2012/1 - European cross country crime statistics, surveys and reports. Brussels: European Crime Prevention Network. http://eucpn.org/research/reviews.asp.

[45] European Crime Prevention Monitor 2012/2 - Public opinion and policy on crime prevention in Europe. Brussels: European Crime Prevention Network. http://eucpn.org/research/reviews.asp.

[46] European Crime Prevention Monitor 2013/1 – Priorities in crime prevention policies across Europe. . http://eucpn.org/research/reviews.asp.

[47] EUCPN (2012a). Sport, science and art in the prevention of crime among children and youth. EUCPN Thematic Paper No.1, European Crime Prevention Network: Brussels.

[48] EUCPN (2012b). The prevention of youth crime through local cooperation with the involvement of the

toolbox on local cooperation[49]. The third paper on community policing[50] was also an academic publication in the framework of the second toolbox 'Community (oriented) policing in Europe: Concepts, theory and practice'[51].

In 2013, two more toolboxes are addressing the evaluation of crime prevention initiatives and the Lithuanian Presidency's theme of domestic violence respectively[52].

Finally, as mentioned before, one of the main aims of the Network is to facilitate the exchange of best practices between Member States. Although there are various ways of achieving this goal, such as the organization of round table discussions and world cafes, thematic seminars, research reviews etc., the highlight is the Best Practice Conference, which is held at the end of each year and which involves the announcement of the winner of the European Crime Prevention Award.

5.3 Best Practice Conference & European Crime Prevention Award (ECPA)

Since 1997, the EUCPN has been organizing a Best Practice Conference (BPC) each year and honouring the best European crime prevention project with the European Crime Prevention Award (ECPA).[53] The aim of the BPC is to share and disseminate experience and knowledge of what is working or not in crime prevention to increase safety and security in the EU Member States. The audience is made up of policymakers, practitioners and researchers from across the EU, from candidate countries and from various national and European organizations. Non-European participants also often join the event as observers.

Since 2004, the European Crime Prevention Award has been officially integrated in the programme of the EUCPN and also turned into an annual activity by linking it to the Best Practice Conference. The ECPA is a competition which aims to publicly award good practices which have proven their success in the field with a prevention prize. It is also a cost-effective instrument to spread good crime prevention ideas from other cities, municipalities and organizations which are faced with similar challenges. Since 2012, the winning initiative is awarded a financial sum of 10.000EUR and the two honourable mentions receive 5.000EUR each.

---

police – A pilot study. EUCPN Thematic Paper No. 3, European Crime Prevention Network: Brussels.

[49] EUCPN Secretariat (eds.) (2012a). Local cooperation in youth crime prevention. EUCPN Toolbox Series, no. 1, European Crime Prevention Network: Brussels. http://eucpn.org/library/results. asp?category=32&pubdate=.

[50] Verhage & Ponsaers (2012). Community policing as a police strategy: effects and future outlook. In: EUCPN Secretariat (eds.), EUCPN Thematic Paper Series, no. 3, European Crime Prevention Network: Brussels. http://eucpn.org/research/reviews.asp.

[51] EUCPN Secretariat (eds.) (2012b). Community (oriented) policing in Europe: Concepts, theory and practice. EUCPN Toolbox Series, no. 2, European Crime Prevention Network: Brussels. http://eucpn.org/library/results.asp?category=32&pubdate=.

[52] All toolboxes are available on the EUCPN website: http://eucpn.org/library/results.asp?category=32&pubdate

[53] More information on the events can be retrieved from: http://eucpn.org/eucp-award/index.asp.

The BPC and ECPA are organized by the Presidency of the Council and revolve around a specific theme. The ECPA is open to all EU Member States who can submit any theme-related project, initiative or package of measures which was successfully implemented to prevent crime. As figure 3 shows, the number of entries has increased over the years from just three in 1997 to no less than 22 in 2012. A continuation of this upward trend can be expected due to the increasing relevance of prevention in crime policies among the Member States.

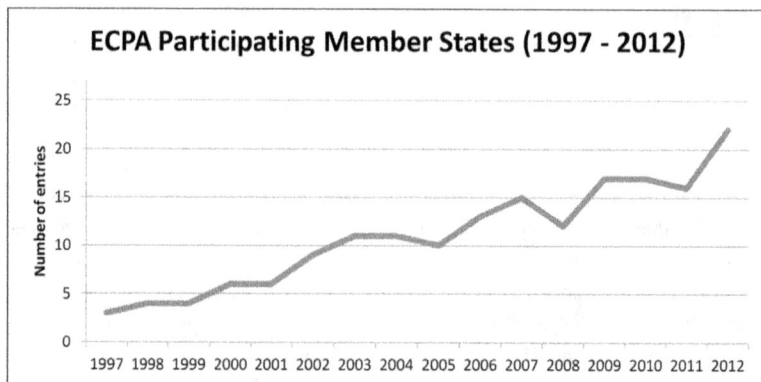

Figure 3: Number of ECPA participants per year 1997 - 2012

5.4 Supporting crime prevention activities at the national and local level

In addition to the substantive support through the development of reports and toolboxes, the third goal, i.e. to support crime prevention activities at the national and local level, is also addressed by providing information on the funding and implementation of crime prevention projects. For example, during Hungary's Presidency in 2011, a short report was circulated among the EUCPN Members and published on the website listing various national and EU funding sources and channels related to crime prevention activities[54]. Information on deadlines for calls to apply for funding are always communicated through the EUCPN's communication channels (e-mail, website, newsletter,...) and the EUCPN Secretariat gives assistance to the applicants' search for partners for projects in other Member States.

Another example of supporting crime prevention activities is the publication of a guide on how to determine costs and benefits of crime prevention, developed in a project led by Denmark. This hands-on guide aims to offer support to policymakers and practitioners who want to conduct reliable cost-benefit analyses of crime prevention programmes in Europe[55].

---

[54] Summary on funding sources and mechanisms of crime prevention activities in the EU Member States, European Crime Prevention Network http://www.eucpn.org/pubdocs/Summary_Board_final.pdf.

[55] Højbjerg Jacobsen, Rasmus (2013). Hands-on Guide to Cost-Benefit-Analysis of Crime Prevention Ef-

Finally, the projects of the Best Practice Conference and the European Crime Prevention Award nominees are being promoted through the website and the three-monthly newsletter. The experts from the winning projects are also promoted through various workshops and/or conferences across Europe to share their experience on other platforms.

5.5 Developing crime prevention throughout the EU

To be able to develop and support crime prevention throughout the EU and to be involved in the EU policy and strategy regarding crime prevention, it is important to firmly establish a good working European Network on Crime Prevention. Hence, the Network is developing and implementing a Network Management Plan, taking into account the results of the external and internal evaluation and developing a structured response to the conclusions and recommendations of these evaluations (see also next paragraph on the outlook of EUCPN).

Additionally, the Network tries to establish partnerships with other relevant bodies, organizations and agencies, based on a stakeholder analysis and meetings with different partners in order to agree on forms of communication and exchange of information. Currently, EUCPN is establishing closer links with EUROPOL, CEPOL and Eurostat, as well as with other international and EU organizations, networks and initiatives.

6. Outlook

As mentioned before and as prescribed in article 9 of the Council Decision 2009/902/ JHA, the European Commission presented an evaluation report to the Council on 30 November 2012 on the EUCPN and its activities. This evaluation laid a special focus on the efficiency of the work of the Network and its Secretariat, taking due account of the interaction between the Network and other relevant stakeholders[56].

The report showed that the EUCPN has been performing well and that many shortcomings have been addressed since the last evaluation in 2009. Nevertheless, some challenges still exist in improving the functioning of the Network, but also in setting the direction in which EUCPN will evolve over the next few years.

These challenges are summarised in 20 recommendations and are related to:

i.   the EUCPN's performance, impact and added value: aligning its priorities with agreed EU priorities, making inputs to EU and Member State policy making in the crime prevention field, allying with other EU entities, developing and disseminating outputs and good practices to key stakeholders and improving the website;

---

forts. CEBR – Centre for Economic and Business Research. Copenhagen. http://eucpn.org/goodpractice/showdoc.asp?docid=308.

[56]   The evaluation was undertaken by the Centre for Strategy & Evaluation Services (CSES).

ii.   its organization and governance: providing guidelines to support the rotating
       EUCPN Presidencies, defining the role of the National Representatives (Board
       Members), observers and Contact Points, and the working of the Secretariat;

iii.   its possibilities to develop towards a 'Crime Prevention Observatory' as sugges-
       ted in the Stockholm Programme (cfr. supra).

Following this evaluation report, the EUCPN has established a working group and
developed a concrete action plan setting out how and when these recommendations
will be implemented. The relevant working groups on EU level are regularly informed
on the further development of the Network. The next evaluation of the EUCPN is
planned in 2016.

Finally, to conclude, the EUCPN developed further towards a real European centre of
expertise on crime prevention over the past decade. This process has been strengthened by the establishment of a permanent Secretariat which is responsible for the administrative, technical and analytical support of the Network. With a variety of activities
and a range of different outputs, such as the toolbox and thematic paper series on
various topics, the organizations of expert workshops, the European Crime Prevention Award and the Best Practice Conference, the EUCPN supports crime prevention
initiatives at the European, national and local level and enhances the links between
these levels.

Through internal and external evaluations of the Network, which are scheduled on a
regular basis, feedback on the functioning of the EUCPN is provided and recommendations are formulated to further professionalize and improve its performance. These
will support the Network in carrying out its long-term mission and turn it into an
important reference when it comes to crime prevention in Europe.

7. References

Centre for Strategy & Evaluation Services (CSES) (2009). Evaluation of the European Crime Prevention Network. Kent. http://ec.europa.eu/dgs/home-affairs/what-we-do/policies/organized-crime-and-human-trafficking/crime-prevention/docs/evaluation_of_eucpn_final_report_(cses_11_03_09).pdf.

Communication from the Commission to the Council and the European Parliament – Crime prevention in the European Union [COM(2004) 165 final, 12.03.2004] http://eur-lex.europa.eu/LexUriServ/LexUriServ.do?uri=CELEX:52004DC0165:EN:NOT.

Communication from the Commission to the Council and the European Parliament. The prevention of crime in the European Union. Reflection on common guidelines and proposals for Community financial support [COM(2000) 786 final - Not published in the Official Journal] http://eur-lex.europa.eu/smartapi/cgi/sga_doc?smartapi!celexplus!prod!DocNumber&lg=en&type_doc=COMfinal&an_doc=2000&nu_doc=786.

Council Decision 2001/427/JHA of 28 May 2001 setting up a European Crime Prevention Network. [OJ L 153, 08.06.2001] http://eur-lex.europa.eu/LexUriServ/LexUriServ.do?uri=OJ:L:2001:153:0001:0003:EN:PDF.

Council Decision 2002/630/JHA of 22 July 2002 establishing a framework programme on police and judicial cooperation in criminal matters (AGIS) [OJ L 203, 01.08.2002] http://eur-lex.europa.eu/LexUriServ/LexUriServ.do?uri=OJ:L:2002:203:0005:0008:EN:PDF.

Council Decision 2007/125/JHA of 12 February 2007 establishing for the period 2007 to 2013, as part of General Programme on Security and Safeguarding Liberties, the Specific Programme Prevention of and Fight against Crime [OJ L 58, 24.2.2007, p. 7–12] http://eur-lex.europa.eu/LexUriServ/LexUriServ.do?uri=CELEX:32007D0125:EN:NOT

Council Decision 2009/902/JHA of 30 November 2009 setting up a European Crime Prevention Network (EUCPN) and repealing Decision 2001/427/JHA [OJ L 321, 08.12.2009, p. 44-46] http://eur-lex.europa.eu/LexUriServ/LexUriServ.do?uri=OJ:L:2009:321:0044:01:EN:HTML.

Crawford, A. (2009). Crime Prevention Policies in Comparative Perspective. Cullompton: Willan Publishing.

Crawford, A. (1998). Community Safety Partnerships. Criminal Justice Matters, 33: 4-5.

EUCPN Newsletter Series http://eucpn.org/newsletter/index.asp

EUCPN's Work Programmes http://www.eucpn.org/work-prog/index.asp

EUCPN's Annual Reports http://www.eucpn.org/key-papers/index.asp

EUCPN (2012a). *Sport, science and art in the prevention of crime among children and youth.* EUCPN Thematic Paper No. 1. European Crime Prevention Network: Brussels. http://eucpn.org/research/reviews.asp

EUCPN (2012b). *The prevention of youth crime through local cooperation with the involvement of the police – A pilot study*. EUCPN Thematic Paper No. 2. European Crime Prevention Network: Brussels. http://eucpn.org/research/ reviews.asp

EUCPN Secretariat (eds.) (2012a). Local cooperation in youth crime prevention. *EUCPN Toolbox Series, no. 1*, European Crime Prevention Network: Brussels. http://eucpn.org/library/results.asp?category=32&pubdate=

EUCPN Secretariat (eds.) (2012b). Community (oriented) policing in Europe: Concepts, theory and practice. *EUCPN Toolbox Series, no. 2*, European Crime Prevention Network: Brussels. http://eucpn.org/library/results. asp?category=32&pubdate=

European Crime Prevention Monitor 2012/1 - European cross country crime statistics, surveys and reports. Brussels: European Crime Prevention Network. http://eucpn.org/research/reviews.asp

European Crime Prevention Monitor 2012/2 - Public opinion and policy on crime prevention in Europe. Brussels: European Crime Prevention Network. http:// eucpn.org/research/reviews.asp

Hebberecht, P. & Baillergeau, E. (eds.) (2012). Social crime prevention in late modern Europe. A comparative perspective. Brussels: VUB Press.

Hebberecht, P. & Duprez, D. (eds) (2002). The prevention and security policies in Europe. Brussels: VUB Press.

Højbjerg Jacobsen, Rasmus (2013). Hands-on Guide to Cost-Benefit-Analysis of Crime Prevention Efforts. CEBR – Centre for Economic and Business Research. Copenhagen. http://eucpn.org/goodpractice/showdoc.asp?docid=308

Keynote to the Multiannual Strategy for EUCPN http://eucpn.org/key-papers/index. asp

Multiannual Strategy for the European Crime Prevention Network http://eucpn.org/ key-papers/index.asp

Multiannual Strategy for the European Crime Prevention Network - Annex 2 http:// eucpn.org/key-papers/index.asp

Presidency Conclusions – Brussels, 4/5 November 2004. Annex 1. The Hague Programme: Strengthening Freedom, Security and Justice in the European Union. [14292/1/04, REV 1, 08.12.2004] http://www.consilium.europa.eu/ uedocs/cms_data/docs/pressdata/en/ec/82534.pdf

Report from the Commission to the Council, Evaluation report on the European Union Crime Prevention Network [COM(2012) 717 final, 30.11.2012] http:// ec.europa.eu/dgs/home-affairs/e-library/documents/policies/organized-crime-and-human-trafficking/crime-prevention/docs/20121130_eucpn_report_en.pdf

Rules of Procedure for the European Crime Prevention Network of 30.08.2010. http://eucpn.org/key-papers/index.asp

Single European Act [OJ L 169, Volume 30, 29.6.1987] http://eur-lex.europa.eu/ JOHtml.do?uri=OJ:L:1987:169:SOM:EN:HTML

Summary on funding sources and mechanisms of crime prevention activities in the EU Member States, European Crime Prevention Network http://www.eucpn. org/pubdocs/Summary_Board_final.pdf

Treaty of Amsterdam amending the Treaty on European Union, the Treaties establishing the European Communities and certain related acts [OJ C *340, 10.11.1997, p. 1–144]* http://eur-lex.europa.eu/LexUriServ/LexUriServ. do?uri=CELEX:11997D/TXT:EN:NOT

Treaty on European Union (Consolidated version 1997) [OJ C 340, 10.11.1997, p.145–172] http://eur-lex.europa.eu/LexUriServ/LexUriServ.do?uri=OJ:C:19 97:340:0145:0172:EN:PDF

The Hague Programme: strengthening freedom, security and justice in the European Union [OJ C 53/1, 03.03.2005] http://eur-lex.europa.eu/LexUriServ/LexUri-Serv.do?uri=OJ:C:2005:053:0001:0014:EN:PDF

The Stockholm Programme — An open and secure Europe serving and protecting citizens [OJ C 115, 4.5.2010, p. 1–38] http://eur-lex.europa.eu/LexUriServ/ LexUriServ.do?uri=CELEX:52010XG0504%2801%29:EN:NOT

The prevention and control of organized crime: a European Union strategy for the beginning of the new millennium [OJ C 124, 3.5.2000] http://eur-lex.europa. eu/LexUriServ/LexUriServ.do?uri=CELEX:32000F0503:EN:NOT

Treaty of Lisbon amending the Treaty on European Union and the Treaty establishing the European Community, signed at Lisbon, 13 December 2007 [OJ C 306, 17.12.2007] http://eur-lex.europa.eu/LexUriServ/LexUriServ. do?uri=CELEX:12007L/TXT:EN:NOT

Verhage & Ponsaers (2012). Community policing as a police strategy: effects and future outlook. In: EUCPN Secretariat (eds.), *EUCPN Thematic Paper Series*, no. 3, European Crime Prevention Network: Brussels. http://eucpn. org/research/reviews.asp

Cecilia Andersson

UN-HABITAT's Safer Cities Programme

UN-HABITAT's Safer Cities Programme was launched in 1996 at the request of African Mayors seeking to tackle urban crime and violence in their cities. The Safer Cities approach embraces a holistic, integrated and multi-sectoral approach to improving the livability of cities and quality of life for all urban residents (especially the most marginalized), predicated on the confidence that good urban governance, planning and management can improve the safety of neighborhoods.The Safer Cities supports cities and other urban stakeholders to develop and implement city-wide crime and violence prevention strategies via two interlinked by distinctive service modes: a network hub (GNSC) and a design service. This bimodality enables work on both a global, normative level, and at the city, operational level, with actions at both levels providing mutual reinforcement, knowledge transfer, amplification of messaging, and added value. To date UN-Habitat has supported programmes in 72 cities in 23 countries worldwide.

The Global Network on Safer Cities (GNSC) was launched during the World Urban Forum in Naples, Italy in September 2012 with the goal of equipping local authorities and urban stakeholders to deliver urban safety, thus contributing towards securing the urban advantage for all. The GNSC represents an international forum for cities and urban stakeholders working to reduce insecurity by stimulating exchange between policymakers and practitioners, facilitating the standardization of principles on prevention at the local level, institutionalizing knowledge, supporting application of proven and promising approaches, spreading a culture of prevention, and increasing coordination and creating synergies among cities and donors. It also promotes the visibility of urban safety, through joint advocacy and communications activities, and leveraging collective policy and political weight to influence other orders of government, especially at the national level. Key activities include:

1. **The Definition of the UN Guidelines on Safer Cities.** A set of internationally accepted and validated standards providing comprehensive guidance to improve the quality and consistency of policymaking and programming by the UN system, Member States, and other partners.

2. **A Global Safer City Award** to celebrate the achievements of local authorities in improving safety and security for all. The Award will become the international benchmark by which local public sector innovation in the safety and security realm is judged.

3. **Urban Safety Monitor** to benchmark urban security. The Monitor is currently in development and will be a composite index, based on comparable indicators including the incidence of violence and crime and other factors. The Monitor will not be a global index, rather foster regional

peer-to-peer comparison

4. **Establishment of a trust fund/funding mechanism for safer cities.** A funding mechanism that will catalyze a wide range of financial resources for specific service lines through a call-for-proposals for format.

5. **Design service.** A locally responsive service for cities and national authorities to assist them in diagnosing and resolving the issues of affecting urban safety.

6. **City-to-city knowledge exchange and training.**

In a survey that was conducted in 2010 on the need and value of a network promoting urban safety, out of the 250 partners that were involved, 228 responses were received. The survey responses affirmed the need for the Network based on the growing number of cities that are adopting safer cities approaches by developing strategic and planned initiatives and the increasing demand for technical assistance to deliver urban safety. This is complemented by the fact that there are also many tools and approaches which have proven their effectiveness in the prevention of urban crime and enhancement of urban safety and social cohesion; and, a tremendous amount of lessons learned from practice. Hence, there is need to:

1) intensify the sharing of experiences, ideas and strategic information across sectors and linguistic barriers, with and among local authorities, of what is working and in what context and what challenges are encountered; and in this way enhance city to city learning and collaboration;

2) consolidate a knowledge repository bringing together experiences, approaches, debates on urban safety so that more cost-effective prevention and intervention policies can be implemented;

3) enhance dialogue among city administrators, other urban stakeholders and citizens in order to create safer and healthier environments for all.

As core resources committed to urban safety continue to dwindle, most city safety interventions are under-resourced. Therefore, there is a need to:

1) leverage additional resources through enhanced partnerships;

2) enhance advocacy and fundraising for safety interventions by seeking out expanded technical cooperation financing from bilateral and multilateral agencies and private sector.

At the global level, the GNSC is designed as a common collaborative platform, a network of networks, which will promote the standardization of principles, indicators and methodologies globally in order to scale up best practices while encouraging the creation of centres of excellence on action-oriented research with emerging issues on urban crime and violence.

At the national level, the Network provides a platform for structured dialogue between local authorities and national government on crime prevention and urban development. The network will also foster the dialogue between various government departments and ministries such as ministries of local government, ministries of housing and urban development and ministries of internal security and justice. At the city level, the network will further encourage community participation and interaction and enhance the link with other ongoing urban processes and developmental programmes.

The GNSC is comprised of 5 key organs:

- The Steering Committee
- The Advisory Panel
- The Partners Consultative Group
- Cities Exchange Assembly/Forum (including local government and grassroots platforms)
- The Secretariat (including the Trust Fund facility and Regional Centres of Excellence)

The **Steering Committee** of the GNSC was constituted to strengthen the international dialogue, advocate for safer more sustainable urban development and provide strategic guidance and advice, across policies, programme of work and budgeting at global, regional, national and local levels on urban safety. The Steering Committee is led by Mayors and other high-level personalities representing the regions:

- Chair of the GNSC: Marcelo Ebrard Casaubón, former Mayor of Mexico City
- North America: Antonio Villaraigosa, former Mayor of Los Angeles, USA
- North America: Annise Parker, Mayor of Houston, USA, representing the United States Conference of Mayors
- Central America: Norman Quijano González, Mayor of San Salvador, El Salvador.
- Andean Region: Gustavo Petro, Mayor of Bogotá, Colombia
- South America: Fernando Haddad, Mayor of Sao Paulo, Brazil (represented by Mr. Roberto Porto, Secretary of Urban Safety)
- Middle East: Bilal Hamad, Mayor of Beirut, Lebanon
- Africa: Parks Tau, Mayor of Johannesburg, South Africa, Chairman of the South African Cities Network
- Africa: François Amichia, Mayor of Treichville-Abidjan, Ivory Coast, President of the National Forum on Urban Safety
- Europe: Guillermo Pintos, Mayor of Matosinhos, Portugal, President of the European Forum on Urban Safety

- Asia/Pacific: Won Soon Park, Mayor of Seoul Metropolitan Government, South Korea

Other Steering Committee members include:

- Germany: Ministry of Economic Cooperation
- Sweden: Swedish International Development Co-Operation Agency (Sida)
- Josep Roig, Secretary General, United Cities and Local Governments (UCLG)
- John De Boer, Director, International Development Research Centre (IDRC) – Canada
- Marisol Dalmazzo , Huairou Commission – Gender representative
- Elizabeth Johnston, Director, European Forum on Urban Security
- Vijay Jagannathan, Secretary General, Citynet
- Private sector representatives

The Advisory Panel is made up of experienced personalities who have worked with UN-HABITAT and partners in the technical field and are experts in the area of urban safety.

The Partners Consultative Group is made up of organizations that have entered into a collaborative arrangement with the GNSC (UN-Habitat) supporting cities through tool development, training, knowledge management and capacity building. The Partners Consultative Group will also work towards joint programming and scaling up of normative and operational work of partners as well as monitor and evaluate the delivery of urban safety in cities.

The Cities Exchange Assembly/Forum is made up of local governments, thematic partner platforms and citizen/grassroots movements (e.g. Youth, Gender, Police, Armed Violence, CPTED, etc.). The Cities Exchange Forum is the World Urban Campaign's Safer Cities Cluster Group and meet to exchange knowledge on policy and practice on urban safety and to enhance city to city cooperation and learning. It will particularly involve city-to-city exchanges and enhanced peer review mechanisms. This will involve cities that have already developed safer cities models (defined as 'resource cities') working with the network of cities. The resource cities will have championed or adopted safer cities approaches that may be replicable in other cities/communities and are willing to share their knowledge with other cities.

The Secretariat serves the GNSC and its members, initiates and facilitates a range of network activities, supports fundraising and collects good practices and tools. The secretariat will also monitor and evaluate implementation of urban safety projects and make available information and relevant tools/methodologies as required to facilitate the work of the cities and partners. UN-Habitat serves as the Secretariat for an incubation period until 2016.

Given that the Network is being established over a four-year horizon, the GNSC architecture, partner database and organization of work will incrementally be built over the period 2012-2016 and be subject to continuous review as it grows in a consultative process alongside the development of UN Guidelines on Safer Cities. The GNSC has adapted a strategy of "starting small" from its launch in September 2012. To facilitate its foundational development, UN-Habitat is entering into partnerships/MoUs with various partners on various themes to provide an impetus to the development of an all-inclusive network architecture and to the assembly of a broader alliance of cities.

Christian Pfeiffer

Parallel Justice – Why Do We Need a Strengthening of the Victim in Society?[1]

Ladies and Gentlemen,

You are aware of the topic of my address. But before I get into that, I ask for your patience. It strikes me as sensible to first of all discuss the main topic of this Congress on Crime Prevention, which is **"More prevention – less victims."** Based on very diverse victim experiences, I would like to begin by discussing where prevention apparently works and how this can be explained. An example of the opposite is intended to illustrate where we urgently need to expand prevention. An analysis of the very diverging victimological findings and prevention policy perspectives then provides the basis for the real topic of my address – Parallel Justice.

1. A Long Journey from the Religiously Motivated Beating of Children to the New Trend of More Love and Less Punishment

I would like to begin with the **prototype** of severe victimization: the beating of children. This method of upbringing follows an old tradition. **"Spare the rod, spoil the child"** is a saying that is attributed to a counselor of the King of Assyria in the seventh century B.C. And in the Bible (Proverbs 13, 24) it says: "He who spares his rod hates his son; but he who loves him disciplines him promptly." This is based on the religious belief in the **innate depravity and original sin of human beings**[2]. It was essential to counteract this with all severity, right from the start. For centuries, "beating the devil out of children" was more than a saying.

But then, **during the Age of Enlightenment**, independent thinkers gained entirely different insights. The French philosopher and humanist Michel de Montaigne stated: "My experience is that the use of the rod makes a child cowardly and more than ever maliciously obstinate."[3] In 1692, in his book "Some Thoughts Concerning Education", the English philosopher John Locke spoke out against the concept of innate depravity that is to be fought with beatings. A quote: "Children are like white paper or wax that one can shape and form positively and negatively."[4] 70 years later Jean Jacques Rousseau countered the Christian concept of original sin with that of **child innocence**. Children were to have the opportunity to develop their creativity and learn step by step from their own experiences.[5]

---

[1]   The version of the address that contains footnotes and literature references is published in the proceedings of the German Congress on Crime Prevention.

[2]   See Pinker, 2011

[3]   De Montaigne, 1998 Edition

[4]   See Wattendorff, 1907

[5]   Rousseau, 1971

It took another 200 years, however, until the wonderful books by Astrid Lindgren lay the groundwork for a fundamental reform in **Sweden** and the Nordic countries.

First, during the fifties and sixties, the right to corporal punishment by teachers was abolished there, and then, between 1979 and 1983, the same thing happened to the corresponding right of parents. When Germany followed Sweden's example in the year 2000, advance empirical research regarding this topic had contributed to this legislation being passed. Among international criminologists, I would like to emphasize David Farrington[6], Terence Thornberry[7] and Dan Olweus[8] and from Germany Friedrich Lösel[9], Hans-Jürgen Kerner[10] and Peter Wetzels[11]. Today, Montaigne's thesis, which was mentioned above, has been empirically validated in many ways. One example is our representative survey of 45,000 ninth grade students, which was carried out in 2007/2008. According to this study, children who had been beaten massively by their parents were five times more likely to become multiple violent offenders than those who had been raised lovingly and without violence. They consumed cannabis five times more often and four times more often they skipped school at least ten times a year.[12]

In addition, our data reveals that **politically relevant effects** result from the corporal punishment of children. Parents who beat their children fail to exemplify positive behavioral alternatives for how to deal with conflict situations. Instead, they send them a false message: The stronger one may and should impose his will with force. It is therefore not surprising that children who have been severely beaten become youths with **extreme right-wing convictions** three times more often than children who have been raised non-violently.[13] The political importance of the culture of upbringing is confirmed by three additional representative surveys of adults that we have conducted since 2004. The more often and the more violently the participants in the survey were beaten by their parents as children and thus repeatedly suffered from feelings of powerlessness, the more they later wished to own a **firearm**. A firearm gives one a feeling of power and fighting strength and stabilizes one's weakened self-esteem. Another thing that was revealed: Those who grew up in constant fear of being beaten by their parents, later often assume that there is a threat of violence from one's fellow humans. They are therefore in favor of **harsh deterrents** against evil, including capital punishment.[14]

---

[6]   Farrington 1992a, Farrington 1992b

[7]   Thornberry et al, 1991

[8]   Olweus, 1980

[9]   Bender & Lösel, 1997

[10] Kerner, Stroezel & Wegel, 2003

[11] Wetzels, 1997

[12] Stadler, Bieneck & Pfeiffer, 2011

[13] ibid.

[14] Baier, Kemme, Hanslmaier, Doering, Rehbein & Pfeiffer, 2011

Another example of the political importance of a country's culture of raising children is provided by an OECD study from the year 2008. A representative study in 20 European countries measured the social skills of students. It turned out that especially youths from Sweden, Finland, Norway and Denmark had by far the highest values regarding **tolerance** and the **extent of their interpersonal trust**.[15] This also seems to be a result of the fact that these four countries were the first worldwide to implement the ideal of raising children in a non-violent, loving way. There, one was convinced of two theses early on. First: raising children non-violently helps them stand tall. And second: raising children in a loving way promotes empathy.

But how has our own culture of raising children developed? Two representative surveys of victims, which we were able to conduct in 1992 and 2011 and which were funded by the Federal German Republic, provide an answer. A comparison of the data confirms a clear trend: **More love, less beatings.** The proportion of those who have grown up entirely without violence doubled from 26 percent to 52 percent during the 19 years between the surveys. Parallel with this, the proportion of those who as children were often held in the arms of their parents and experienced intense cuddling with them, increased from 53 percent to 71 percent. In contrast, the number of mild and severe acts of violence was significantly lower. Furthermore, among the 9,500 Germans who participated in the survey, we looked separately at those who were between 16 and 20 years old at the time of the survey. Among these, all four points provide even more positive findings. The proportion of this younger age group who were raised non-violently was 63 percent. The proportion who were beaten severely was only seven percent.[16]

---

[15] Van Damme, 2012

[16] Pfeiffer, 2012a, Pfeiffer, 2012b, Pfeiffer, 2012d

Figure 1: The development of parental devotion and parental violence 1992 - 2011

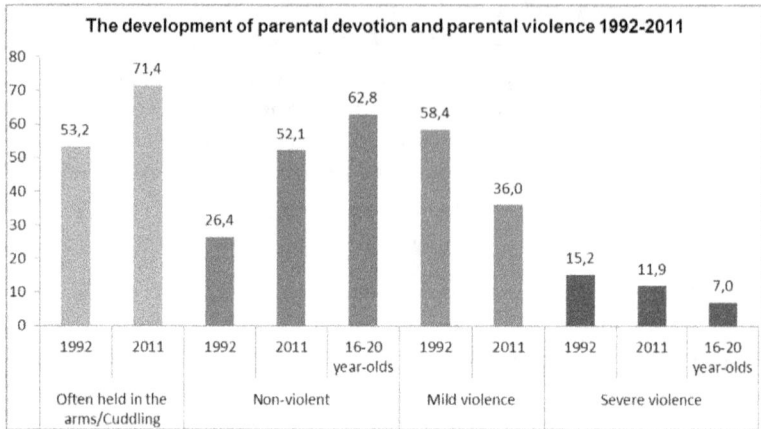

The new production of youth violence because of parents who beat them has thus de-creased greatly. What we find in our statistics is therefore not surprising. An example is the data from the health insurance funds regarding the frequency of severe fighting injuries at schools, where the victims had to be admitted to hospital. Since the height of the violence in schools in the year 1997, the number of such cases per 10,000 stu-dents decreased from 16 to 7 (in 2010), i.e. by 60 percent.[17] The reason why this data is so convincing is because there are virtually no unreported cases when the schools report to the state health insurance funds. Fittingly, the student surveys that the Crimi-nological Research Institute of Lower Saxony [hereafter called by its German acro-nym KFN] has carried out in eight cities and administrative districts since 1998 show a stable **decrease in youth violence.**[18] And finally, the police criminal statistics since 2007 also confirm this positive trend – and this, although the willingness of young victims of violence to report the violence has increased. Youth violence in this age group has decreased by 33,3 percent per 100,000.[19]

The result of all this data fits perfectly with the topic of the conference: More preven-tion – less victims. One could also formulate it as follows: **More resilience, more power of resistance – less victims.** With this, I would for the first time like to use a concept that fits naturally here. There is a proven insight in the psychology of deve-lopment which states: Children, who are raised in a non-violent and loving way and who have developed a strong bond to their primary caregiver, thereby gain the power

[17]   Baier, Kemme, Hanslmaier, Doering, Rehbein & Pfeiffer, 2012

[18]   Bundeskriminalamt, PKS 2013

[19]   Bundeskriminalamt, PKS 2013

to master their lives, even when things become difficult.[20] Today, the word resilience is used to describe this quality – i.e. the ability of a person to deal constructively with onerous life circumstances by accessing his/her own resources.[21] It goes without saying that resilience generates preventive power.[22] On the other hand, it is also important for how people process a victim experience. I will provide two concrete examples of this later. But first I would like to return to an aspect that played an important role in the beginning of my address: The importance of the Christian religion for the way parents raise their children.

2. Christian Religion and the Culture of Upbringing Today

It seems reasonable to include religion, because it was against the church's tradition of raising children that the Age of Enlightenment was focused. We therefore asked ourselves if Christian congregations still today hold these century-old convictions and if so, what the effects of this may be.

Our analysis was based on data from almost 23,500 native German youths from West Germany, who, according to their own statements, belonged to a Christian congregation. Almost half of them were Protestant. Among these, 431 stated that they belonged to an **Evangelical Free Church congregation**. We undertook a special evaluation of this group.[23] In an article on September 30, 2010, two editors of the Süddeutsche Zeitung, Florian Götz and Oliver Das Gupta[24] had attested that such congregations had an extremely repressive culture when it comes to the parental raising of children. As an example, they referred to an American parenting guide by the fundamentalist pastor Michael Pearl and his wife, which evidently is very popular among evangelical parents.

The following quote describes one of the central messages of the text:

"When the time comes to apply the rod, take a deep breath, relax, and pray, "Lord, make this a valuable learning session. Cleanse my child of illtemper and rebellion. May I properly represent your cause in this matter." No jerking around. No raised voice. The child should be able to anticipate the coming rod by your utterly calm and controlled spirit. […]If you have to sit on him to spank him then do not hesitate. And hold him there until he is surrendered.[…] Sometimes, with older children, usually when the licks are not forceful enough, the child may still be rebellious. If this occurs, take time to instruct and then continue the spanking. A general rule is to continue the disciplinary action until the child is surrendered."

---

[20]   Suess & Kißgen, 2005, Daigle, Beaver & Turner, 2010

[21]   Werner & Smith, 1992, Lösel & Bender, 2007, Pianta, Stuhlmann & Hamre, 2007, Greve, Hellmers & Kappes, 2012

[22]   Matt & Siewert, 2008, Wegel, Kerner & Stroezel, 2011

[23]   Pfeiffer & Baier, 2013 (Manuscript in preparation)

[24]   Götz & Das Gupta, 2010

The German version of the book was published in 2008 and approx. 4,000 copies were sold. Then, in the autumn of 2010, it was banned by the Federal Review Board for Publications Harmful to Young Persons.[25] A similar message is provided by the book "Shepherding a Child's Heart".[26] The author is the American pastor Tedd Tripp. Here a quote: "The rod is a parent, in faith toward God and faithfulness toward his or her children, undertaking the responsibility of careful, timely, measured and controlled use of physical punishment to underscore the importance of obeying God, thus rescuing the child from continuing in his foolishness unto death. [...]The use of the rod is an act of faith. God has mandated its use."

But last week the Federal Review Board made a decision concerning the prohibition of this book, too. The publisher has already been informed. The indexing will be published in the German Federal Gazette on April 30, 2013.[27]

Figure 2 shows what can be learned about spanking children if one differentiates between whether the families of the surveyed youths belong to a Catholic, Protestant or Evangelical Free Church congregation. Furthermore, a distinction is made depending on the degree to which the youths classify their parents' level of religiousness.

Figure 2: Parental violence in childhood depending on the religious group and religiousness; non-academic families, student survey 2007/2008[28]

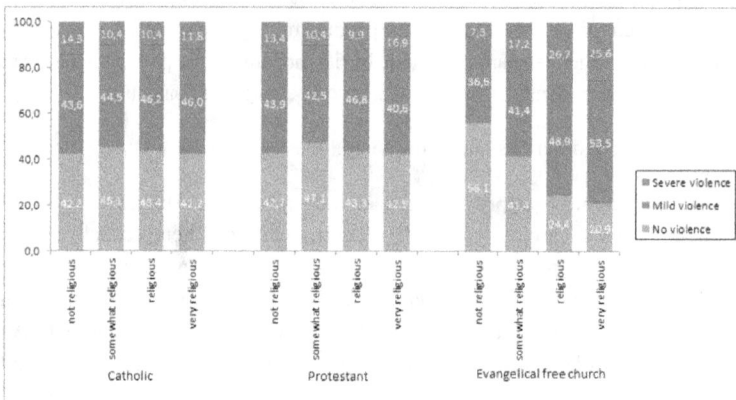

---

[25] Bundesprüfstelle für jugendgefährdende Medien, Entscheidung vom 06.08.2010, Entscheidung Nr. 9389 (V); BAnz 2010, Nr. 130.

[26] Tripp, 1995

[27] Bundesprüfstelle für jugendgefährdende Medien, Entscheidung vom 05.04.2013, Entscheidung Nr. 10919 (V); BAnz 2013 AT.

[28] Pfeiffer & Baier, 2013 (manuscript in preparation)

When it comes to Catholic families, children in parental homes that are not religious were beaten the most – 14 percent. In the religious or very religious families it was only 10 and 12 percent, respectively. The situation is similar in Protestant families. Here, however, most beating (17%) is done by the group of very religious parents. The findings regarding the **Evangelical Free Church families** do not fit the pattern at all. Here, **the stronger the parents are rooted in their beliefs, the more they spank.** The proportion of severely beaten children increases from 7 percent for non-religious parents to 26 percent for those highly religious. It should also be noted that, compared to the four groups, the proportion of children who are brought up non-violently here decreases from 56 percent (non-religious parents) to 21 percent (highly religious parents).[29]

We used the opportunity we had in 2011 to survey 11,500 adults to carry out this study a second time. This again confirmed the results of the student survey. Those questioned who came from Evangelical Free Church congregations and whose parents were very religious, suffered from massive beatings twice as often as the comparison group whose parents were not or only somewhat religious.[30] Here, too, due to the small number belonging to this religious minority, it was not possible to differentiate between the different types of congregations.

These different patterns of upbringing of course leave their traces in the children concerned. Clear, consistent findings thus emerge for Catholic and Protestant respondents. The more religious they are, the more seldom do they resort to violence. 16 percent of non-religious youths are perpetrators of violence, but only 6 percent of those who are very religious. This connection is, however, much weaker for Evangelical Free Church youths (12% non-religious, 8% very religious). Furthermore, it turns out that the satisfaction with life, especially for Catholic, but also Protestant youths increases strongly, the stronger their belief is. This trend is especially clear for young Catholics (35 % of non-believers are very satisfied, 52 % of strong believers are very satisfied). No such connection could be found for the Evangelical Free Church youths. A further finding corresponds with these insights. Especially for Catholic youths, the following applies: the more religious they are, the fewer of them report having thoughts of suicide. For Evangelical Free Church youths, however, there is a slight trend in the opposite direction.[31]

3. The Repressive Culture of Upbringing in the United States

Only one percent of the youths surveyed by KFN belonged to Evangelical Free Church congregations. In the United States, however, the proportion of the population that are evangelical Christians is 26 percent; in the Southern states sometimes even more

---

[29]   ibid.

[30]   Pfeiffer, 2012a; Pfeiffer 2012b

[31]   Pfeiffer & Baier, 2013 (manuscript in preparation)

than 50 percent.[32] This fits with the findings of a study by Human Rights Watch. In the United States, in the year 2009, more than 200,000 students, most of them in the Southern states, were beaten with a rod by their teachers. This is permitted in 21 states.[33] In addition, American parents nationwide have the right to use corporal punishment. Two overview studies that were undertaken in 2010 by Gershoff and Strauss showed that only 15 % of American children are raised non-violently by their parents[34] (as a reminder: this now applies to 63% of German children). Furthermore, 70 percent of American parents agreed with the statement: "It is sometimes necessary to discipline a child with a good hard spanking."[35] The numbers document the extent to which there is still a repressive culture of upbringing in the United States, under the strong influence of fundamentalist Christian groups. It is obvious that this also has political consequences.

The domestic political division within the nation, the power of the Tea Party, the intolerance of the reactionary conservatives toward liberal groups, the substantial aggression potential of American society, coupled with people's urge to arm themselves and their extreme desire to punish – all this is strongly promoted by the repressive culture of upbringing in families and schools. The United States is paying a high price for this: there are eight to ten times more people in prison per 100,000 citizens than in Germany and the Northern European countries.[36] Furthermore, 18 times more killings with firearms occur in the United States than in Germany.[37] In addition, the rate of other homicides in the United States is more than three times higher than in Germany.[38] Of course other factors play a role in this, such as the tough fight for survival by those experiencing poverty in the United States or the historically evolved tradition of owning guns. But the influence of the antiquated tradition of upbringing is obviously very strong.

All this is important also for us. It is simply a fact that the United States is a leading culture on this Earth. It is therefore important that the reaction to the latest killing spree is not limited to the attempt to reduce the private possession of firearms. What the United States above all needs is disarmament of the mind. But this requires a radical change in the culture of upbringing. We should therefore not only watch passively; instead, we should appeal to this strong, great nation and its President: abolish the right to corporal punishment for parents and teachers.

---

[32] Pew Forum on Religion & Public Life, 2008

[33] Human Rights Watch & American Civil Liberties Union, 2008

[34] Gershoff, 2010

[35] Straus, 2010, p. 17.

[36] United Nations Office on Drugs and Crime (UNODC), 2011

[37] The numbers are based on the publications regarding homicides with firearms 2010 by the FBI and the U.S. Department of the Interior and the corresponding population figures. In the United States, there were 2.84 homicides with firearms per 100,000 residents; in Germany there were 0.19.

[38] ibid.

4. Sexual Child Abuse and Violence against Women – Two Examples of the Great Importance of Resilience

Ladies and Gentlemen, after this excursion into global politics, I would now like to continue with what I already mentioned: the two examples of the great importance of resilience. The first concerns **sexual child abuse**. In this regard, our two representative surveys from 1992 and 2011 show a similar trend as that concerning violence against children within the family. Among those under the age of 16, the risk of becoming a victim of abuse has also diminished greatly – from 7.1 to 4.4 % (abuse with physical contact).[39] When seeking an explanation for this, a finding from the survey data from 1992 gives us an important clue. According to this survey, children who are neglected and beaten by their parents have an especially high risk of abuse.[40] Those who have not received their fill of parental love radiate insecurity. Pedophiles have an antenna for this; they offer such children devotion and take possession of them. But those who were able to become self-confident and strong at home and who developed distinct powers of resilience are less in danger of being abused by their uncle, neighbor, priest or a stranger.

And if, in spite of this, it still happens, those victims who today are more self-confident and more active have much more power than before to put an end to the abuse, get help and report it. The survey of 2011 shows this especially clearly in comparison with the three age groups that we surveyed. Those who were between 31 and 40 years old at the time of the survey had reported the abuse only between 5 % and 13 % of the time, depending on the type of abuse, whereas those between 16 and 20 years of age reported it between 28 % and 41 % of the time. The percentage for those between the ages of 21 and 30 lies between these values. Whereas in the 1980's only about every twelfth perpetrator could count on criminal proceedings, today this applies to every third one.[41] This obviously dampens the enthusiasm for taking action among potential abuse offenders.

But here, too, there is no mono-causality. There are obviously other factors that can explain the increase in the willingness to report abuse. The sense of shame has changed in the course of the last three decades. In addition, the committed work by a large number of organizations for the aid of victims has borne fruit and has encouraged those concerned to step out of their passivity.[42] And finally, public attention and the sympathy for those concerned have increased markedly during the last three decades. All this has encouraged them to break their silence and get help.

---

[39] Stadler, Bieneck & Pfeiffer, 2012

[40] Pfeiffer & Wetzels, 1997

[41] Stadler, Bieneck & Pfeiffer, 2012

[42] Stiftung Opferhilfe Niedersachsen, 2011

My second example concerns **physical violence against women** within and outside the household and family. Figure 3 below shows what proportion of women were victims of physical injury during the five years preceding the surveys and compares the results of the survey in 1992 with the one in 2011. Overall, we find a decrease from 22.8 % to 16.6 %. When comparing the places of injury, however, we find the opposite trend. The proportion of women, who became victims of physical injury exclusively at home, sank during the 19 years from almost 18 % to 10 %. Parallel to this, since 1992, women are increasingly exposed to the risk of experiencing violence outside the family and household. Here, the proportion of victims increased from 1.7 % to 4.1 %.[43]

Figure 3: Physical violence against 16- to 40-year-old women within and outside the family

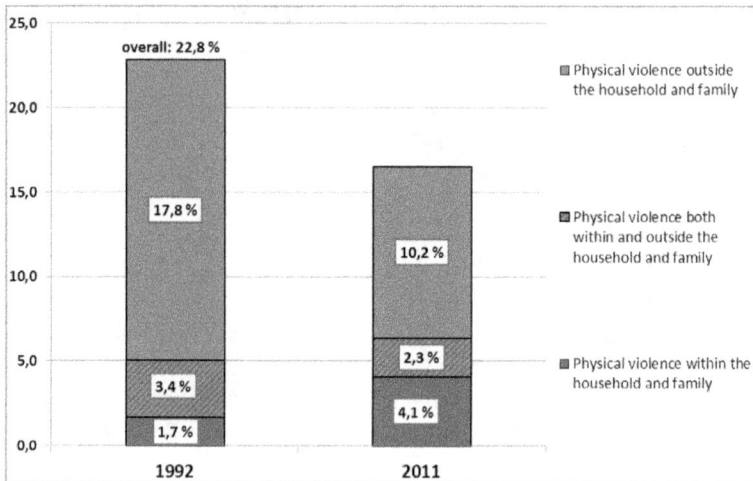

But why did the incidence of domestic violence fall so sharply? An initial explanation is obvious: The committed implementation by the police of the Protection against Violence Act. But a different aspect seems to be equally important: Girls have profited from the change described above much more than boys. When comparing the age groups in our survey in 2011 with that from the 1980s, the massive parental spanking of girls thus decreased from 17 to six percent – for boys it only decreased from 14 to eight percent.[44] On the other hand, in contrast to earlier years, the girls, as compared with the boys, received considerably more devotion and love not only from their

---

[43]   Pfeiffer & Thoben, 2013

[44]   Pfeiffer, 2012a, Pfeiffer, 2012b

fathers, but also from their mothers.[45] All this strengthened their self-confidence and contributed to increased success rates in their education and profession. They thereby became more independent and no longer let themselves be dominated as much as previously. Today, they have a greater amount of resistance against any claims to dominance by their partner and more often set limits when necessary. All this considerably reduces their risk of becoming a victim of intra-family violence.[46] More resilience means more prevention.[47]

But why did the proportion of women who became victims of physical injury in public areas increase so much? Here, too, the increased self-confidence of women seems to have been an important factor. The more they freed themselves from their earlier role as housewives, the more their leisure time behavior also changed. Today, they go outside much more than before. This goes hand in hand with taking higher risks. The result is that the public life of women has become more exciting, but also a bit more dangerous.

5. A Counter-example to the Positive Trend: Domestic Burglaries

Ladies and Gentlemen, at the beginning of my lecture I announced that I would provide a counter-example to all these positive stories of prevention. This concerns domestic burglaries. Police crime statistics registered an increase of 25 percent in the number of domestic burglaries between 2006 and 2011. Parallel to this, the clear-up rate sank from 20 to 16 percent.[48] The data from so far eleven federal states available from the year 2012 indicate that the situation has continued to worsen. As compared with 2011, an increase can be expected of 10 percent in the number of cases and a further decrease in the clear-up rate. In addition, the data from the police sugarcoats the situation a lot. The reason for this is that only in every fifth case that the police declares to be cleared up do the attorneys general have enough evidence to charge the suspect. The result is that, based on the cases that were reported in 2011, there is only a two percent risk of being convicted for a burglary.[49] This is a clear message to the burglars. In Germany, with a certainty of 98 percent, they can count on going unpunished for their criminal work. That is a true invitation for organized gangs of criminals to act – no matter if they live in Germany or in our neighboring Eastern European countries.

We at KFN used the opportunity of the large representative survey from 2011 to survey the 11,500 persons also regarding domestic burglaries. The findings match the bleak picture of the official statistical figures. There were many problematic messages from the five percent who stated that they had once been victim of a domestic

---

[45]   Pfeiffer, 2012d

[46]   Pfeiffer & Thoben, 2013

[47]   Walklate, 2011

[48]   Bundesministerium des Innern, 2012

[49]   ibid.

burglary. The average amount of damages was approx. 3,200 Euros. 38 percent were not insured and therefore had to cover the costs for the damages themselves. Many, however, stated that something else distressed them much more: **this burglary into the intimate sphere and security of their apartment.** Every second person suffered emotionally from it for a long time. Especially women tell of persistent, strong feelings of anxiety (37 %) and complain about massive sleep disorders (27%). Overall, every fifth person moved out of their apartment due to the burglary. Furthermore, three quarters of the victims (77 %) described the fact that the perpertrator could not be identified by the police as very unsatisfactory and disappointing.[50]

Faced with this shocking data regarding domestic burglaries, one of course asks oneself if such findings describe an exception or if there are any other negative examples from a victimological point of view. Here are a few key facts concerning this:

1.   Human trafficking has increased considerably.

2.   Many girls and possibly also boys become victims of pedophile men who aggressively try to come on to them while chatting in children's forums.

3.   The subculture of motorcycle gangs such as Hells Angels, Bandidos or Mongols is obviously growing rapidly.

6. Parallel Justice – Justice for all Victims

These highlights are a part of the overall picture. But they can only in a limited way supplement what Wiebke Steffen has presented within the framework of her extremely differentiated report regarding the **state of victims of crime in Germany**.[51] She justifiably points out that the overall situation has improved in many ways. Beginning with the Victims Compensation Act of 1976 and the Protection of Victims Act of 1986, the State has little by little strengthened the legal position of victims of crime. Regarding **criminal law proceedings** alone, there have been nine victim-related reforms since 1986 – from the injured party's right to inspect the records, via victims' attorneys at the State's expense, to the improvement of the adhesive procedure.[52] A final example deals with the recently adopted law regarding the strengthening of the rights of victims of sexual abuse, through which, for example, the injured party is granted extended rights of declaration and avenues for appeal.

We also have 13 changes in the **substantive criminal law** – from different regulations regarding victim-offender mediation, via the tightening of criminal law in the area of the penal code for sexual offences, to new regulations for the protection against human trafficking or the punishability of stalking.

---

[50]   Pfeiffer, 2012c, see also Görgen, 2012

[51]   Steffen, 2013

[52]   Böttcher, 2012, Schöch, 2012

Many of these legal regulations are justifiably welcomed by Wiebke Steffen, because they have contributed to preventing a re-victimization of the victim during the criminal proceedings and to supporting him/her against inappropriate attacks by the offender and his/her lawyer during these proceedings. I also agree with her in her criticism that these reforms only affect the 12 % of the victims whose cases have led to prosecution. Steffen also justifiably criticizes the fact that these laws for the protection of victims are not based on a clear, systematic concept. They often originated as a result of current events, sometimes had a populist orientation and should be seen as the result of lobbying by the associations for the protection of victims. But what can especially be criticized is a gross lack of empirical research regarding the experiences and true needs of the victims.

Legislators always claim to act in the interest of the victim, but they have almost never taken the trouble to carefully determine if their assumptions are correct. In addition, they are not very interested in if the intended strengthening of the rights of victims has had the desired effect and what experiences the different parties to the proceedings have made with the practical application of the new legal regulations. There are certainly good reasons to undertake an encompassing evaluation in this regard. This applies to the concern, expressed by many critics of the legislation concerning the protection of victims, that it would impede an effective criminal defense of sexual offenses. Another example is the prosecution of sexual offenses. The statement by many victims that they, in retrospect and in view of the experiences they gathered during the legal proceedings, would never again press criminal charges, should cause lawmakers to empirically investigate the assumptions that underlie the legislation.[53]

I will return to these research deficits later. But they can only be correctly assessed if we first expand our perspective. At this point in my lecture, I would finally like to introduce the concept of the protection of victims into the analysis, a concept which has been discussed for a few years under the term **"Parallel Justice."** With her book with the same name, Susan Herman, Professor of Criminal Justice at Pace University in New York City, has triggered a fundamental criminal policy discussion that goes far beyond the boundaries of the United States.[54] Her theses are on the one hand based on a wealth of empirical, victimological studies. On the other hand they are founded on her broad range of experience from over 30 years of helping victims in a practical way. She thus headed up the National Center for Victims of Crime in Washington for seven years and before that she was the head of the Aid to Victims of Domestic Abuse in New York.

Her theses can be summarized in four points.[55]

---

[53]   See Krahé, 2012, Volbert, 2012
[54]   Herman, 2010
[55]   ibid.

1. Criminal law and criminal procedural law are primarily focused on the offender. If he/she has received his/her rightful punishment and, if needed, has received help to reintegrate into society, we assume that justice has been done.

2. There is no comparable forum for the victims of crimes, in which justice can be organized for them by the State. It is true that the State, by introducing legislation regarding the protection of victims, has tried to take the needs of the victims into consideration within the framework of criminal proceedings. But it thereby limits itself to a small minority of victims, i.e. those whose offenders are taken to court. The vast majority of the victims come away empty-handed. And for the others, too, in spite of the legislative efforts, the role of the witness often entails very unsatisfactory and negative experiences.

3. In view of this blatant disregard of the interests of victims, we should decouple the effort to ensure justice for offenders from that of ensuring justice for victims. **Justice for victims** is thereby afforded an **importance of its own.** As a separate procedure, a plan of action consisting of three elements should be implemented – the determination that the victim has been wronged; effective protection of the victim against re-victimization; and finally support of the victim when it comes to dealing with the consequences of the victimization and regaining control over his/her life.

4. There should be no hierarchy of victim claims that grants special rights to **certain** victims as opposed to others. That would contradict our basic concept of justice. There is thus no sufficient reason to grant the victims of violence more rights than, for example, victims of burglary, stalking or fraud. Moreover, it should not matter if an offence occurred on the street, in a prison, a nursing facility or a psychiatric ward. Finally, the implementation of the concept of Parallel Justice should not depend on if the offender has ever been investigated or convicted.

In respect to the topic of our Congress on Crime Prevention, Susan Herman's book contains two clear messages, which she can substantiate through various empirical studies. First: Anyone who has been a victim has a significantly higher risk of becoming a victim again. Second: Parallel to this, there are also clear indications that victims often become perpetrators. Among youths, the strongest predictor for future criminality is thus that one has oneself been a victim of an attack.

From this, Susan Herman draws several conclusions for the work for the aid to victims. She thus demands that people who have been victims of crime receive fast and concrete support so as to actively prevent a repetition of their victim experience. I would like to illustrate this based on an example concerning our Protection against Violence Act. A policeman, who has been called by the neighbours, prohibits the husband, who has been beating his wife, from using his apartment for 14 days. He also informs the woman that the family court that has jurisdiction has the possibility to extend this expulsion for up to half a year. That would be an effective strategy for preventing re-victimization. But Susan Herman also justifiably points out that aid to victims should bear in mind the wishes of many of those concerned to hit back and to overcome the deep-seated frustration regarding the humiliating victim experience through aggression[56]. Such needs should then be addressed openly, so that together a way can be found to solve the problem constructively. That, too, would constitute highly effective prevention.

Finally, a further point is of key importance to Susan Herman. The help to victims should provide their support measures as soon as possible after the offence, also because the victim then has the opportunity to overcome the consequences of the offence quickly and can again look ahead. Staying with the example of inner family violence mentioned above, it is important that the woman concerned soon receives urgently needed psychotherapy and not years later, once a time-consuming expert opinion process based on the Victims Compensation Act finally has given the green light for it. The aid to victims should thus not tie those concerned to the role of weak, needy people, thereby contributing to them seeing themselves and behaving as such. On the other hand, Susan Herman also points out that it is up to those concerned to determine how long a time period they see and define themselves as victims. She consciously avoids the use of the term "learned helplessness," which to some extent has been used in this connection. On the one hand she feels that the term is often used to make the victims responsible for not "getting back on their feet" faster. On the other hand, she justifiably points out that the term awakens the false impression that there is a predictable period of time specifying how long someone suffers from the consequences of a criminal offence. "Some people transcend the crime quickly, others more slowly, and others not at all".[57]

But who are the actors involved in Parallel Justice? The answer is: Everyone! First of all, it is everyone who, within the context of schools, youth welfare, aid to victims or social work, is confronted with the fact that someone has become the victim of a crime. Second, it also concerns everyone who in everyday life is confronted with such a situation – for example, a neighbor who has heard that someone has become the victim of a burglary or a fight. All of them and all of us can and should contribute to the stabilization of the victim, in terms of the action strategies mentioned above.

I would like to explain this using **the police as an example**. For them, Parallel Justice means that they no longer may limit themselves to fulfilling their customary role. In the context of a criminal prosecution that is characterized by Parallel Justice, they have two functions of equal importance. On the one hand, they continue to be

---

[56] See Dutton& Greene, 2010; Barton, 2012

[57] See Herman, 2013 in a mail to C. Pfeiffer, in which she presents convincing arguments to protest against an ambiguous use of the term "acquired helplessness", which was used in the first version of the lecture manuscript.

responsible for indentifying the perpetrator of a crime that they have become aware of. In addition, however, and entirely independent of if they succeed in this, they also have the task of turning to the victim to first of all deliver a clear message: "You are not the victim of an accident. No, you have suffered injustice at the hands of an offender. We do not accept that." The police should thereby show respect, sensibility and empathy toward every victim. And they should, on principle, consider every victim to be credible. It is only if there is concrete evidence that gives rise to doubt that this rule does not apply.

It is subsequently the task of the police to determine in detail how great the resulting damages are. Later, this is important, especially if it does not succeed in identifying the perpetrator. In addition, during this first contact with the police, it is crucially important that the victim receives detailed information regarding two points. First, he/she should be informed of what it can expect during the criminal proceedings. Second, the police should provide comprehensive and very concrete information regarding what support offers are available – from the "Weisse Ring" [German for "White Ring," an independent non-profit organization in support of victims of crime and their families] to any State victim aid and specific offers of support, such as those available for victims of sexual violence, intra-family violence or stalking.

Police officers who are present could now turn to their neighbors and say: "But we are doing this already." "Really?" I answer. Does that apply without any restrictions, i.e. also to immigrants who have become victim of a crime, convicts, the homeless, drunk victims and those who are strongly agitated emotionally and seem to be difficult to communicate with? In such difficult communication situations, is the information that is necessary for the victim to have really provided later? There are not yet any satisfactory answers to these questions. The questions point toward initial research deficits that I would like to discuss in closing.

Here, I do not have time to go through, in detail, all that Parallel Justice means to all parties to the proceedings. For this I simply recommend reading Susan Herman's truly inspiring book and then asking yourself what her recommendations mean in detail if we translate them into our system of criminal prosecution. But I would like to mention a special issue.

Under point 3 in the Parallel Justice concept, I stated that Susan Herman recommends a **special procedure to determine the victim status**. In my opinion, if this recommendation were to be implemented, new perspectives would open up that would clarify many issues that exist between associations of victims and other groups. This applies, for example, to the problem of the statute of limitations.[58]

---

[58]   See Albrecht, 2011, Barton, 2012

Representatives of the victims are requesting that the statute of limitations for sexual abuse in part be repealed completely. Legal scholars and representatives of defence lawyers are against such requests, arguing that the resulting criminal proceedings that occur a long time after the abuse cannot lead to reasonable results. Here, the concept of Parallel Justice offers more flexibility. The system could remain the way it is regarding criminal proceedings against the offender. Entirely independent of this, there would be a procedure to determine that somebody has become the victim of such a crime. Here one could consider setting a statute of limitations of 30 years or even eliminating it entirely. This could, for example, contribute to intra-family witnesses to an abuse no longer remaining silent because they are freed from the burden of putting a family member in jail with their testimony.

7. Evaluation and Research – the Driving Force for a Gradual Implementation of Parallel Justice in Practice and Legislation

Two points appear to be important for the gradual implementation of Parallel Justice into our legal culture: First, we need a strict orientation toward the real needs of the victims, and second, we must take these needs into consideration in practice and in the legislation regarding victim compensation. For the **practical implementation of the concept**, this results in the need to constantly review its quality. I wish to explain this again using the example of police work.

Mr. Müller, who is slightly drunk, is beaten up and robbed by two fellow drinkers on his way home from his pub. He therefore immediately files charges at the nearest police station. Three days later he is called up by an evaluation agency that is cooperating with the police. It is explained to him that he is one of 50 victims who have been selected randomly in order to evaluate the work of this police station. He can now grade how satisified he is with the style of communication of the police officer and how he assesses the investigation of the harm he has suffered. He can also grade the advice he received regarding aid for victims and any claims he might have to crime victim compensation. The police station and the police directorate, in turn, get differentiated feedback in the form of the complete results of the 50 responses from the victims.[59] Such an **evaluation** should be carried out regularly and nationwide. This would be an important contribution to the gradual implementation of Parallel Justice.

But **victimological research** is here also of key importance. It thus appears essential to regularly carry out representative surveys in order to raise public awareness about the victimization risks that people have in the various areas of crime. It is only through such **research on unreported cases**, together with the crime statistics of the police, that it becomes possible to evaluate the security situation of the population. Only then will we be able to systematically review the viability of various prevention approaches. We then finally have the chance to review the victim risks of the various

---

[59] See Herman, 2010

population groups. We should therefore welcome the fact that the German Federal Office of Criminal Investigation and the Max Planck Institute in Freiburg together succeeded in surveying almost 35,000 people regarding their victim experiences.[60] It is only by surveying such a great number of people that we can expect to get reliable findings regarding rare victim risks. One can only hope that this will become a continuous, ongoing project.

We also need a **second victimological approach: the immediate survey of victims**, i.e. of persons who one knows have become victims of a certain crime. Only then is it possible to formulate questions regarding the consequences of the victimization in such a differentiated way that sufficiently well-founded evaluations of victim justice are possible on the basis of such a survey. In the following I would like to explain this, using the **Victim Compensation Law** as an example.

Since the introduction of the Victim Compensation Law (German acronym: OEG), which took effect in 1976, it has helped thousands of victims of violent crime receive considerable compensation payments.[61] In spite of this, there are critical questions regarding two aspects. On the one hand, they concern **access justice**, i.e. point number 4 in the concept of Parallel Justice described above. Why are the victims of a physical assault privileged? Which groups of victims appear to be equally severely affected as the current benefit recipients and should therefore also be eligible to apply? But clarifying the issue of access justice also involves asking questions of victims who, in principle, are eligible to apply but have not used the chance to receive compensation as provided by the OEG. Were they falsely advised or not advised at all? Are there peculiarities regarding their social status or certain types of offenses (for example intra-family violence)? How can the very large regional differences in the frequency of applications be explained that the White Ring is referring to?

On the other hand, the **application justice** of the OEG is increasingly being discussed. The question arises if the criticism is justified that the White Ring and different media have expressed, i.e. that many victims come away empty-handed in spite of applying and fulfilling the legal prerequisites.[62] Here, a broad-based **analysis of the records** could determine where possible problems arise when applying the OEG and how they can be solved in the interest of the victim justice that is being sought. It should also be investigated why the OEG procedure in part takes a very long time and why applications for preferred, quick aid obviously seldom have any chances of success.

It will not be easy to convince the responsible ministries and authorities of the necessity of such research approaches. But guarded optimism seems to be warranted,

---

[60] Module 4 of the project "Barometer Sicherheit in Deutschland" (BaSiD), which is being carried out by the Max Planck Institute in cooperation with the German Federal Office of Criminal Investigation.

[61] Stiftung Opferhilfe Niedersachsen, 2011

[62] Weißer Ring e. V., 2012

especially concerning one group of victims. The **roundtable regarding sexual child abuse** has been dealing with the problems mentioned here concerning the application of the OEG in a critical and constructive way.[63] In addition, at the final session of the roundtable, a clear signal was sent by policymakers. Dr. Niederfranke, the undersecretary of the Federal Ministry of Labor and Social Order, expressed the wish to clarify the remaining open questions regarding the application of OEG with the help of a scientific investigation.

Ladies and Gentlemen, what I have presented here as an example of the right to victim compensation leads to two conclusions. On the one hand, there is a need to answer Susan Herman's appeal to us, both for an improvement in the practical application of the law and for legislation reform. On the other hand, however, it is clear that we need broad-based scientific studies in order to deal with both issues.

8. Research on Victims of Abuse by Priests – Does the Church Want to Back Out?

But what has been mentioned above certainly does not sufficiently describe the **purpose of victimological research**. For the victim such research has an immediate value of its very own. Dealing scientifically with the suffering that victims have been subjected to brings both acknowledgment and appreciation to those concerned. The victims are taken seriously. They are listened to. What they have experienced is thoroughly registered, analyzed and finally published. It can no longer be swept under the rug.

I emphasize this point also because there are currently a large group of victims that could miss out in this regard. I mean the people who were sexually abused as children by priests, members of orders or deacons of the Catholic Church. In this regard, the **German Bishops' Conference** initially agreed contractually with us on a research concept that would have provided the victims with truly significant opportunities to play a constructive role. But then the project failed, because the Church suddenly wanted to push through broad-based control and censorship wishes through contractual changes that we could not accept.[64] It is now an open question what **importance the victims will have in any follow-on project**. In this regard, in a press release of Feb. 21, 2013, the Bishops' Conference writes: "One of the main objectives continues to be the collecting of reliable data and a review of the personnel files. The intent is to gain insights into the number and actions of the perpetrators and a deeper understanding of the behavior of those responsible in the Church during past decades."

Here, the victims are not mentioned with a single word. I ask myself if that has anything to do with the fact that many documents have obviously been destroyed.

---

[63] Final report of the roundtable "Sexueller Kindesmissbrauch in Abhängigkeits- und Machtverhältnissen in privaten und öffentlichen Einrichtungen und im familiären Bereich" ["Sexual Child Abuse in Relationships of Dependence and Power in Private and Public Facilities and within the Family Sphere."]

[64] Pfeiffer, Mößle, Baier, 2013 (manuscript in preparation)

It is true that the Church has stated that in case of the destruction of documents, the operative provisions of the judgment and a summary of the facts of the case are to be saved. These facts, which continue to be available in an offender's personnel file, were to make it possible to realize the research project. But in my mind that is highly doubtful. When documents are destroyed, it is specifically the information regarding the suffering of the victims that is lost. From a victimological point of view, such personnel files no longer have anything to offer. Should the project truly be re-started, then in my opinion, the Church should reveal in advance how many documents have been destroyed in each individual diocese. Only then can it be assessed if the research still makes any sense from the point of view of the victims. It would therefore be helpful if the victims' associations would demand three things: First, the future project may not contain any censorship regulations, whether in the contract or in additional, hidden agreements. Second, the suffering of the victims must remain a main focus of the project. And third: The Church should not try to wait out the affair and do without a research project entirely.

9. Outlook – a Special Research Project on the Victim-Perpetrator Constellation in Child Abuse

But I do not wish to end my lecture with this appeal. The end should consist of something entirely different: a brief look at a really interesting **research project** by the University of Stuttgart **regarding the topic of sexual abuse**. Based on 490 prisoners' personnel files, and using a methodologically excellent method of data analysis, Dieter Urban and Joachim Fiebig[65] were able to determine something that of itself is not very surprising. Men, who during childhood were abused by a pedophile offender, later in life have a significantly increased risk of themselves becoming abuse offenders. Their second insight, however, is very exciting. If such abused boys during the rest of their childhood attracted attention through especially aggressive behavior, then the probability that they later would become pedophile offenders was substantially lower. The authors offer a plausible explanation for this finding. The agressive behavior of such a boy can be seen as a strategy to overcome the trauma of the abuse he experienced. By proving himself as an agressive fighter, he compensates for the loss of self-worth and self-efficacy that was triggered by the abuse.

What does this teach us? In parting, I will give you two thoughts to reflect on: First, we should be very careful how we treat aggressive children. There can be many reasons for their behavior. One of them could be an early abuse experience.

Second: Simply punishing and preventing wrongdoing by children is the wrong way to go. We should not let up in our attempts to show especially such children ways how they can gain self-worth and self-efficacy. The corresponding program title is called awakening a passion for life through a broad range of challenges in the areas

---

[65] Urban & Fiebig, 2011

of sports, music, playing theater, circus and similar activities. If the children then develop a true passion for such an activity, then this experience of self-efficacy gives rise to what I mentioned earlier: the power of resistance and resilience. That would then constitute both effective prevention and an increased ability to cope well with victim experiences.

Bibliography

Albrecht, H.-J. (2011). Sexualstrafrecht – Reformen und Ergebnisse. *Recht der Jugend und des Bildungswesens*, 59 (2), 148-162.

Baier, D., Kemme, S., Hanslmaier, M., Doering, B., Rehbein, F. & Pfeiffer, C. (2012). *Kriminalitätsfurcht, Strafbedürfnisse und wahrgenommene Kriminalitätsentwicklung. Ergebnisse von bevölkerungsrepräsentativen Befragungen aus den Jahren 2004, 2006 und 2010. (KFN-Forschungsbericht Nr. 117).* Hannover: KFN.

Barton, S. (2012). Strafrechtspflege und Kriminalpolitik in der viktimären Gesellschaft. Effekte, Ambivalenzen und Paradoxien. In: S. Barton & R. Kölbel: *Ambivalenzen der Opferzuwendung des Strafrechts. Zwischenbilanz nach einem Vierteljahrhundert opferorientierter Strafrechtspolitik in Deutschland. (Interdisziplinäre Studien zu Recht und Staat, Band 53).* Baden-Baden: Nomos, 111-140

Bender, D. & Lösel, F. (1997). Risiko- und Schutzfaktoren im Prozeß der Mißhandlung und Vernachlässigung von Kindern. In: U. T. Egle, S. O. Hoffmann & P. Joraschky (Hrsg.) *Mißbrauch, Mißhandlung, Vernachlässigung.* Stuttgart: Schattauer, 35-53.

Boers, K., Feltes, T., Kinzig, J., Sherman, J., Streng, F. & Trüg, G. (Hrsg.) (2013) *Festschrift für Hans-Jürgen Kerner* . Tübingen: Mohr Siebeck. (Manuscript in preparation).

Böttcher, R. (2012). Perspektiven für den Opferschutz in Strafverfahren. *Neue Kriminalpolitik, 24 (4),* 121-164.

Bundesprüfstelle für Jugendgefährdende Medien. (2010). Entscheidung Nr. 9389 (V) vom 06.08.2010; bekannt gemacht im Bundesanzeiger 130 vom 31.08.2010.

Bundesprüfstelle für Jugendgefährdende Medien. (2013). Entscheidung Nr. 10919 (V) vom 05.04.2013; bekannt gemacht im Bundesanzeiger AT vom 30.04.2013.

Daigle, L. E., Beaver, K. M. & Turner, M. G. (2010). Resiliency against victimization: Results from the National Longitudinal Study of Adolescent Health. *Journal of Criminal Justice,* 38, 329-337.

De Montaigne, M. (1998). *Essais.* Frankfurt am Main: Eichborn GmbH & Co. Verlag KG.

Dutton, M. A. & Greene, R. (2010). Resilience and Crime Victimization. *Journal of Traumatic Stress,* 23 (2), 215-222.

Farrington, D. (1992a). The need for longitudinal experimental research in offending and antisocial behavior. In: J. McCord & R. E. Tremblay (Hrsg.). *Preventing antisocial behavior.* New York: Guildford Press, 353-376. 23

Farrington, D. (1992b). Psychological contributions to the explanation, prevention and treatment of offending. In: F. Lösel, D. Bender & T. Bliesener (Hrsg.). *Psychology and law: international perspectives.* Berlin: De Gruyter, 35-51.

Gershoff, E. T. (2010). More Harm Than Good: A Summary of Scientific Research on the Intended and Unintended Effects of Corporal Punishment on Children. *Law and Contemporary Problems*, 73 (2), 31-57.

Görgen, T. (2012). Zum Stand der internationalen viktimologischen Forschung. In: S. Barton & R. Kölbel: *Ambivalenzen der Opferzuwendung des Strafrechts. Zwischenbilanz nach einem Vierteljahrhundert opferorientierter Strafrechtspolitik in Deutschland. (Interdisziplinäre Studien zu Recht und Staat, Band 53)*. Baden-Baden: Nomos, 89 109.

Götz, F. & das Gupta, O. (2010). Erziehung mit der Rute. Liebe geht durch den Stock. *Süddeutsche Zeitung*, Jhg. 66 (39), Nr. 273

Greve, W., Hellmers, S. & Kappes, C. (2012). Bewältigung krimineller Opfererfahrungen: Entwicklungsfolgen und Entwicklungsregulation. In: S. Barton & R. Kölbel: *Ambivalenzen der Opferzuwendung des Strafrechts. Zwischenbilanz nach einem Vierteljahrhundert opferorientierter Strafrechtspolitik in Deutschland. (Interdisziplinäre Studien zu Recht und Staat, Band 53)*. Baden Baden: Nomos, 89 109.

Herman, S. (2010). *Parallel Justice for Victims of Crime*. Washington, DC: The National Center for Victims of Crime.

Human Rights Watch & American Civil Liberties Union (Eds.). (2008). *A Violent Education. Corporal Punishment of Children in US Public Schools*. New York: Human Rights Watch.

Kerner, H.-J., Stroezel, H. & Wegel, M. (2003). Erziehung, Religion und Wertorientierungen bei jungen Gefangenen. *Zeitschrift für Jugendkriminalrecht und Jugendhilfe*, 14 (3), 233-240.

Krahé, B. (2012). Soziale Reaktionen auf primäre Viktimisierung: Zum Einfluß stereotyper Urteilsmuster. In: S. Barton & R. Kölbel: *Ambivalenzen der Opferzuwendung des Strafrechts. Zwischenbilanz nach einem Vierteljahrhundert opferorientierter Strafrechtspolitik in Deutschland. (Interdisziplinäre Studien zu Recht und Staat, Band 53)*. Baden-Baden: Nomos, 159-176.

Lösel, F. & Bender, D. (2008). Von generellen Schutzfaktoren zu spezifischen protektiven Prozessen. Konzeptuelle Grundlagen und Ergebnisse der Resilienzforschung. In: G. Opp & M. Fingerle (Hrsg.) *Was Kinder stärkt. Erziehung zwischen Risiko und Resilienz*. München, Basel: Ernst Reinhardt Verlag, 279-298.

Matt, E. & Siewert, S. (2008). Resilienz, Lebenslaufperspektive und die Frage der Prävention. Einige kriminalsoziologische Betrachtungen zur Jugenddelinquenz. *Zeitschrift für Jugendkriminalrecht und Jugendhilfe*, 19 (3), 268-275.

Olweus, D. (1980). Familial and temperamental determinants of aggressive behavior in adolescent boys: A causal analysis. *Developmental Psychology*, 16 (6), 644-660.

Pew Forum on Religion & Public Life (Eds.). (2008). *U. S. Religious Landscape Survey. Religious Affilation: Diverse and Dynamic*. Washington, D. C.: Pew

Research Center. 24

Pfeiffer, C. & Wetzels, P. (1997). *Kinder als Täter und Opfer. Eine Analyse auf der Basis der PKS und einer repräsentativen Opferbefragung. (KFN Forschungsbericht Nr. 68).* Hannover: KFN.

Pfeiffer, C., Wetzels, P. & Enzmann, D. (1999). *Innerfamiliäre Gewalt gegen Kinder und Jugendliche und ihre Auswirkungen. (KFN-Forschungsbericht Nr. 80).* Hannover: KFN.

Pfeiffer, C. (2012a). Mehr Liebe, weniger Hiebe. *Süddeutsche Zeitung*, Jhg. 68 (2), Nr. 14, S. 2.

Pfeiffer, C. (2012b). Weniger Hiebe, mehr Liebe. Der Wandel familiärer Erziehung in Deutschland. *Centaur*, 11 (2), 14-17.

Pfeiffer, C. (2012c). Einbruch in die Seele. *Centaur*, 11 (5), 2-5.

Pfeiffer, C. (2012d). Zu wenig Liebe für unsere Söhne? Teil 1. *Centaur*, 11 (8).

Pfeiffer, C. & Baier, D. (2013) *Christliche Religiosität und elterliche Gewalt. Ein Vergleich der familiären Sozialisation von Katholiken, Protestanten und Angehörigen der evangelischen Freikirchen.* (Manuskript in Vorbereitung).

Pfeiffer, C., Mößle, T. & Baier, D. (2013). *Kontrolle und Zensur statt Kooperation und Forschungsfreiheit. Der Konflikt zwischen der deutschen Bischofskonferenz und dem Kriminologischen Forschungsinstitut Niedersachsen (KFN).* (Manuskript in Vorbereitung).

Pianta, R. C., Stuhlmann, M. W. & Hamre, B. K. (2008). Der Einfluss von Erwachsenen- Kind-Beziehungen auf Resilienzprozesse im Vorschulalter und in der Grundschule. In: G. Opp & M. Fingerle (Hrsg.) *Was Kinder stärkt. Erziehung zwischen Risiko und Relienz.* München, Basel: Ernst Reinhardt Verlag, 279-298.

Pinker, S. (2011). *Gewalt. Eine neue Geschichte der Menschheit.* Frankfurt am Main: S. Fischer. (Original published in 2011: The Better Angels of Our Nature. Why Violence has Declined).

Rousseau, J. J. (1971). *Emile oder über die Erziehung.* Paderborn: Ferdinand Schöningh.

Schöch, H. (2012). Opferperspektive und Jugendstrafrecht. *Zeitschrift für Jugendkriminalrecht und Jugendhilfe*, 23 (3), 246-254.

Suess, G. J. & Kißgen, R. (2005). Frühe Hilfen zur Förderung der Resilienz auf dem Hintergrund der Bindungstheorie: das STEEPTM –Modell. In: M. Cierpka (Hrsg.). *Möglichkeiten der Gewaltprävention.* Göttingen: Vandenhoeck & Ruprecht, 135-152.

Stadler, L.; Bieneck, S. & Pfeiffer, C. (2012). *Repräsentativbefragung Sexueller Missbrauch 2011. (KFN-Forschungsbericht Nr. 118).* Hannover: KFN.

Stiftung Opferhilfe Niedersachsen (2011). *Hilfe schenkt Freiheit. Festschrift anlässlich des 10-jährigen Jubiläums der Stiftung Opferhilfe Niedersachsen.* Hannover: Stiftung Opferhilfe Niedersachsen.

Straus, M. A. (2010). Prevalence, Societal Causes, and Trends in Corporal Punishment by Parents in World Perspective. *Law and Contemporary Problems,* 73 (2), 1-31.

Thornberry, T. P., Lizotte, A. J., Krohn, M. D., Farnworth, M. & Jang, S. J. (1991). Testing interactional theory: An examination of reciprocal causal relationship among family, school and delinquency. *Journal of Criminal Law and Criminology,* 82 (1), 3-33.

Urban, D. & Fiebig, J. (2011). Pädosexueller Missbrauch: wenn Opfer zu Tätern werden. Eine empirische Studie. *Zeitschrift für Soziologie,* 40 (1), 42-61.

Van Damme, D. (2012). Non cognitive Skills Surveys in OECD. Vortrag anlässlich der ESP conference in Amsterdam, 3.-4. 12. 2012.

Volbert, R. (2012). Geschädigte im Strafverfahren, positive Effekte oder sekundäre Viktimisierung? In: S. Barton & R. Kölbel: *Ambivalenzen der Opferzuwendung des Strafrechts. Zwischenbilanz nach einem Vierteljahrhundert opferorientierter Strafrechtspolitik in Deutschland. (Interdisziplinäre Studien zu Recht und Staat, Band 53)* Baden-Baden: Nomos, 197-212.

Walklate, S. (2011). Reframing criminal victimization: Finding a place for vulnerability and resilience. *Theoretical Crminology,* 15 (2), 179-194.

Wattendorff, L. (1907). *John Lockes Gedanken über die Erziehung.* Paderborn: Ferdinand Schöningh.

Wegel, M., Kerner, H.-J. & Stroezel, H. (2011). Mobbing und Resilienz in Schulen. Zusammenhänge des Opferwerdens und dessen möglicher Vermeidung. *Kriminalistik,* 8-9, 526-532.

Weißer Ring e. V. (Hrsg.). (2012). *Moderne Opferentschädigung. Betrachtungen aus interdisziplinärer Perspektive. Dokumentation des 21. Mainzer Opferforums 2010. (Mainzer Schriften zur Situation von Kriminalitätsopfern, Band 48).* Baden-Baden: Nomos.

Werner, E. E. & Smith, R. S. (1992). *Overcoming the Odds. High Risk Children from Birth to Adulthood.* Ithaca and London: Cornell University Press.

Wetzels, P. (1997). *Gewalterfahrungen in der Kindheit. Sexueller Mißbrauch, körperliche Mißhandlung und deren langfristige Konsequenzen. (Interdisziplinäre Beiträge zur kriminologischen Forschung Band 8).* Baden-Baden: Nomos.

Online sources

Final report of roundtable: „Sexueller Kindesmissbrauch in Abhängigkeits- und Machtverhältnissen in privaten und öffentlichen Einrichtungen und im familiären Bereich".

http://www.rundertisch-kindesmissbrauch.de/documents/AB%20RTKM_barrierefrei.pdf

Barometer Sicherheit in Deutschland:
http://basid.mpicc.de/basid/de/pub/projekt.htm

German Federal Ministry of the Interior: Police criminal statistics 2010
http://www.bmi.bund.de/SharedDocs/Downloads/DE/Broschueren/2011/PKS2010.
pdf?__blob=publicationFile

German Federal Ministry of the Interior: Police criminal statistics 2011
http://www.bmi.bund.de/SharedDocs/Downloads/DE/Broschueren/2012/PKS2011.
pdf?__blob=publicationFile

Federal Bureau of Investigation (FBI): Murder Victims by Weapon, 2006-2010
http://www.fbi.gov/about-us/cjis/ucr/crime-in-the-u.s/2010/crime-in-the-u.s.-2010/
tables/10shrtbl08.xls

Steffen, W. (2013). Expert opinion for the 18th German Congress on Crime Prevention, Apirl 22 & 23, 2013 2013 in Bielefeld „Mehr Prävention – Weniger Opfer".
http://www.praeventionstag.de/kriminalpraevention/Module/Media/Medias/18-DPT-
Gutachten_267.pdf

Wiebke Steffen

Report for the 18th German Congress on Crime Prevention
Bielefeld, 22-23 April 2013
"More Prevention, Fewer Victims"

Victim orientation in society, research, criminal justice and crime prevention: Status, problems and perspectives

Wiebke Steffen
Heiligenberg (Baden) / München

Content

Preface

From around the late 1970s, German society, research, criminal justice and crime prevention began to show an increasing orientation towards victims of crime, "to the point of a renaissance of the victim, a renaissance that is now also underway in the public perception of victims … [because it] … not only affects specific sectors, but cuts right across society" (Barton/Kölbel 2012, 11, 14).[1]

To cite just a few milestones and sectors involved: WEISSER RING e.V., a not-for-profit association for victim support and crime prevention, was founded in 1976. Child welfare organisations and the feminist movement began lobbying for better treatment of women and children who had become victims of sexual offences. In the academic domain, victimology became established during the last 25 years as a separate sub-discipline of criminology.[2] An important year in lawmaking was 1984, when the 55th Congress of German Jurists elected as its principal topic "The legal position of the injured party in criminal proceedings." Germany's first Victim Protection Act (Opferschutzgesetz) came into force at the end of 1986. For over 40 years now, the German Police Crime Prevention Programme has issued advice for the public on how to protect against crime. Increasingly, other governmental and non-governmental organisations, too, have acknowledged their responsibility to help people avoid becoming victims of crime as part of the overall societal task of crime prevention.

In recognition of these developments, the 18th German Congress on Crime Prevention took as its principle topic "More Prevention, Fewer Victims." This report, "Victim orientation in society, research, criminal justice and crime prevention: Status, problems and perspectives", takes stock after a quarter century of victim orientation. It begins by reviewing current empirical knowledge about victimisation and what victims need and want – the basis for victim-oriented responses by society and the criminal justice system. It then enquires into the current status, problems and perspectives of victim orientation in criminal justice and society, before finally discussing consequences for crime prevention.

---

[1]   The increased victim orientation is thus by no means restricted to criminal law and the law of criminal procedure, even if the debate about the status of the injured party in criminal proceedings is carried on in a more heated, controversial way in that discipline than in other social domains, and not without sceptical voices. See, for example, the proceedings of the 4th Bielefelder Verfahrenstage (Bielefeld Congress on Procedural Law) under the heading of "Zwischenbilanz nach einem Vierteljahrhundert opferorientierter Strafrechtspolitik in Deutschland" ("Taking stock after a quarter century of victim-oriented criminal law policy in Germany").
The 'rediscovery of the victim' is also by no means specific to Germany; similar changes are to be seen in many Western legal orders (Barton/Kölbel 2012, 11 ff; Weigend 2012).

[2]   For example with the publication in 1986 of "Soziologie des Opfers. Theorie, Methoden und Empirie der Viktimologie" ("Sociology of the victim: Theory, methods and empirical methods of victimology") by Kiefl and Lamnek.

0

Summary and conclusions

From about the late 1970s, German society, research, criminal justice and crime prevention began to show an increasing orientation towards victims of crime. Today, in all of these areas, the victim has long ceased to be what prior to this 'renaissance' of the crime victim could still be fittingly referred to the "forgotten man." There is even talk of an "era of the victim."

The time is therefore ripe for an **interim assessment** of the status, problems and perspectives of victimisation. What is the current status of empirical research on victimisation, victims' needs and victims' wishes? Which victims are in the focus of attention and which are overlooked? What has changed for victims in society and in criminal justice over the last 25 years? What are the perspectives – is it not true that the best way to protect victims is to prevent crime?

A note on terminology: Labelling the **injured party in a crime** a 'victim' is not entirely without problems. Firstly, in society at large, the word 'victim' makes people both want to help and to turn away. Secondly, it is at odds with the criminal law presumption of innocence. It is nonetheless used in the following because it is the established term, notably in legislation, and is in universal use both nationally and internationally.

Between perceptions and empirical knowledge: Which victims are in the focus of attention and which are overlooked?

The increased orientation towards victims mostly relates to victims of violent crime, but by no means all. The focus of attention is on 'ideal' victims: Children, women (but only if they do not 'have themselves to blame'), old people, and people in nursing care. This does not include men – especially not young men.

Yet this focus does not fit the facts of victimisation in society, as reflected by analysis of reported crime statistics and findings from victimological self-report surveys. Sexual offences excepted, men are far more frequently victims of violent crime than women, and young people are more frequently victims of violence than older people.

There is **insufficient data**, however. Reported crime statistics still centre on offenders, suspects and institutional responses and either take no account of victims at all (German criminal prosecution statistics) or only give limited account to victims of specific (violent) crimes along with a small range of victim and offender data (German Police Crime Statistics). The field of view must be widened to take in all victims of crime and at least the same set of variables as are collated for offenders; this is best done in the Police Crime Statistics.

Knowledge about unreported crime is even less satisfactory, with a particularly large share of sexual and violent offences staying below the surface because of victims' unwillingness to report. **Victim surveys** have been done to close this knowledge gap, but mostly restricted to specific regions or victim groups. The latest nationwide victim surveys date from 1997 (a representative national victim survey by the Federal Criminal Police Office (BKA) is currently in analysis).

More victim surveys are urgently needed, both quantitative and qualitative – not just on victimisation and willingness to report crimes, but also on the effects of victimisation and what victims want and expect from support systems and the criminal justice system.

One thing is clear: There is no such thing as the typical victim

There are few empirical findings, and scarcely any recent findings, on victimisation, the effects of victimisation, and what victims want and need. Most surveys were carried out around 1990/1991 and international findings do not readily transfer across national borders. Despite this, one thing is clear: There is no such thing as the typical victim, and victimisation, victim behaviour and victims' wishes are very individual indeed.

Not all victims suffer, yet some suffer their whole life long. And the effects cover a broad range: Psychological, physical and financial impacts, fear of crime, revictimisation, personal risk of delinquency – all of these can apply. Yet knowledge about how frequently and in what circumstances they apply is very limited.

The same goes for victims' **wants and needs** after a crime. Here, too, there are scarcely any recent findings, and victims' wishes are highly individual. Victims can be generally assumed to want social support, information and advice, and acknowledgement of the wrong done to them. Relative to these needs, victims' wishes in terms of punitiveness and retribution play more of a minor role, and certainly a lesser one than is often assumed. The need for retribution can be reduced to victims' interest in acknowledgement of the wrong done to them and in that wrong being suitably responded to. Many victims desire restitution of the harm done and are also prepared to take part in conflict mediation arrangements such as victim-offender mediation.

Victim wants and needs are also another area where there is urgent need for empirical victimological research. This is the only way to avoid deciding over victims' heads and to give them (or give them back) their self-determination and autonomy.

The criminal justice system is inherently unable to serve the interests of victims

The German Code of Criminal Procedure has seen several victim-oriented reforms since 1986 with the aim of improving victim protection, but it is hard to make out a clear, systematic concept behind them. It has also been disputed from the outset whether victims can be subjects of criminal proceedings with rights of their own.

Whether victims of crime actually wanted the new rights and protection in criminal proceedings and whether the German victim protection acts actually achieved their express aim of preventing **secondary victimisation** cannot be determined: The reforms have not undergone any evaluation and there are no findings on whether they are what victims want and need.

Going by what we know so far, most victims are less interested in having an active part in a trial than in three relatively simple things:

- Being kept informed about the course of the proceedings
- Compensation for the harm done
- To be treated respectfully as witnesses.

In a criminal justice system based on the rule of law and oriented to victim needs, all of that should be a matter of course without any need to create additional rights and powers for victims.

In any case, the criminal justice system is inherently unable to serve the needs and wishes of victims. Firstly, it is and remains offender-oriented; secondly, giving testimony always places a burden on the victim; and thirdly, only a very small percentage of victims make it to court. Most criminal investigations are dropped by the prosecution service and only about 12 percent lead to charges being brought.

All involved should keep in mind that certain pressures on victims are unavoidable in proceedings under the rule of law, and for that very reason, burdensome aspects not necessary to the conduct of a fair trial should be changed.

Social support, help and recognition for victims must come from outside the criminal justice system – from family and friends and from victim support organisations

When victims speak about what they have experienced – and they by no means always do – then the first and most important people they turn to are close family and friends. That is often enough to stabilise the victim and give them a sense of safety and security.

Otherwise, victims can turn not just to psychotherapists, crime victim lawyers and similar providers of psychosocial and legal help and advice, but most of all to victim support organisations. Such organisations embody the increasing victim orientation of society, and they presided over a 'renaissance' of the crime victim long before the victim was 'discovered' by the criminal justice system. They provide help both in material form and in kind, but first and foremost they provide care und support after a crime.

There are now a wide range of publicly and privately organised and funded victim support organisations in Germany. The oldest and best known, which operates nationwide and with an entirely volunteer staff, is WEISSER RING e.V. ('White Ring').

A victim's help and support needs can be met in a day, but it can also take years. The goal is to help victims rebuild their lives as quickly as possible after the traumatic event, always with the aim of maximum autonomy for the victim. This is because any act of support for someone who has been victim to a crime also labels that person a victim. Help for victims is only helpful if it helps them move beyond the state of needing help.

The increased orientation towards victims in society has taken victim support and assistance quite some way. The **Parallel Justice** framework, developed by Susan Herman in the USA and in part already implemented, could bring further improvements. Parallel Justice is rooted in the conviction that society has an obligation to exercise justice for victims, and aims to create a new framework for responding to crime: Two separate, parallel paths to justice – one for victims, one for offenders.

More prevention, fewer victims

However efficient and effective the criminal justice, victim protection and victim support systems are made, it is always better to stop crimes and consequently victimisation from happening in the first place. No criminal justice system, however victim-oriented, and no victim support system, however well-established and capable, can hope to make good, let alone undo, the physical and material harm to victims and the often severe psychological impacts of a crime. The best way to protect victims is thus to prevent crime.

Victim-oriented crime prevention is concerned on the one hand with the implications of findings on the effects of victimisation. On the other hand, it is concerned quite conventionally with preventing and reducing victimisation. While victim-oriented crime prevention, as the name suggests, places the emphasis on the victim, it does not mean the kind of prevention that has to be or can be put into practice by victims themselves, but crime prevention in the usual comprehensive sense taking in victims, offenders and situations.

Victim-oriented crime prevention must take special care on two counts, however: To avoid raising (unnecessary) fears of victimisation or revictimisation, and to avoid giving victims any part of the blame for their victimisation.

1
Between perceptions and empirical knowledge of crime victims

"Public (i.e., media) discourse increasingly revolves around victims of crime.[3] The press, radio and television report on the fates of victims; victims and their relatives appear in talk shows. It does not seem too much to speak of an era of the victim ... Solidarity with the victim unites the community; society is becoming the 'victim society'" (Barton/Kölbel 2012, 14).[4]

While in the 'victim' society attention and interest are said to have switched from accused to victim (thus Barton 2012, 112), and while victimology is now an established sub-discipline of criminology[5] – with key research topics including "questions of the phenomenology of victimisation events and processes and of the prevalence and incidence of reported and unreported victimisation" (Görgen 2012, 91) – this is not to say that the people who society perceives as victims actually are victims of crime. There is a distinct discrepancy between the 'ideal' victim[6] and 'real' victims. But before going on to explore the territory "between perceptions and empirical knowledge of crime victims," first a few necessary remarks about the concept of victim.

1.1
Notes on problems with the concept of victim

There are a number problems with the concept of victim.[7] Firstly at both individual and societal level because of inherent ambivalence, and secondly at the level of criminal law and the law of criminal procedure because of the provisional nature of role attribution in criminal proceedings (Schöch 2003, 19).[8]

---

[3] Weigend had already noted the 'high status' accorded to the problems of the victim some years previously, saying, "A number of years ago when the idea for this present paper was born, any exploration into the role of the injured party in criminal proceedings, if not exactly a venture into unknown territory, at least represented a journey to a largely neglected tract bearing little fruit of academic research and attracting little interest in its cultivation. The scene has changed fundamentally in a short space of time. The field of victim studies is well tilled and even in the narrower bounds of criminal procedure research, the victim long ceased to be what only a few years ago could still be fittingly termed the 'forgotten man'" (1989, 13 f.).

[4] On the term and concept of the victim society see also Kunz: "Society becomes the 'victim' society by regarding potential victimhood as a point of reference for individual attributes and thus electing not the superior victor, but the weak, suffering victim as the basic model for the classification of individuals" (2011 a, § 31, at 59). For an in-depth discussion of the victim society see Barton 2012.

[5] For Barton, criminology has "more or less become a victimology. Not of course the old victimology, in which the victim is primarily seen in terms of partial blame for the committing of crimes, but a victimology that is not about blame but about victimisation" (2012, 119).

[6] Term coined by Nils Christie, cited by Barton 2012, 116.

[7] See also Steffen 2012 a, 142 f.

[8] Sessar (2012, 264) notes a very basic problem, writing, "The use of the term 'victim' is, however, highly problematic as it grafts an abstract criminal law definition onto an individual experience, so to speak 'without asking'. Criminologically, it would be better to distinguish self-declared and extraneously declared victims, thus respecting the freedom of the individual affected by a crime to regard themselves or not to regard themselves as a victim."

Ambivalence in the concept of victim

"Victim status is always something attributed – by the individual themselves or by people around them and by society – ... [and this attribution] is not free of ambivalence. At individual level the associated attitudes oscillate between sympathy and the urge to help on the one hand and disparagement and rejection on the other" (Görgen 2012, 90).

Becoming the victim of a crime does not necessarily enhance an individual's social status. On the contrary,[9] connotations that go with the concept of victim – 'weak', 'dependent', 'vulnerable' and 'in need of protection'[10] – not only communicate empathy and support, for example in connection with victim support services, but also denigration and disparagement, and not just in youth-speak.[11]

"People who become victim of a violent crime experience powerlessness, helplessness, vulnerability, and weakness. But it is wrong to reduce them to this experience; it does not necessarily make them powerless, helpless and weak in themselves ... The goal of working with victims must therefore be to strengthen their autonomy and self-esteem" (Ladenburger 2012, 290).[12]

The interests of crime victims "tend to be dilemmatic," writes Reemtsma (2006, 18): "People who become victims of crimes want those around them to take that into account – yet do not want to be cast in the role of victim."

This finding is directed especially at victim support organisations, whose – well-meaning – efforts to help and protect victims can reduce them to their victimhood rather than enabling them to say goodbye to the victim role, regain their autonomy and ability to act, and develop their own resistance and resilience (Steffen 2012 a, 143).

---

[9]   "Victims are embarrassing, they remind us of our own weakness and downfall" (Margarete Mitscherlich, cited by Maercker 2006, 53).
      Anders Barton (2012, 117): "Victimhood is associated in the victim society with prestige, recognition, attention, rights and privileges ... Slightly exaggerating, the victim society can even be said to be a society in which 'everyone wants to be a victim.'"

[10] See also Baurmann 2000, 3; Seilaff 2010, 264. Further connotations, of a kind rarely helpful to the victim, follow from the sacred, religious origin of the victim concept.

[11] It is common among boys and young men to use the word 'victim' as an insult ('You victim!'). "The term 'victim' ... is used to gain assurance of the individual's own identity and to push away all that is associated with victimhood: weakness, loss, fears, failure – everything to do with being or becoming a 'loser'" (Voss 2003, 58).
      For Barton (2012, 117), "'You victim!' as an insult from the mouth of a young outlaw means ... 'I don't abide by your rules.' Thus, from an outsider position, the youth deliberately derides the basic social consensus and the victim society.

[12] On the "problematic gains of victimisation" see also Barton, who with reference to Nils Christie notes that the attribution of victim status can amplify suffering and delay healing processes; there is also the risk that victim protection measures can cause victims to cease believing in their own ability to cope with the situation. This could lead to acquired helplessness – a disastrous outcome. Further, a victim could find the gains of victimisation so enriching that they prefer being a lifelong victim over other roles (2012, 134).

Problems of the victim concept in criminal law and the law of criminal procedure
"As the accused in a trial is presumed innocent, it is not established that the accused has done harm until the court establishes guilt … In criminal proceedings, therefore, the accused as potential offender has a logical complement in the form of 'potential' victimhood" (Kunz 2011 b, 2).

It is doubtless hard to dismiss the argument that designating someone the victim[13] of a crime implies that there is also an offender and hence is at odds with the presumption of innocence[14], a central pillar of criminal procedure. It is necessary to agree with Weigend, however, when he writes that most legal systems uphold a fiction that the individual identified in a trial as the injured party is indeed and not merely apparently the victim of a crime.[15] "Yet this means the rights granted to victims in criminal procedure are explicitly also granted to individuals who will later prove to be non-victims. This cannot be seen – as is sometimes claimed – as a breach of the presumption of innocence, for the guilt or innocence of the accused is unrelated in principal to whether he or she has harmed the specific individual who appears in the trial as the victim[16] … The experience, too, that it is fairly rare for someone wrongfully to usurp the role of victim speaks in favour of a certain generosity in according victims' rights in criminal proceedings" (2012, 31 f).

Besides, the very frequency with which criminal proceedings are dropped shows that labelling one person 'victim' and the other 'offender'[17] has minimal or zero prejudicial effect. In any case it is the established term, most of all in the law.[18]

---

[13] Using the term 'injured party' ('Verletzter', as predominates in German law of criminal procedure) instead of victim poses the same problems; the two terms are therefore often used synonymously (see Weigend 2012, 31 and Weigend 1989, 13).

[14] The presumption of innocence is enshrined in Article 6 (2) of the European Convention on Human Rights, which stipulates that anyone charged with a criminal offence must be presumed innocent until proved guilty according to law. In German law, the presumption of innocence also follows from the rule of law under Article 20 (3) and the first sentence of Article 28 (1) of the German Basic Law.
The presumption of innocence also applies in Germany for the press (Section 13 of the Press Code).

[15] It is thus consistent that a 'victim' is defined in Article 65 (1) of the Austrian Code of Criminal Procedure as "a person who may have been exposed to violence or dangerous threat or whose sexual integrity may have been compromised through an intentional criminal offence" (Weigand 2012, 31).
The term 'victim' is also used without any qualification in Directive 2012/29/EU of the European Parliament and of the Council of 25 October 2012 establishing minimum standards on the rights, support and protection of victims of crime, and replacing Council Framework Decision 2001/220/JHA. Under the Directive, 'victim' means "(i) a natural person who has suffered harm, including physical, mental or emotional harm or economic loss which was directly caused by a criminal offence; (ii) family members of a person whose death was directly caused by a criminal offence and who have suffered harm as a result of that person's death."
The OpferFibel – a guide for victims of crime – published by the German Federal Ministry of Justice likewise speaks throughout of 'victims of crime' without questioning the term in any way.

[16] For Schünemann, 'victim' in the context of criminal proceedings is "an expression that implicitly negates the presumption of innocence" (cited in Pollähne 2012, 8, fn. 17).

[17] Or in police investigation proceedings 'suspect' or 'accused'.

[18] 'Opfer', the German word for victim, is found for example in 'Opferschutzgesetz' (Victims Protection Act), 'Opferrechtsreformgesetz' (Victim Law Reform Act), 'Opferanwalt' (a lawyer representing victim

Actual and potential victims

When therefore the phrase 'victims of crime' – rather than 'putative victims'[19] – is used in the following, then it is used in the sense of actual rather than potential victims. That is, "Persons who have reason to assert of themselves that they have been harmed by a criminal act. They are 'actual' victims of a crime ... Besides 'actual' victims, however, there are also 'potential' victims ... Anyone who is not the victim of a crime but fears becoming a victim of crime is in a wholly different position to an 'actual' victim ... they do not demand rights in specific criminal proceedings, but may demand a specific type of crime policy[20] designed to meet their rights as potential crime victims. They also have no victim experience; instead they have victim fantasy" (Hassemer/Reemtsma 2002, 100 f.).[21]That is, a **narrow definition of the term 'victim'** is used, based on the standards applied in criminal law:[22] Victims are individuals who are registered as victims of crime in the reported crime statistics or have stated in victim surveys that they have been victims of crime ('self-declared' victims). In either case, only direct victims are included – individuals targeted in or directly harmed as a result of a prosecutable act.[23]

1.2
Perceptions of crime victims: The 'ideal victim'

When we speak of an increased victim orientation in society, research, criminal justice and crime prevention, while that orientation is seen to be broadly and publicly welcomed (Barton/Kölbel 2012, 14) and "acknowledgement of victim status" is seen to confer "attention, rights and privileges" (Kunz 2011 a, 367), this by no means applies to all victims of crime. Those who are perceived and recognised as victims in the described sense are mostly, if not almost always 'ideal' victims who in fact make up only a (small) fraction of people who become victims of crime.

---

interests), the OpferFibel (guide for victims) published by the Justice Ministry, and so on (see also Steffen 2012 a, 142). The German term 'Opfer' is thus the established term nationally and across all government departments, just as 'victim' is the established English term internationally.

[19] Or 'potential victims' as advocated by Kunz (2011 b, 2).

[20] This 'specific type of crime policy' relates to policy in which actual or alleged fears of victims are 'abused' to advocate repressive criminal law policy. See also Barton/Kölbel 2012, 15; Steffen 2012 b.

[21] "Virtual crime victims do exist and they have real influence on the criminal justice system and its policies. The current phenomenon of victim orientation uses not so much a concept of actual as of virtual victims. A basic right to safety, for example, is conceived most of all as a guarantee to potential victims of crime" (Hassemer/Reemtsma 2002, 101).

[22] Feldmann-Hahn notes criticisms of this narrow definition and calls for a criminological/victimological definition of the victim that places the focus of victim-related research on the subjective perspective and bases the classification as victim on the victim's sensibilities alone: A victim is whoever feels they are a victim (2011, 11). Likewise Sessar 2012 (Fn. 8).

[23] And not indirect victims, individuals affected by another's experience of victimisation by virtue of being in some way especially close to them (on terminology see Sautner 2010, 164). On the impacts on indirect victims such as family see also Sielaff 2010.

As so frequently happens, perceptions and empirical findings diverge[24], raising the question of which victims are in mind when asserting, describing and observing an increase in victim orientation, and which victims are overlooked.

Nils Christie aptly coined the term 'ideal victim': The ideal victim, says Christie, is weak – that the concept of victim connotes 'weak', 'dependent', 'vulnerable' and 'in need of protection' has already been mentioned; it is someone going about their morally or socially respectable business; they are somewhere they cannot reasonably be blamed for being; the offender was big and bad; the offender was unknown and there is nothing to connect them personally with the victim.[25]

Anyone who does not match this 'ideal' will not, or at least not readily, be recognised as a victim. The focus when it comes to victims of crime is therefore on children, women (but only if they do not 'have themselves to blame'), old people, and people in nursing care. This does not include men – especially not young men.[26]

That this selective focus does not fit the facts of victimisation in society is shown by criminological and victimological findings on the prevalence and incidence of reported and unreported victimisation.

1.3
Empirical findings on the prevalence and incidence of reported and unreported victimisation

First, a **preliminary remark**: Considering the 'renaissance' of the victim in the last quarter of a century, the recognition given to victim support services, the improved position of the victim in criminal proceedings, the marked shift in attitudes towards more sensitivity for the concerns of victims and – of particular relevance for the present section of this report – the establishment of victimology as a sub-discipline of criminology, it is remarkable **how little empirical knowledge there is about victims of crime**. For Germany at least, there are few findings – and none from the recent past – on key aspects of victimisation, including:

- Prevalence and incidence of (primary) victimisation

- Impacts/effects of victimisation experiences, including the nature and extent of

---

[24] See, for example, the findings under the heading "Jugendkriminalität zwischen Wahrnehmung und empirischen Befunden" ("Juvenile Crime: Between Perceptions and Empirical Findings") in Steffen 2008.

[25] Cited in Barton 2012, 116.

[26] Accordingly, the increased victim orientation, the special attention paid to victims in the last 25 years, has primarily focused on specific *victim groups* and their protection:
Maltreated children were 'discovered' first, later came women who were victims of violence and rape, and finally children who had been subject to sexual exploitation. The numerically largest group of victims of crime, on the other hand, continue to be overlooked and not regarded as victims: Men and boys (likewise, Baurmann 2000, 3).

secondary victimisation[27] through criminal proceedings and from family, friends and acquaintances

- Victim needs, expectations and wishes.

There is a distinct lack of data and empirical research is urgently needed.

One thing is clear, however: There is no such thing as the typical victim, and victimisation, victim behaviour and victims' wishes are very individual indeed.[28]

The findings on both reported and unreported victimisation presented in the following mostly relate to victims of violent or 'contact' crimes: Crimes involving contact between offender and victim and emotional, physical or sexual violence.[29] In the German Police Crime Statistics on reported crime, these are in any case the only crimes for which information on victims is recorded. Most victim surveys additionally take in other types of crime, notably crimes against property.[30]

1.3.1
Victims of police-reported crime in the German Police Crime Statistics

In the German Police Crime Statistics, victims – "the natural persons against whom the punishable act was specifically directed"[31] – are only included for specific offences or groups of offences.[32] This reflects the fact that the police statistics and other official crime statistics are focused to this day on offenders, suspects and the institutional response to offences (Görgen 2012, 100).[33]

In total, the **number of victims** – like the number of crimes[34] – has fallen continuously for some years. For violent crime[35], 257,257 victims were recorded in 2007 and

---

[27]   'Secondary' victimisation refers to victimisation subsequent to that experienced through the crime itself in the form of responses from agencies of the criminal justice system and from friends and acquaintances.

[28]   See, for example, the study findings in Kilchling 1995, 621 ff.

[29]   Baurmann/Schädler rightly note that the situation of victims of violence is often wrongly generalised to include all crime victims. In fact, about 94 percent of victims of reported crime are not victims of violence. Kilchling surveyed victims of contact offences comprising robbery and attempted robbery, sexual offences, assault and threat, victims of non-contact offences comprising car offences, motorcycle/bicycle theft, theft of personal property, and as an in-between category, victims of burglary. This matches the categories used in the International Crime Victim Surveys (see below).

[30]   On limits as to the offences able to be included in surveys and the resulting lopsided selectivity of research on unreported crime, see Feldmann-Hahn 2011, 33 ff.

[31]   This is the definition given in the Definitions section of the Police Crime Statistics for the Federal Republic of Germany.

[32]   Presented in Table 91 (Victim classification by age and sex) and Table 92 (Victim-suspect relationship); the crimes involved are primarily violent, sexual and robbery offences.

[33]   The bias is even stronger in criminal prosecution statistics, which do not include any information on victims at all.

[34]   Except a small increase of one percent between 2010 and 2011.

[35]   The category-level classification key 89200 'Violent crime' encompasses murder; manslaughter and killing another at his or her own request; rape and sexual coercion; robbery, extortion accompanied by vio-

233,950 in 2011. The number of victims per 100,000 population went down from 312.5 to 286.2, meaning that approximately 0.3 percent of the German population were recorded in the Police Crime Statistics as victims of violent crime in 2011 as in 2007.

As to **gender**, just over a quarter (27.4 percent) of all victims of violent crime were female in 2007, compared with 29.2 percent in 2011 (although here again the absolute figures have gone down). The number of victims per 100,000 population was significantly higher for men, at 412.9, than for women, at 164.1 (2007: 463.2 versus 168.0).

Looking at specific violent offences, two-thirds of all police-recorded victims of murder and manslaughter, robbery and bodily injury are male; for dangerous and serious bodily injury the figure is no less than three-quarters.

Only in offenses against sexual self-determination are female victims in the majority, at over 90 percent.

For offenses against personal freedom, the ratio is roughly 50:50.[36]

Comparing **age groups**, adolescents and young adults are registered with disproportionate frequency as victims of bodily injury, robbery, offences against personal freedom and offences against sexual self-determination[37] – categories in which the same young age groups also account for the largest number of offences.

The German Police Crime Statistics data confirm findings from victimisation research that **victimisation risk is linked to key demographic attributes** – in this instance age and gender[38] – and that at least for reported crime as presented in that data, the reality of victimisation is at odds with 'ideal victim' of popular perception: With the exception of sexual crimes, women are far less frequently victims than men[39]; similarly, it is relatively rare for children and older people aged 60 upwards to be recorded as victims.

---

lence, and assault on motorists with intent to rob; bodily injury resulting in death; dangerous and serious bodily injury; hostage taking; and attacks on air and sea traffic.

[36] Victim-suspect relationships can incidentally likewise be said to be gender-specific, with victims mostly being male in cases of violence by offenders having no previous relations with the victim and cases of violence in public places; victims of violence by relations and acquaintances close to the victim are predominantly female.

[37] For example, the number of victims of bodily injury per 100,000 in each group was recorded in 2011 as 2,822 for young adults and 2,014 for adolescents, versus only 894 for adults aged between 21 and 60 and as few as 133 for adults aged 60 and above.

[38] Other demographic factors are economic and social status in society (Görgen 2012, 93), on which no information is recorded in the Police Crime Statistics.

[39] For Treibel et al., it is not possible to say from the available data whether women are more frequently and more severely affected by violence than men: The reported crime data in the German Police Crime Statistics show that men overall are more frequently victims of crime than women; however, women are more frequently affected by offences with low reporting rates, such as domestic and sexual violence (2008, 459).

Those at risk, on the other hand, are male adolescents and young male adults: Violence by (young) men is most of all violence against other (young) men – and offender-victim role reversal is not the exception, but the rule (Steffen 2008, 241).

1.3.2
Willingness to report crimes and motives for reporting

The central problem in any assessment of victimisation risk based on police-reported crime statistics is that it depends on victims' willingness to report a crime and make it public. Over 90 percent of the offences officially recorded in the German Police Crime Statistics come to the notice of the police and so make it into the statistics through crimes being reported by private individuals, mostly victims and injured parties. Yet far from being the 'normal' response of victims and injured parties to an inherently prosecutable wrongdoing, reporting to the police is in fact very much an 'exclusive' response.[40]

Findings from research on unreported crime show that only a certain proportion (variable by type of offence[41]) of criminal offences are reported by victims to and registered by the police. In terms of overall crime, it can be assumed that by far the majority of inherently prosecutable wrongdoings stay unreported – and with them their victims (Steffen 1993, 33).

There are no recent nationwide findings on reporting rates for specific offences in Germany.[42] The following figures were determined for contact and non-contact offences in the two most recent (1997) nationwide victim surveys:[43]

- Burglary and attempted burglary: 88.3 and 80.5 percent (at victim prevalence rates of 1.8 and 1.7)

- Robbery: 57.1 percent and 59.9 percent (at victim prevalence rates of 1.1 and 0.8)

- Physical assault: 37.9 percent and 32.7 percent (at victim prevalence rates of 2.0 and 1.5)

- Sexual assault: 44.4 percent and 61.4 percent (at victim prevalence rates of 0.3 and 0.2)

- Sexual harassment: 20.6 percent and 19.2 percent (at victim prevalence rates of 2.1 and 1.5).

---

[40] Steffen 1976 and 1982, cited in Steffen 1993, 33.

[41] In a victim survey, Kilchling determines a reporting rate of 76.9 percent for victims of burglary; the figure for victims of non-contact offences was 62.6 percent and that for victims of contact offences was 31.8 percent (1995, 211 f).

[42] Van Dijk 2012, 31 gives a reporting rate of 62 percent for burglary in Germany for 2009/2010.

[43] PSB 2006, 19. The first set of figures relate to reporting rates among respondents age 18 and above, the second set to respondents age 16 and above. Likewise for the victim prevalence rates. Reporting rates for shoplifting and damage to property are far higher, not least due to insurance requirements.

In 2004, the Federal Ministry of Family Affairs, Senior Citizens, Women and Youth (BMFSFJ) conducted a representative survey on the prevalence of violence from age 16 among over 10,000 women aged 16 to 85 and determined reporting rates ('police brought in') of 14 percent for all situations of physical violence and 21 percent for serious forms of such violence (Müller/Schröttle 2004, 189). The police were brought in for 11 percent of all cases of sexual violence and for 15 percent where the offender was a partner, ex-partner or lover of the victim (Müller/Schröttle 2004, 208 f).

For sexual abuse, a representative survey by the Criminal Research Institute of Lower Saxony in 2011 (with some 11,000 respondents) arrived at reporting rates ranging from 11.9 percent to 18.4 percent for the various forms of abuse, with female victims reporting somewhat more frequently than male victims with one exception ('anal/ vaginal penetration') (Standler et al. 2012, 42).[44]

For adolescents of an average age of 15, in a representative survey (with close to 45,000 respondents) conducted in 2007 and 2008, the Criminological Research Institute of Lower Saxony measured reporting rates of 24 percent for all violent offences; respondents reported robberies in 40.2 percent of cases, severe bodily injury in 36.8 percent of cases, and other violent offences (extortion, sexual violence, and slight bodily injury) in about 18 percent of cases (Baier et al. 2009, 42).[45]

The most frequently cited **reasons for not reporting** a crime:[46]

- Offence not very severe/not so serious
- Not appropriate to bring in the police/police would not have been able to do anything
- Informal conflict resolution
- Wanted peace and quiet
- Shame – offence too intimate
- Scared/fear of vengeance
- (Presumed) police ineffectiveness/inactivity; did not want anything to do with the police

If a victim does bring **charges**, it marks the "final step in what is often a conscious decision process. Especially in the interpersonal domain, victims use the bringing of

---

[44] Schöch (2012, 247) notes in connection with sexual abuse in institutions "that it was partly fear of criminal proceedings that contributed to the wall of silence."

[45] The victimisation rate (victimisation in the last 12 months) for violent offences as a whole is 16.8 percent; male respondents: 20.2 percent; female respondents: 13.0 percent; sexual harassment is the only offence for which female respondents (11.9 percent) state a higher victimisation rate than male respondents (1.9 percent) (Baier et al. 2009, 39).

[46] See PSB 2006, 19; Müller/Schröttle 2004, 190, 210.

charges instrumentally, not infrequently after a failed attempt at resolution. It is thus the victims themselves who in almost all instances "determine the process of prosecution and hence select (or at least preselect) the offences to be prosecuted" (Kilchling 1995, 25 f).[47] Kilchling assumes that "in a very broad sense, criminal prosecution has the character of a service for victims, or can take on or reassume that character" (1995, 24).

Whether **charges are brought** also depends on other factors (aside from insurance terms and conditions). Such other factors include:

- Nature and severity of the crime or injury
- Offender characteristics
- Victim characteristics
- Offender-victim relationship
- Third-party influence
- Social tolerance (Schwind 2011, § 20, at 9).

When it comes to **motives for bringing charges**, a key factor is the type of crime: "What victims want most is to get help and avoid a repeat occurrence. With property-related crime and robbery, the hope of recovering the property dominates along with the fact that charges often have to be brought so as to claim on insurance. Across all offence types, a part is played by hopes that the offender will be caught and punished, by the perceived severity of the crime, and by the extent to which the victim feels obliged to bring a committed crime to official notice" (Görgen 2012, 98).

Whether such an obligation is 'felt' can also depend on the – estimated or perceived – effectiveness of the criminal justice system and on victims' prior experience with the system if they have brought charges in the past.[48]

---

[47] Schwind speaks in this connection of the "victim's power of selection" (2011, § 20, at 2).

[48] See also Schwind 2011, § 20, at 10a; Feldmann-Hahn 2011, 6.

1.3.3
Victims of unreported crime[49]

1.3.3.1
Victims of unreported crime: Methods and limitations of victim surveys

Studies on the prevalence, nature and incidence of victimisation in relation to unreported crime are a central research topic in victimology. Most such studies take the form of surveys (Schwind 2011, § 2, at 44).[50]

Whereas the first systematic surveys of unreported crime were offender surveys[51], "the rise of victimology and the 'rediscovery' of the victim in the sense of increased focus on neglected victim interests" brought a shift in emphasis towards victim surveys (Feldmann-Hahn 2011, 17).

Kilchling distinguishes two basic types of victim survey: Crime surveys to measure crime levels and victim surveys enquiring into broader issues of victimology (1995, 55 f.; the same definitions are taken up in Sautner 2010 and Feldmann-Hahn 2011).

Research on the victim side began with **crime surveys**, "whose main aim was, or is, to record the nature and extent of victimisation in the population ... although the main focus of such studies (remains) criminal behaviour per se. Victim aspects come second" (Sautner 2010, 146). The focus of such surveys, which that parallel the official crime statistics,[52] is on crime rates and crime rate measurement and on precisely measuring prevalence and incidence rates (Feldmann-Hahn 2011, 4).

Victim surveys are studies "that set out from a victimological standpoint to investigate the underlying circumstances of victimisation and the multifaceted victim perspective" (Sautner 2010, 146). They make up the majority of present-day surveys; their focus is on victims themselves and victim-related issues such as reporting rates, regard for the police, and fear of crime (Feldmann-Hahn 2011, 4).[53]

---

[49]   'Unreported crime' is taken to mean all offences for which charges are not brought and therefore neither come to the notice of the criminal investigation authorities nor feature in the Police Crime Statistics (Schwind 2011, § 2, at 34). A further factor is police recording practices: It may be assumed that some reported crimes are not included in the Police Crime Statistics as a result of selectivity in recording (Feldmann-Hahn 2011, 14).
For a fundamental treatment of the status of research on unreported crime, see Heinz 2006; for an overview of the status and perspectives of research on unreported crime in Germany and internationally, see Stock 2012.

[50]   On other methods of research into unreported crime, such as participant observation and experiments, see Schwind 2011, § 2, at 37-43.

[51]   See the figures in Schwind 2011, § 2, at 46-52.

[52]   On the status of debate about periodic victim surveys in Germany and the benefits of ongoing unreported crime research of this kind, see Feldmann-Hahn 2011, 158 ff. See also Stock 2012.

[53]   An intermediate form between crime surveys and victim surveys consists of **victimisation surveys** – effectively crime surveys from the victim perspective that also incorporate the consequences of victimisation into the research programme (Kilchling 1995, 56).

Victim surveys are generally implemented as population surveys, with the effect that they cover non-victims as well as victims. This creates the problem of how to distinguish the two, or means that respondents must identify themselves as victims (**self-declaration**).[54]

Sautner (2010, 165 ff) points to the problems in connection with self-declaration as victims. A degree of misclassification is to be expected. Non-victims might declare themselves as victims, although according to Sautner this is quite rare. Far more common, in Sautner's analysis, is non-assertion of victim status by failing to report experiences of victimisation in the survey. A range of causes are identified:

- Forgetting
- Suppression of experienced victimisation
- Deliberate withholding, e.g. out of shame
- Considering it a private matter
- Conscious rejection of the victim role, e.g. because the incident involved is thought too minor
- What is in fact a crime is not thought of as one by the person affected.

In summary, "non-victims are individuals who have either not experienced a crime or have forgotten or do not wish to remember."[55]

Most victim surveys relate to victimisation experiences in a given **reference period**, usually 'in the last 12 months' before the survey but sometimes during a period of several years or in the victim's lifetime ('at any time in your life'). With longer reference periods, there appears to be a bias towards reporting offences of greater severity. Responses involving such offences, and particularly violent offences, also appear to display a telescoping effect, i.e. that respondents falsely attribute the timing of the victimisation. Victimisation can be falsely attributed into the reference period (forward telescoping) or out of it (backward telescoping) (Feldmann-Hahn 2011, 44 f; Sautner 2010, 167 f).

Another methodological problem with victim surveys[56] relates to their limits in terms of **offences capable of being surveyed**. It is not possible to ask about offences that

---

[54] In population surveys, the need for such self-declaration is obvious. But even with 'victim-only' surveys, i.e. surveys of people already recorded as victims in police or court files, there is a need for self-declaration, because the known (on file) victimisation incident may be overlaid by earlier or later experiences of victimisation, whereas responses are wanted on a specific type of incident (Sautner 2010, 165). Such 'victim-only' surveys include the studies by Baurmann/Schädler (1991) and Richter (1997).

[55] On the information value of responses and the willingness of respondents to provide information, see also Feldmann-Hahn (2011, 44).

[56] For a comprehensive discussion of this and other methodological problems and limitations to the usefulness of victim surveys, see e.g. Feldmann-Hahn 2011, Schwind 2011, § 2, at 44 ff, and Steffen 1993.

are not directed against private individuals or that go unnoticed by the victim. Offences in the context of interpersonal relationships, such as intrafamilial violence, child maltreatment and child sexual abuse, are capable of being surveyed "only with major limitations" (Feldmann-Hahn 2011, 34).[57] Offences for which victim surveys are well suited include theft, burglary, robbery and bodily injury (outside of the family context) (Schwind 2011, § 2, at 54b). For Feldmann-Hahn (2011, 33) this leads to a "lopsided selectivity of research on unreported crime."[58]

Victim surveys are therefore subject to non-trivial methodological problems that limit their usefulness. Görgen (2012, 100) is nonetheless right in saying that "empirical victimological research ... [is] an indispensable corrective for police-reported crime statistics." But it is also no more than that: Surveys of unreported victimisation are not better or more useful by definition than official crime statistics. The two are merely different ways of obtaining data on crime and victimisation, "neither of which is more 'accurate' or 'precise' than the other, but each of which leads to specific findings and conclusions" (Steffen 1993, 46).[59]

Another reason victim surveys are 'indispensable' in victimology is because the Police Crime Statistics contain little information on victimisation (see above) and none on reporting rates and reporting motives or on victims' needs and wishes. The "shift in emphasis from crime surveys to victim surveys in modern victimology" (Feldmann-Hahn 2011, 27) is therefore to be welcomed. It means the focus of research is no longer on finding out the extent of unreported crime (which is impossible anyway) but on victims and the consequences of victimisation (Steffen 1993, 46; Feldmann-Hahn 2011, 27).[60]

---

[57] According to Schwind, "Research into unreported crime is inherently incapable of capturing offences committed within the family or in the immediate social environment (such as offences in the context of an interpersonal relationship) (2011, § 2, at 53a). However, this assertion can be considered to have been refuted by studies on violence (by partners) against women (Müllser/Schröttle 2004) and on child sexual abuse (Standler et al. 2012).

[58] Limitations are also necessary for cost reasons; only 'basic' data can be surveyed (Heinz 2006, 251). It is not possible either on a qualitative or on a quantitative basis to survey all crimes included in the German Police Crime Statistics.

[59] Or as Kiefl and Lamnek noted as early as 1986: "Official crime statistics, offender surveys, unreported crime surveys and victim surveys each have their pros and cons, and none of these methods captures all occurrences of victimisation. The best approach is a combination of offender and victim studies in a specific geographical area" (1986, 53).
     Kunz is likewise critical of the ability of unreported crime surveys to map reality, notably in pointing out that population surveys on offences suffered (victim surveys) or committed (offender surveys) reflect how respondents answer surveys, "which is not the same as criminal acts suffered or committed. Such surveys are not about self-reported criminal behaviour and victimisation, but about **self-reports** concerning criminal behaviour and victimisation." They are about "a narrative that does not simply report facts but presents experience in a form rendered suitable for the survey setting" (2011, § 21, at 23).

[60] "The knowledge gain from modern research into unreported victimisation therefore lies not only in contrasting the findings against those from reported crime data (something that can only be taken so far), but in obtaining information that is not and cannot be gleaned from official crime and criminal justice statistics" (Heinz 2006, 245).

1.3.3.2
Victims of unreported crime: Victim survey findings

Although many victim surveys have now been carried out in Germany[61], there is still far from enough data, and most of all there is a glaring lack of recent empirical findings from victimological research. This is mostly because there are scarcely any representative nationwide surveys for Germany – representative, that is, for the entire population and all offences capable of being surveyed, not just for specific population groups or groups of offences,[62] and at least in principle allowing comparison with the nationwide police-reported data from the Police Crime Statistics.

There have long been calls for nationally representative victim surveys of this kind, and notably for **studies of unreported crime paralleling official crime statistics.**[63] This is not just to learn more about victimisation experiences, but also serves crime policy purposes. An ongoing need is felt – mainly from experience in other countries[64] but also based on findings from mostly urban self-report surveys in Germany[65] – for the ability to contrast official crime statistics with data on unreported crime. Official crime statistics are very hard to interpret without information on unreported crime. Most of all, rational crime and criminal justice policy needs a sound empirical footing. Evidence-based crime policy requires regular nationally representative population surveys (Heinz 2006, 251), otherwise the result could well be crime policy "flying blind."[66]

---

[61] Feldmann-Hahn most recently brought together the victim surveys carried out in the Germany or the former West Germany that are representative of the resident population age 14 and above and at least include questions on how the victimisation came about (2011, 78). The analysis took in 30 "general, regionally restricted victim surveys" carried out between 1973 and 2010, 13 "nationwide, internationally comparative victim surveys" carried out between 1981/1982 and 2004/2005, and 22 "victim surveys in the context of criminological regional analyses" carried out between 1987 and 2007 (listed in Feldmann-Hahn 2011, 185 ff).

[62] For example surveys of 15-year-old school students (Baier et al. 2009), on partner-inflicted violent victimisation of women (Müller/Schröttle 2004), on victimisation in the 40-to-80 age group (Görgen et al. 2010), on sexual abuse (Standler et al. 2012) and on violence against police officers (Ellrich et al. 2011).

[63] See, e.g., Schwind 2011, § 2, at 76-79b; Heinz 2006.

[64] In the USA, for example, comparing data from the Uniform Crime Report with data from the annual National Crime Victimization Surveys shows an increase in severe violent crime in the crime statistics but a marked decrease according to the survey data (Feldmann-Hahn 2011, 159).

[65] In repeat surveys in Bochum (in 1975, 1986 and 1998), two-thirds of the increase in police-reported bodily injury offences merely related to a change in the willingness of victims to report offences (Feldmann-Hahn 2011, 159).
    Similarly, in a representative survey of 15-year-old school students by the Criminological Research Institute of Lower Saxony (KFN), findings on the willingness of victims to report violent offences "put the information value of the Police Crime Statistics in a different perspective on several counts ... reporting rates among victims of violence ... increased for bodily injury offences by 20 to 50 percent ... This increasing shift of cases from the domain of unreported to reported crime suggests that the recorded increase in juvenile violence since 1998 ... is substantially due to a change in victims' reporting behaviour" (Baier et al. 2009, 11).

[66] Heinz, cited in Feldmann-Hahn 2011, 160; Schwind 2011, §2, at 76: "Statistikbegleitende Dunkelfeldforschung als Postulat" ("Necessity of unreported crime surveys paralleling official crime statistics").

Few studies of unreported crime in the form of nationally representative population surveys have been carried out at all in Germany[67], none in recent years and certainly none on a 'parallel', i.e. periodic basis in step with the official crime statistics. This means it is impossible to say if the prevalence and incidence of victimisation is the same for unreported crime as it is for reported crime. And it is also impossible to say in respect of offences not brought to the notice of and not recorded by the police whether victims of violent and contact offences (other than sexual offences) are indeed predominantly young and male (see section 1.3.1).[68]

An insight into this latter point is expected from a joint study of **victimisation experiences** carried out by the Bundeskriminalamt and the Max Planck Institute for Foreign and International Criminal Law as part of a consortium project, *Barometer of Security in Germany (BaSiD)*, from June to October 2012.[69] In a computer-aided telephone interview (CATI) survey, close to 35,000 respondents were asked about their victimisation experiences, sense of security/fear of crime, and willingness to report crime. The interviews averaged 20 minutes. The questionnaire was based for comparability on the items used in the International Crime Victim Surveys (ICVS) (see below). Data analysis is currently in progress and initial findings are expected beginning in May 2013.[70]

For the recent past, nationally representative data on victimisation in relation to unreported crime in Germany is only available in connection with surveys carried out as part of the International Crime Victim Survey (ICVS)[71] – perhaps the best known international comparative study. The ICVS has gone through five iterations so far. Germany took part in the first ICVS (in 1989, albeit for the territory of former West Germany only) and in the most recent ICVS (2005)[72]; it also took part in the ICVS

---

[67] For an overview, see Feldmann-Hahn 2011, 98 ff.
The most recent national **victim surveys** in Germany were carried out in 1997 with two samples of different sizes (and a 12-month reference period) in research commissioned by the Federal Ministry of Justice. For the range of crimes they surveyed, the two studies arrived at overall prevalence rates of, respectively, 15.9 and 19.5 percent of respondents. The prevalence rates for victims of simple theft ranged from 9.2 and 11.5 percent; for burglary and attempted burglary between 1.5 and 1.6 percent; and for violent crime between 2.2 and 2.9 percent (PSB 2006, 17 f and Heinz 2006, 254).

[68] A survey carried out in early 2005 under the leadership of the Criminological Research Institute of Lower Saxony (KFN), in which individuals in the 40 to 85 age group were asked about victimisation involving crimes against property, violent crime and sexual offences, found that, as with the Police Crime Statistics, "the findings of this nationwide survey, too, do not paint a very dramatic picture with regard to risk in old age" (Görgen et al. 2010).

[69] See Haverkamp 2012/www.basid.mpicc.de and Steffen 2012 b.

[70] Christoph Kirkel and Nathalie Guzy from the Bundeskriminalamt reported on the study design and pre-test findings at the European Society for Criminology conference in Bilbao on 14 September 2012.

[71] See van Dijk 2012 und Feldmann-Hahn 2011, 115 ff.

[72] Van Dijk et al. 2007. The European Crime and Safety Survey (EU ICS 2005) was co-financed by the European Commission and is methodologically integrated into the ICVS, i.e. it is essentially part of the fifth iteration of the ICVS (Feldmann-Hahn 2011, 116 f).
The 2005 survey wave covered 18 countries and focused on household crimes (such as vehicle theft and

2010 pilot in 2010.[73]

Findings of the ICVS 2010 pilot compared with ICVS 2005:[74]

- In the last twelve months, 16.7 percent of respondents in Germany were victims of twelve offences[75] asked about in the survey; compared with other participating countries[76], this is the second lowest figure for both survey years. Respondents in 2010 were least frequently victims of vehicle theft in the last twelve months, at 0.3 percent, and most frequently victim of bicycle theft, at 4.8 percent.

- In the last five years, 44.5 percent of respondents in Germany were victims of the offences asked about in the survey – once again the second lowest figure compared with other participating countries. In 2005 the figure had been 43.1 percent, the lowest for that year. Respondents in 2010 were again least frequently victims of vehicle theft in the last five years, at 1.5 percent, and most frequently victims of bicycle theft, at 18.7 percent.

- In contrast, fear of crime, with 17.5 percent of respondents "feeling unsafe or very unsafe walking alone in the dark" in the area where they lived, was second highest compared with the other countries, after the United Kingdom. However, this compared with a figure of 30.6 percent in 2005, which was likewise second highest after the United Kingdom.

- Germany scores a low figure of 13.4 percent on the other hand for the number of respondents who worried about becoming a victim of burglary in the next twelve months (with only Canada and the Netherlands scoring lower at 12 percent). This was down from 22.8 percent in 2005, when only Canada and the United Kingdom recorded a higher figure.

Overall, therefore, the findings for Germany do not give cause for alarm – least of all in light of the findings of the EU ICS 2005 on reporting to and satisfaction with the police. Germany is fourth out of 18 countries for the frequency with which burglaries are reported (there is no analysis by country for other offences on this point) and sixth for satisfaction with the police.

---

burglary) and personal crimes (such as robbery, theft of personal property, physical assault, threat and sexual assault). Approximately 1,200 individuals across the country were surveyed (by telephone), plus another 800 in Berlin (Goergen 2012, 96).

[73]   www.crimevictimsurvey.eu and www.int-cvs.org

[74]   See also van Dijk 2012; findings from the EU ICS 2005 are also to be found in Görgen 2012, 97 ff.

[75]   Theft of a car, theft from a car, theft of a motorcycle/moped, bicycle theft, burglary, attempted burglary, robbery, theft of personal property, sexual offences against women, sexual offences against men, assault and threat.

[76]   The ICVC 2010 pilot was carried out in Canada, Denmark, Germany, the Netherlands, Sweden, and the United Kingdom.

Scope for analysis by variables other than those mentioned – such as by victim age and gender – is evidently limited, or at least the relevant data is not available.

1.3.4
Effects of victimisation

Another focus of victimological research is on the effects of victimisation. This line of research confirms a conclusion stated at the beginning: There is no such thing as the typical victim, and the same also goes for the effects of victimisation experiences. Not every victim suffers – yet some suffer their whole life long. Not every victim of a crime experiences "deeper or lasting injury beyond the immediate impacts of the crime … But there are many, many thousand cases every year here in Germany where a crime victim suffers severe emotional harm as a result of the crime" (Böttcher 2012, 122).[77]

So the effects of victimisation are a very subjective thing: Objective criteria – such as offence severity in terms of physical harm, financial loss or counselling needs – are by no means enough "when it comes to probing the nature and impact of harm to victims, because this significantly depends on the victim's subjective perception,[78] which is affected by a wide range of factors" (Sautner 2010, 179).[79]

1.3.4.1
Psychological, physical and financial impacts

Görgen (2012, 95) points to a "wide range of possible effects." These include:

- Health impacts
- Psychological impacts
- Behavioural impacts
- Financial impacts both for the victim and for society.[80]

---

[77] Barton 2012, 115 estimates, however, that people do not argue so finely: "A final piece of received wisdom in the victim society is the idea that crime always leads to trauma, criminal proceedings lead to renewed trauma, crime victims suffer their whole life long, and violent and sexual crime is on the rise in Germany."

[78] Likewise Baurmann/Schädler (1991, 299): "The study showed generally that there is no such thing as 'the' victim. Different crime victims with similar experiences have very different ways of dealing with their victimisation."

[79] Kilchling quite rightly not only criticises the use in victimology of attempts to fit offender characteristics on a severity scale (e.g. the Sellin-Wolfgang scale), but also notes a general weakness in much victimological research to date, in that questions are mostly asked in relation to fictional cases and not to personal experiences of victimisation (1995, 129 f).

[80] At personal level loss and devaluation of property, at societal level healthcare and nursing costs, productivity loss, institutional costs and expenditure on victim support and victim compensation.

Psychological impacts are likely to be more common than physical impacts,[81] "something that public perceptions of crime probably do not get right. The proportion of victims who suffer no harm from criminal victimisation is probably under 10 percent." Also, violent and contact offences are not the only ones that can have psychological and physical impacts; non-contact offences and burglaries can too (Sautner 2010, 180 f).[82] By the same token, it is necessary to agree with Kilchling that from the victim's standpoint, it makes a crucial difference whether or not the victimisation involved an encounter with the offender (1995, 106).

While men suffer physical harm from criminal victimisation significantly more frequently than women, women experience psychological impacts somewhat more frequently than men.[83] Psychological impacts, due to "the many different forms they take and because they are sometimes not recognised at all as (serious) impacts, are [likely to be] far harder to detect than physical or material harm to victims. On top of this, it ... heavily depends on the individual whether criminal victimisation has any psychological impacts at all and if so what kind ... However, a common cause of such impacts can be sought in the fact that for those affected, victimisation experiences mark a violation of their own identity ... [and] severely challenge their personal integrity ... In some crime victims, the experience of victimisation causes them to lose their 'belief in a just world' ... Overall, however, how people deal with victimisation is a very individual process" (Sautner 2010, 186 f).[84]

---

[81]   Baurmann/Schädler (1991, 299): "When there is express talk of victims of violence, then the especially debilitating emotional injuries tend to be neglected and it is pretended that physical injuries and damaged clothing matter most." According to Kilchling's findings, subjectively perceived severity is most pronounced in victims of sexual offences (1995, 158, table: "Persönliche Beeinträchtigung nach Einzeldelikten" ("Personal harm by type of offence").

[82]   The psychological impacts of burglary in particular have long been underestimated: "For many people, burglary, an intrusion into their own four walls, is a big shock. Victims often have a harder time dealing with the violation of their private sphere, lost sense of security and attendant psychological problems than with the purely material loss" (WEISSER RING: Thema Wohnungs-Einbruch. 11/2010). See also Deegener 1996 and the K-Einbruch publicity campaign launched by the German police in October 2012 (www.k-einbruch.de).
        Sautner (2010, 174) similarly notes that because it is a violation of the victim's private sphere, burglary also has features of violent crime, putting it halfway between crimes against property and violent crimes.

[83]   According to Kilchling, physical impacts are suffered by men in 62.5 percent and by women only in 37.5 percent of cases, whereas psychological impacts are suffered by men in 44.9 percent and by women in 55.1 percent of cases (1995, 134). This probably also relates to the fact that men are the predominant victims of physical violence, while women are also victims of sexual violence.

[84]   Fewer than half of victims, incidentally, are compensated for the harm inflicted on them. With victims of violent and contact offences this figure is even smaller, with only 10 percent and 30 percent of victims respectively receiving **compensation** (Sautner 2010, 182 f).
        Victims relatively rarely turn to **institutional assistance**. In a 2004 survey of women who had experienced physical/sexual violence since age 16, only 16 percent accepted medical and as few as 11 percent psychosocial care (Müller/Schröttle 2004, 159).
        In a study on **stalking** by Voß/Hoffmann/Wondrak – an online survey in which 543 victims took part in 2002 – 43 percent of victims obtained professional treatment: Two-thirds took psychotherapeutic treatment, one in two turned to a physician, only one in five sought victim counselling and no more than six percent went to a self-help group (2006, 145). Yet as the study made clear, "stalking victims suffer massive physical, psychological and social effects with a negative impact on all areas of their lives" (2006, 149).

A distinction must be made here between immediate and short-term effects of victimisation experience (such as shock or shame) and potential longer-term effects (Görgen 2012, 95).[85] In particular, there may be symptoms of post-traumatic stress disorder (PTSD).[86]

The likelihood of PTSD increases with the severity of the traumatic experience. Victims of violent crime are at greater risk with about a 20 percent prevalence rate, and victims of rape at greatest risk with a 50 percent prevalence of PTSD (Sautner 2010, 189).[87]

Maercker (2006) points to social conditions for long-term psychological effects of this kind, to "social components of coping," and picks out "lack of social support" as the key risk factor for PTSD.[88] Maercker distinguishes two aspects of social support following victimisation: The response of family members and being recognised and acknowledged by other people and institutions as "someone who has gone through something bad" (2006, 53). Also, social handling of victimisation trauma "today often has to deal with **media** reporting", it being "not right from a psychological point of view ... for severely traumatised victims to be given media exposure, as severely traumatised victims tend to perceive the impact of the media on themselves as negative" (2006, 56 f).[89]

1.3.4.2
Fear of crime[90]

That fear of crime is partly or even primarily driven by personal experience of victimisation has long been assumed in research. Studies in this connection, however,

---

[85] On the long-term effects of sexual abuse of minors, for example, see Görgen et al. 2011 and Bergmann 2012, 41.

[86] See, for example, a leaflet published by WEISSER RING in 2007 with the title "Gewalt erleben – was nun? Informationen und Hilfen zu psychischen Belastungen" (on information and assistance with the emotional impacts of violent victimisation): "After a violent crime, besides physical injury, victims and also witnesses and family members may sooner or later also develop **emotional trauma**. This is a common stress response to extreme events." In the same connection, the 22nd WEISSER RING Victim Forum called for the establishment of a nationwide network of outpatient trauma units.

[87] On the symptoms, see Sautner 2010, 188 f and Maercker 2006.

[88] Other risk factors: General stress level in ordinary life, trauma severity, low socioeconomic status, female gender (2006, 52).

[89] Also see Böttcher: "Media reporting on proceedings can add to victims' fear ... There are victims who are not afraid of media reporting and there are victims who, despite their fears, want the media to report about their fate as victims so that what was done to them is made public. There are victims who voluntarily seek media publicity" (2012 a 187 ff).
Reemtsma (2006, 18) notes the general inability of victims to cope with the added stress of dealing with the media – and to one of the key challenges for victim support in the future: "Media training for lawyers in the interests of victims – generally meaning media abstinence."

[90] For findings and further references on fear of crime in Germany and possible influencing factors, notably with regard to the connection between generally increased insecurity and loss of sense of security, see Steffen 2012 b.

have produced contrasting results. This probably depends on the aspect or dimension of personal fear of crime selected in a study:[91]

- The cognitive aspect, expressing the individual's personal assessment of their risk of becoming the victim of a crime in the near future ("How likely do you think it is that – in a specific period – you will become the victim of a crime?").

- The affective or emotional aspect, reflecting emotional worry about crime risk in the individual's home surroundings ("How safe do you feel when you are out alone at night in the area where you live?").

- The conative aspect, relating to behavioural responses in the form of avoidance behaviours and protective measures ("How often have you – in a specific period – taken action to protect yourself from crime?").

Studies show that in the cognitive dimension, there are links between past experience of victimisation and fear of (once again) becoming the victim of a crime.[92] However, according to Sautner (2010, 192), the differences are not big enough to support a presumption of psychological harm to the victim.

In the affective dimension, the differences between victims and non-victims tend to be small. Someone who counts victimisation among the risks they face need not develop a fear of crime if they believe they have the resources to cope[93] (Ziegleder u.a. 2011, 35).

As PSB 2006 found in this regard, "In sum, explanations of fear of crime based on experience of victimisation do not prove universal and adequate either at individual or at aggregate level" (2006, 514).

1.3.4.3
Re-victimisation

According to Schneider (2010, 628), victims have a high risk of re-victimisation, i.e. the risk of becoming victims of crime for a second time: "Past victimisation is the best predictor of future victimisation. Repeat victimisation substantially depends on the psychological harm, the trauma of victimisation. Victimisation can alter the psychological processes of thinking, feeling and behaviour ...Victimisation can operate to result in acquired helplessness, vulnerability, insecurity, loss of control and self-accusation in victims." Victimisation confirms a belief in personal helplessness that

---

[91] See Sautner 2010, 190 ff and Ziegleder et al. 2011, 28 ff.

[92] This matches the experience of victim support organisations that many victims are anxious, at least in temporal proximity to the crime. "Suddenly, a lot of things are fear-ridden. Confined by fear, victims lose their basic sense of inner security" (WEISSER RING 22 a, 38).

[93] The individual's own resources for coping with victimisation.

grows with each further victimisation (Sautner 2010, 193).[94]

According to international victimisation studies, 4.3 percent of victims who have been victimised five or more times in one year experience 43.5 percent of reported crime.[95] There is an especially high risk of re-victimisation with crimes against the person, such as intrafamilial violence, sexual victimisation, maltreatment of children and old people, racial attacks and bullying. In particular, all forms of childhood victimisation go with a higher risk of lifetime victimisation (Schneider 2010, 630).

Just as with offenders, where a small number of repeat offenders account for the majority of crime, so with victims, with a small number of repeat victims experiencing a large proportion of all victimisation that occurs.

1.3.4.4
Enhanced delinquency risk (the 'cycle of violence')

Among the possible consequences of victimisation, the question also presents itself of "whether victimisation experiences increase the risk of victims becoming delinquent themselves" (Sautner 2010, 192).

This role reversal from victim to offender – which is by no means automatic – is empirically confirmed at least for children and adolescents subjected to violence and abuse (Sautner 2010, 193). For Schneider (2010, 633) victimisation in childhood or adolescence can be pivotal to the child's or adolescent's subsequent biography. It may become the start of a career as victim or offender. Dudeck, too, notes that experience of sex and violence-related victimisation in childhood marks a serious risk to the developmental psychology process and could set off a 'cycle of abuse', "i.e. be a risk factor for later sexual offences ... Childhood sexual abuse increases the risk of becoming a sex offender in later life by almost five times relative to other early traumas" (2012, 122 f).

The Criminological Research Institute of Lower Saxony accordingly sees the fact that adolescents are less exposed to violence-fostering factors – and notably the decrease in parental violence[96] – as a key explanation for the decline in youth violence (Baier et al. 2009, 10).

---

[94] Based on findings of the studies she draws upon, Sautner likewise estimates the rate of multiple victimisation "as relatively high" (2010, 170).

[95] Herman (1010, 13 f) presents National Crime Victimization Survey data on re-victimisation or repeat victimisation in the USA: 4 percent of victims experience 44 percent of all crimes. Repeat victimisation accounts for 49 percent of all sexual offences, 43 percent of all cases of assault and threat, 33 percent of all burglaries, and 15 percent of all theft of personal property.

[96] Risk factors for later violent delinquency not only include the experience of parental violence, but also being confronted with violence between parents.

Preventing victimisation is thus a vital part of preventing crime – in this instance of avoiding or reducing the risk of victims becoming offenders.

2
Needs and wishes of victims

The foregoing findings on the consequences of victimisation for victims and society mean that as well as preventing crime and victimisation wherever possible, it is also essential to lessen the impacts of crime on victims by fostering greater victim orientation in society and criminal justice.

2.1
No such thing as the typical victim

If the aim is to avoid deciding over victims' heads – assuming helplessness and vulnerability at the risk of amplifying the helplessness and weakness experienced particularly by victims of violent crime – and instead to promote victims' self-determination and autonomy[97], then it is important to know what victims want, need and expect from support systems and to the criminal justice system.[98] This applies even if there is "no such thing as the typical victim," but a "diversity of personal experiences" resulting in a "many-layered pattern of victim interests and attitudes" (Kilchling 1995, 621 f).

Or as Reemtsma asked in an address on the 25th anniversary of WEISSER RING in Hamburg, "What actually are the interests of a crime victim? Let's start by asking, what are their wishes? Their wishes are many and varied, as human wishes always are. One victim wants things one way, the next another way. One has revenge fantasies, another has none, one wants material compensation for the harm done, another finds that thought uncomfortable ..., one wants publicity, another wants to withdraw, one is strongly interested in the case's prosecution, another is uninterested, one wants a prominent appearance in court, another wants to avoid appearing if at all possible, and so on" (2006, 17).

But even if we bow to the law of averages when it comes to victim needs and allow that individual cases can vary widely, even our knowledge of the 'average' is not much better now than Schädler et al. described in their report to an April 1989 congress on assistance for crime victims: In Germany, on an international comparison, knowledge "about victims' needs has so far remained patchy and is limited to only a small number of studies" (1990, 3).

---

[97] Enhancing victim autonomy must accord with Kilchling's basic call for a victim-oriented reform of the law of criminal procedure.

[98] Empirical victimology has heightened awareness not only of what an upheaval victimisation represents in many people's lives, but also of the direction taken by what victims want from the state in dealing with the crime (Weigend 2010 a, 40).

Little has changed since, and there is still insufficient data. Most of all there is a lack of new findings for Germany. Most studies on victim interests and victim needs, and on their assistance and support requirements, were carried out in 1990/1991, nearly a quarter of a century ago.[99] With regard to violence experienced by women there are findings for the years 2004 and 2011;[100] concerning sexual abuse there are the findings of the Independent Commissioner on Sexual Abuse (Bergmann 2012) and the findings of a 2011 study by the Criminological Research Institute of Lower Saxony (Stadler et al. 2012).[101]

One thing is clear: The victim's intrinsic interest in making the crime undone cannot be fulfilled. "Nothing in the world can reverse or make good the fact that someone has become the victim of a crime" (Reemtsma 2006, 17).

But attempts can be made to lessen, or at least not to compound, the impacts of victimisation by taking into account "victims' wishes after the event."[102]

2.2
Victims' willingness to tell

Taking into account victims' wishes requires victimisation to become known – that victims speak about what has happened.[103] Yet victims of crime by no means always speak out, least of all victims of sexual or indeed physical violence: Almost half of all women who have been victims of sexual violence (47 percent) and over a third of victims of physical violence (37 percent) do not talk to anyone about the violence inflicted on them (Müller/Schröttle 2004, 162 f); for victims of sexual abuse with physical contact the figure is still one in four (Standler et al. 2012, 51).[104]

---

[99] Baurmann/Schädler's findings were published in 1991 (survey of 203 crime victims, mostly immediately after charges were brought; 29.1 percent were victims of violent crime); Kilchling's in 1995 (1990 written survey of victimisation experiences – both contact and non-contact offences – with 3,213 respondents who had previously taken part in the ICVS 1989 international telephone survey on victimisation mentioned earlier; Deegener's findings were published in 1996 (written survey of 716 robbery and burglary victims recorded by the police between March 1990 and February 1991) and Richter's findings came out in 1997 (1991 written survey of a sample of 342 victims of violent crime from WEISSER RING records); these and other findings are discussed in Sautner (2010).

[100] A 2004 representative survey by Müller/Schröttle of over 10,000 women between 16 and 85 on experiences of violence and recourse to support; and a 2001 representative survey (as part of a multi-topic survey) of 1,138 women from 16 to 65 on knowledge of and recourse to counselling and on experience of violence (Helfferich et al. 2012).

[101] A 2011 representative survey of 11,428 individuals aged 16 to 40 on exposure in particular to sexual abuse within the family.

[102] With regard to victims' needs, a basic distinction must be made according to the type of crime and the type of **harm suffered**: In the immediate aftermath of victimisation, victims of non-contact offences and burglaries mainly seek restitution (60.8 and 36.8 percent respectively), whereas victims of contact offences predominantly want to forget (31.8 percent); the wish to see the offender punished is also most prevalent in these victims (28.4 percent), particularly after assault or threat (Sautner 2010, 203; detailed figures in Kilchling 1995).

[103] It has already been seen that bringing charges is the exception rather than the rule, especially for victims of violence.

[104] Yet according to the Independent Commissioner on Sexual Abuse, "being able to speak about it ... was

When victims do speak to someone, then the first and the most important points of contact are individuals from their immediate social environment – friends, acquaintances, neighbours and family – with professional sources of help some way behind (Müller/Schröttle 2004, 159, 163).[105] These findings are confirmed in the 2011 survey: If counselling is not sought despite an experience of violence, then it is because the victim has confided in someone in their private surroundings and is trying to deal with the questions and problems in that way, to cope without counselling – for "The private nature of experiences of violence is a high barrier to divulgence" (Helfferich et al. 2012, 203). Victims of sexual abuse, too, if they speak to anyone at all, tend most of all to speak to family and friends (Standler et al. 2012, 51).[106]

Not just the private nature of many experiences of violence, but also the fear of not being believed means victims are not likely to speak about violence inflicted on them (Bergmann 2012, 40)[107] – not to family or friends and certainly not to the police or the judiciary: The willingness to report is exceptionally low, most notably when the offender and the victim knew each other before the offence.[108]

The findings of the 2011 representative survey on child sexual abuse are therefore remarkable in showing a significant increase in the willingness to report child sexual abuse within the family: "Whereas ... in the 1980s on average only one in twelve offenders could expect criminal prosecution, today that applies to about one in three. This circumstance may have curbed the proclivities of potential offenders and contributed to the decline in the forms of sexual abuse surveyed here" (Standler et al. 2012, 54).

2.3
Desire for social support, information and advice

When victims of crime – and especially violent crime – speak about their experiences, in most cases they are driven to do so by the desire for social support, in the form of

---

hugely important for all" (Bergmann 2012, 42).

[105] See also the findings on recourse to institutional support related in footnote 86.

[106] Baurmann/Schädler have if anything a negative appraisal of the 'benefit' to victims of speaking to family and friends: "In most cases, experienced victimisation (was) first spoken about with close family members ... In few instances, however, did victims find in such conversations the support and stabilisation they needed. Victims [overcame] the consequent isolation ... partly through 'cries for help' to institutions such as the police and victim support organisations. This may also be related to the finding from our study that victims, and particularly victims of violence, desired assistance from the state far more frequently than private support" (Baurmann/Schädler 1991, 291).
Bergmann notes that it was helpful for dealing with what had happened if victims found support in the family or in their social surroundings (2012, 42).

[107] On the relationship between doubts about victims' credibility and their secondary victimisation primarily in investigation and prosecution proceedings, see below, section 3.

[108] According to the findings of Müller/Schröttle, 13 percent of women victims of violence from past/current partners brought in the police and eight percent pressed charges. These figures increase to 19 percent for police involvement and 11 percent for the bringing of charges if the sample is restricted to women who have experienced violence resulting in injury or are in fear of serious/life-threatening injury (2004, 237).

corresponding responses from family, friends and acquaintances, and from the criminal justice system.[109]

A key facet of this desire for social support is acknowledgement of the wrong done, that the offence and the offender be called by name, to be accorded recognition and respect as someone who has gone through something bad, to receive clear acknowledgement of victim status, including in particular by the criminal prosecution authorities.[110] Or as Reemtsma put it: "Acknowledging criminal liability means acknowledging that wrong has been done. The victim has not just had back luck – the victim has been attacked, not struck by a falling branch. What the offender did was not allowed. The victim not only suffered injury but was wronged" (2006, 17).[111]

Social support also includes information and counselling, and these are important for victims: Information and advice can impart a sense of security and of being able to do something – and this is an area where there are glaring deficits.[112] "Crime victims who come to the police or have to appear in court are mostly poorly informed. Victims generally know little about how an investigation and prosecution proceed" (Baurmann 2000, 3; Frederking 2007) – but they do want more information, for example on the rights and duties attached to the role of the victim (Richter 1997, 94).

Providing such information is a task largely undertaken by victim support and counselling organisations. In preparations for a trial, for example, staff from WEISSER RING work closely with lawyers to inform victims about their rights in criminal proceedings, to turn victims into witnesses – because being a victim is a passive role, a powerless role, whereas being a witness in a trial is an active role (Hartwig 2012, 57).

---

[109] Richter's study from as early as 1997 thus came to the conclusion that what the surveyed victims of violence needed most of all (63.4 percent) in the aftermath of the offence was concrete assistance in the form of psychological and social support and that this desire was primarily directed at the "agencies and servants of the official criminal prosecution system." Because fulfilling this role "is not, however, first priority in the performance of [the latters'] work ... the mismatch between victims' expectations and the actual official response ... may be experienced by victims as a problem" (Richter 1997, 86 ff).

[110] See also Baurmann/Schädler 1991; Baurmann 2000, 4; Richter 1997, 86 ff ; Kilchling 1995, 222; Bergmann 2012, 42.
Sautner (2010, 218), too, notes the need of victims for acknowledgement of their own victim status right through the criminal prosecution system and the courts (more on this point in section 3).
For Maercker, social support is "absolutely pivotal" in coping with the trauma of victimisation and avoiding long-term psychological effects (2006, 52 f).

[111] Likewise Hassemer/Reemtsma (2002, 130 f) regarding the great importance of the offence being recognised as a wrong and not an unlucky accident. "Nobody is responsible for an accident, nobody is to blame. Wrongdoing should not have been allowed to happen ... The suffering inflicted on me is an outcome of the other's freedom to injure me. The offender could have refrained from doing it. That the offender could have refrained from doing it is given expression in the court judgement, which labels it a wrong."

[112] Richter 1997, 92 ff; see also the papers on awareness of victims' rights in "Opferschutz – unbekannt," Mainzer Schriften zur Situation von Kriminalitätsopfern, Vol. 44 (WEISSER RING (Eds.), 2007); Seidler 2006.

2.4
Victims' wishes in terms of punitiveness and retribution

Relative to the needs referred to so far, victims' wishes in terms of punitiveness and retribution play a **comparatively minor** role, and certainly a lesser one than is often assumed: "When people think about the role of the injured party in a trial, they usually assume that the crime victim's main interest will be to see the offender punished ... This premise is the only way to explain the widespread calls for the injured party to be given a greater say (i.e. to better assert their interest in redress), as also assumed by the powers that be in the Victim Protection Act (Opferschutzgesetz). Oddly, these considerations lack any empirical support that crime victims indeed seek retribution ... The British and German empirical studies that exist on this topic show victims to have strikingly relaxed and moderate attitudes towards offenders and their punishment ... There is much to indicate that victims typically leave the nature and extent of the state response to the discretion of the criminal prosecution system on the basis of prevailing law, and are in agreement with the outcome if they are involved in the proceedings to a subjectively and emotionally satisfactory extent – primarily through information and consultation" (Weigend 1989, 408 ff).[113]

This assessment corresponds with that of Sautner in light of empirical research since carried out into victims' wishes in terms of punitiveness and retribution: "If victims are asked what they think should be the response to the criminal conduct in question, it becomes clear that a majority prefer state criminal justice intervention – and also that this does not always mean punishment of the offender in the sense of a criminal sentence" (Sautner 2010, 235).

As Weigend goes on to explain, retribution could be reduced to the victim's interest in acknowledgement that they have been done wrong, that this wrong is recognised and appropriately reacted to, thus giving the victim (symbolic) assurance that nothing of the kind will happen again. The victim's legitimate wish that the crime should not be let go without an official reaction must not be equated with a thirst for revenge. The formal reprobation inherent in a sentence also has the function of saying to the victim that they have been done wrong and are not obliged to accept the offender's conduct (Weigend 2010 a, 43).

---

[113]   See also Gelbert/Walter 2013, 75.

"The injured party – any injured party, not just those who have suffered especially serious injury – can demand that their fate not be marginalised, and that it be acknowledged that they have been done wrong. But that is not necessarily to say such acknowledgement much come in the form of a penal sentence" (Weigend 2010 b).

Likewise Reemtsma: "The victim's interest in hearing confirmation that they have been done wrong and the public interest in it being established that a norm has been breached but continues to apply despite the breach – as confirmed by the handing down of a sentence ("You should not have done that!") – those interests converge ... Yet the injured party does not have a right to see the court accept their view of things, they only have a right for the court to consider their view and to do so competently ... Justice cannot heal anything, but where justice is not done, new, irreparable harm occurs" (2006, 17).

2.5
Restitution

Many victims desire restitution of the harm done to them and view restitution as a suitable condition to be imposed for the termination of proceedings, although they also tend to regard the imposition of such conditions as a form of criminal sanction (Sautner 2010, 239).

It is important to victims, however, to see that restitution comes from 'their' offender. For many victims, it matters that the offenders themselves fulfil their debt to them (Weigend 1989, 404; Baurmann 2000, 4). The way victims view restitution as having a sanction aspect is through the offender having to face up to the crime and its consequences. In such circumstances, victims can also envisage taking part in conflict **mediation** arrangements such as victim-offender mediation (Sautner 2010, 240, 261).

Victim-offender mediation (VOM) gives victims and offenders an opportunity to reach a satisfactory resolution of conflicts out of court in the presence of a neutral facilitator. It generally comprises counselling and/or mediation, an agreement on restitution, and incorporation of the outcomes as input into the criminal justice process.[114] VOM is an important tool for autonomous conflict resolution between victim and offender. Its merits are considered first and foremost to be "that it is better suited to serving victim interests than normal criminal proceedings[115] while also improving offenders' prospects for positively influencing the future ... That victim interests are adequately served in practice here can be seen from the high victim participation rates and the large number of mutual agreements that come out of such mediation. This encourages greater use of victim-offender mediation in future, including in cases of severe crime that are suited to mediation of this kind (in this context naturally only as a means of conflict resolution alongside a sentence to be imposed in criminal proceedings)."[116]

---

[114] Bundesverband Mediation e.V. (Federal Mediation Association, wwwmbmev.de.

[115] Although empirical proof of this is largely lacking. Whether and to what extent victims – and not just offenders – benefit from out-of-court mediation is currently being investigated for Germany and Austria in a European Commission-funded project on out-of-court mediation as a victim support tool. Using qualitative methods and focusing on violent crime in the individual's immediate social surroundings, the study asks how out-of-court mediation influences or is capable of influencing both adolescent and adult victims in the process of dealing with a crime, and what factors are important in helping this process take a positive course in a way that prevents long-term traumatisation in the direction of tertiary victimisation (www.mediation-im-strafverfahren.de).

[116] Federal Ministry of Justice: "Täter-Opfer-Ausgleich" (Victim-Offender Mediation") (www.bmj.de; viewed 17 February 2013).
Given the very low reporting rates for physical and sexual abuse of women and children by family or close acquaintances, Schneider suggests that thought should be given to whether reparation and mediation proceedings along restorative justice lines are not a better solution than criminal proceedings (2010, 633 f).

Victim-offender mediation was first incorporated into German juvenile criminal law (1990) and later into adult criminal law.[117] "In contrast to the more 'lightweight' sanctions under the heading of diversion in the Juvenile Justice Act (Jugendgerichtsgesetz), this legislative provision also made it possible to apply victim-offender mediation without restriction in severe offences, as a 'mitigating category'" (Schädler 2012, 54). "Since then, victim-offender mediation and restitution are recognised as two forms of reparation that can lead to a discharge or a mitigated sentence. The legislature aimed in this way to promote recognition of guilt, restitution and the peace-making effect of mediation, including with severe crimes" (Schöch 2012, 250).[118]

Schädler doubts that this has succeeded, however: "In the minds of practitioners, victim-offender mediation has made the transition from juvenile to adult criminal law, if at all, at best in mangled form: Courts and the prosecution service tend to apply victim-offender mediation as before with less serious crimes, sometimes with severe bodily injury. Victims of sexual offences in particular, however, are troubled by the fact that victim-offender mediation with the aid of a neutral facilitator was not made mandatory by law yet can be launched into at any stage of the proceedings. One upshot of this is that conflict resolution is often sought very late, after the evidence-taking part of the proceedings has failed, is then gone at hastily in the corridor or sometimes even in court, and in most cases resolution is only sought on a financial basis. This is almost always to the detriment of victims" (2012, 54).[119]

Other problems connected with the offender's 'apology' are noted by Schöch: An apology is a key part of the peace-making effect of almost all reconciliation agree-

---

[117] And inserted into section 46a of the German Criminal Code. In juvenile criminal law, victim-offender mediation or 'restitution' was added to the list of conditions and directions available to be imposed on an offender by a court (Schädler 2012, 53).

   According to national **VOM statistics** collated by Kerner et al. since 1993 (most recently for 2010), the type of injury suffered was bodily injury in 36 percent (slight bodily injury 75 percent) of cases, psychological harm in 19 percent and material harm in 21 percent. The type of conflict was relationship conflict in 57 percent of cases, neighbourhood conflict in 21 percent, domestic violence in 16 percent and stalking in 6 percent of cases.

[118] WEISSER RING, the victim support organisation, advocated restitution as early as 1996 as part of both criminal investigation proceedings and court sentencing. Article 2 of its Articles of Association was amended to include support of restitution and victim-offender mediation projects as an object and purpose of the organisation.

   On victim-offender mediation, see also the position papers in 'Spektrum der Mediation', the professional journal of the German Federal Mediation Association (www.bmev.de); 'TOA-Infodienste' published by the VOM and mediation service bureau of the Association for Social Work, Criminal Law and Criminal Policy (DBH) (www.toa-servicebuero.de). The Federal Ministry of Justice also publishes an annual report on victim-offender mediation statistics (www.bmj.de; Kerner et al. 2012).

[119] Kerner et al. note that VOM is not truly established nationwide and there are still both guarded and outspoken reservations among some parts of the public, and also among members of the judiciary and (defence) lawyers. This goes with the fact that quantitatively, VOM cases still, or so far, only account for a modest share of all cases dealt with in prosecution and sentencing in any one year. Austria is far ahead in this regard, VOM having become established there as a valid alternative to conventional responses (2012, Vorwort).

ments.[120] Many victims, according to Schöch, are willing to accept such an apology but not to 'forgive' the offender, least of all with severe crimes. Many understand 'forgiving' as rendering the crime undone as if nothing had happened. That goes too far for them, Schöch writes, because they do not generally want to view the crime as not having happened. But on the other hand restitution does not require that (2012, 250).

3
The criminal justice system and victims' wishes

"In conflict resolution through criminal justice today ... the position of the individual victim rightly appears to be that of a quantity independent of the legal community and of the state entrusted by the latter with criminal prosecution. The call for the state right of punishment to be exercised across the board in a more victim-friendly way is now uncontested" (Kunz 2011 a, Ch. 5, at 49).

3.1
Victim orientation in criminal justice

'Today' – in other words, criminal justice has by no means always been exercised in a 'victim-friendly' way and that was not always 'uncontested' and self-evident. Indeed, the increasing orientation towards victims in criminal justice only took hold some 25 years ago.[121]

"Historically,[122] the injured party in a crime had a strong status in trials up to the Middle Ages ... That status was lost with the emergence of the state monopoly on violence and the rise of modern criminal justice under the rule of law ... To the same extent as the state took over conflict resolution, the injured party gave up their role as an autonomous actor in criminal proceedings, and for the most part only featured in the practical exercise of the law as a source of evidence, namely as a witness. The victim thus became an object of the trial. Outside of criminal process, too, little attention was given to the injured party (Barton/Kölbel 2012, 11).

The criminal law and the law of criminal procedure focus on the offender: "Only a few years ago, for many people who had to do with issues of guilt and sentencing, the real victim in the guilt and sentencing complex was the offender, namely as the victim of state retribution measures. The protective guarantees of criminal justice based on the rule of law were directed at the offender alone, and the victim of the crime did not feature in the argument ... Things are very different today. When the word 'protection' is mentioned in a criminal justice context, we associate it not with the offender

---

[120] According to the TOA statistics for 2010, an apology is by far the most frequent form of agreement reached, at 43 percent (Kerner et al. 2012).

[121] This is regarding – with others such as Kilchling (1995, 4) – the 1986 Victim Protection Act (Opferschutzgesetz) as the point where the legal position of victims in criminal proceedings began to be strengthened. Weigend, too, considers this act the "key step towards the victim" (2012, 52).

[122] On historical aspects of victim protection and victim participation, see e.g. Weigend 1989 or Rössner 1990.

but with the victim, and what we are concerned about today is protecting from the offender rather from the state" (Hassemer/Reemtsma 2002, 14 f). A crime is no longer seen foremost as a rebellion against state precepts or a violation of an abstract legal construct, but as a violation of the legally protected interests of a specific individual – real harm to a real person (Weigend 2010 a, 41; Böttcher 2012, 123).

In any event, both in criminology and in criminal justice, the injured party is no longer the 'forgotten man', as the victim was still able to be termed in the 1970s (Weigend 1989, 13; Barton/Kölbel 2012, 11).[123] According to Weigend, however, the wind has turned in recent years; today, the tendency is more to warn of a change in the public character of criminal proceedings by the injured party being granted all-too autonomous status with far-reaching active rights (Weigend 2010 a, 53).

3.1.1
Reasons for the increased victim orientation in criminal justice

The reasons for the increased victim orientation in criminal justice partly have to do with fundamental arguments relating to the rule of law and partly with practical considerations.

The **'rule of law' argument** draws on the state monopoly on violence,[124] the renunciation of violence by the individual, and the resultant guarantee by the state under the rule of law to look after the safety of its subjects.[125] If the state cannot deliver on that guarantee – and given the large numbers of crime victims it evidently cannot – then it should at least protect victims from suffering harm in investigation and criminal proceedings (see also Baurnann 2000, 2).[126]

Reemtsma, too, advocates a "measure of fair play" while also stressing the negative consequences of construing the "reciprocal obligation" that goes with the state mo-

---

[123] "These days, the crime victim drives criminal policy ... The victim has stepped out of the shadows that an offender-focused criminal justice system kept them in for decades, indeed for centuries. We are witnessing a shift ... Our attention, our interest and also our sympathies are moving from offender to victim" (Hassemer/Reemtsma 2002, 13).

[124] "The state monopoly on violence means the sole legitimacy of the state to exercise and threaten physical violence under the framework of prevailing law to the extent that the law does not grant such legitimacy to the individual by way of exception ... [the monopoly on violence corresponds to] a reciprocal obligation to enable subjects to live without fear of threat, actual or presumed (including threat of crime) (Schwind 2011, § 18, at 33; § 20, at 13). This 'reciprocal obligation', however, is not uncontested as it can lead directly to the preventive state (see Steffen 2012 b).

[125] Weigend (2010 a, 45), however, only finds this inference persuasive at first sight: The state authorisation to punish, he says, can no longer be understood as the outcome of an imaginary transference of responsibilities by potential crime victims; instead, that authorisation is legitimised by lawmakers in the democratic decision making process. This means the injured party does not have any entitlement in compensation for the loss of some archaic right of self-'justice'.

[126] The CDU/CSU party's draft of the Victim Compensation Act (Opferentschädigungsgesetz) passed in 1976 refers to a duty of the state, reciprocal to its assumed monopoly on violence, to stand by the victim of a crime in the event that crime fighting fails (cited in Schädler 2012, 53).

nopoly on violence as meaning that the state must enable subjects to live without fear of actual or presumed threat: "A victim does not have a claim against the community – the state – merely because they have become the victim of a crime. They have not become a victim because the state has not given adequate protection – except where that is the case in a specific instance ... Anyone who thinks the state has failed whenever a crime is committed must want a state that is actually capable of preventing crime everywhere – and that would have to be a state that not only watches everywhere but is omnipresent with the means of immediate intervention. That would not just be impossible: Anything approaching such a condition would be unbearable.

"Crime-free conditions are in the interest of almost everyone – but we cannot bring such conditions about, nor would we like what it takes to achieve them. But it is in the general *interest of all citizens* – and this interest can indeed be met – to have assurance that if they find themselves in the role of victim (or aggrieved party), then their fate will be governed by a certain degree of fair play" (2006, 17).

This call for investigation and criminal proceedings in which the victim does not suffer additional harm (the 'secondary victimisation' already mentioned) is one of the most important **practical arguments** for a professional way of dealing with the victims of crime that avoids (unnecessary) distress.[127]

"The state, a security coalition comprising all individuals, has a duty to safeguard individuals from violations of their legitimate spheres of interests. If this fails in a given instance, the affected party can at least expect that the damage done will not be made bigger or worse by the state" (Weigend 1989, 19).[128]

Victim orientation is also "correlative with the fact that the state makes victims serve duty as witnesses and exposes them to considerable stress in doing so" (Weigend 2010 a, 55). Special rights can be inferred for victims not only because suffering the crime itself and the (consequent) intensive demands of the criminal justice process imposes a special sacrifice compared with other citizens. The state has cause to minimise or make good this special sacrifice by providing an appropriate framework and compensation (Weigend 1989, 379). Because victims have to fulfil their witness duty – sometimes against their own sensibilities and against their own needs (Baurmann 2000, 2). "The victim must bring a special sacrifice for the community. That virtually cries out for support and help" (Böttcher 2012, 123).

---

[127] A further line of argument follows from the fact that by bringing charges, crime victims are the initiators of police investigations, and through their readiness to provide information and the quality of that information they also influence the success of those investigations – whether crimes are cleared up and whether offenders are arrested and put on trial.

[128] Likewise the German government in the 2009 draft version of the second Victim Law Reform Act (Opferrechtsreformgesetz): "The constitutional order under the German Basic Law obliges the organs of the state not only to clear up crimes and determine the guilt or innocence of the accused in fair proceedings under the rule of law, but also to place themselves protectively in front of victims and respect victims' concerns" (cited in Sielaff 2010, 213).

When victims opt to press charges in cases where the proceedings are likely to put a great strain on them – say out of a wish for justice to be done, so the crime does not go unpunished or to save other people the same fate – then "they are doing a service for the state under the rule of law, a service that deserves recognition. That service makes it all the more urgent to minimise the distress to victims and to give them the opportunity to be party to the process of discovering the truth and arriving at a fair judgement" (Böttcher 2012, 123).

3.2
Victim orientation in the police

Because in most cases charges are first brought before the police, the increased victim orientation in the criminal justice system starts with the police service and not just at the point where a case passes on to the judiciary.[129] Efforts to meet the call for professional treatment of victims parallel a general heightened sensitivity to victims of crime and to their needs and expectations.[130]

For the police, victim protection – looking after victims of crime and of road accidents with the aim of minimising the consequences of an incident for those affected – is a part of police crime prevention. Under the police approach to prevention, "this task falls first of all to every police officer in the course of their everyday duty" (Programm Polizeiliche Kriminalprävention).

Promoting "professional information practices"[131] – and helping to satisfy the above-mentioned information needs and requirements of crime victims – is an aim of VIKTIM, an interactive training tool on police conduct towards victims. A module on what victim protection means for the police thus gives in-depth information on the need for and aims of victim protection. The many other topics include victim expectations, [132] rights, and sources of support: "Looking after the victims of crime is ... today part and parcel of police work." And: "Professional victim protection is fundamentally important to the entire criminal justice process. Going by the maxim that people only put trust in a professional, the quality of victim statements can be decisively improved."[133]

---

[129] With regard to the following, see also Steffen 2012 a.

[130] The call for professional treatment of victims and for increased victim orientation in the police service was also furthered by the 2002 Protection Against Violence Act (Gewaltschutzgesetz), which effectively gave the police victim protection responsibilities in relation to domestic violence and violence in the victim's immediate social environment (Sielaff 2010, 217).

[131] As called for by Baurmann 2000, 3.

[132] According to a victim survey by the Technical University of Darmstadt Institute of Psychology, what victims want and expect of police officers is a quick response, a good manner, continuity (the point of contact and interviewing officer stay the same), provision of an appropriate situation for interview, acceptance, information, and consideration (source: VIKTIM).

[133] The application of "professional information practices" by the police is also visible in the public information the police provide for (potential) crime victims: On the German Police Crime Prevention Programme

Speaking generally, victim protection has now become an integral part of police work and part of the duties of every police officer throughout Germany. Almost everywhere, victims' commissioners have been established – specially trained police officers who not only serve as a point of contact and provide help for victims, but also champion victim protection within the service (Steffen 2012 a, 146).[134]

This increased victim orientation in the police seems to have paid off. In the study cited earlier on violence against women in Germany (Müller/Schröttle 2004), satisfaction with the work of the police was found to have increased in the preceding 15 years: "In summary, it is possible to say that positive changes with regard to police handling of violence against women have become visible in the present study, most notably in victim protection and victim support, and in the communication of information. In investigation proceedings, too, there are indications of cases being investigated more diligently" (2004, 197).

In an assessment of support provision for female victims of violence (Helfferich et al. 2012) in which women were also asked about their knowledge and use of counselling on experienced violence,[135] there were few who did not know somewhere they could turn to. Of the named sources of help, the police came first (74 percent would recommend going to the police in cases of sexual violence and 63 percent in cases of maltreatment). The police thus enjoy considerable trust, followed by medical practitioners (recommended by 45 percent for cases of sexual violence and 36 percent for cases of maltreatment). Counselling services were recommended far less frequently in comparison. Evidently, with acute violence, the priority is more on protection and medical treatment than on psychosocial counselling (2012, 188 ff).

3.3
Victim protection in criminal proceedings

Victim protection in criminal proceedings relates to two things:

- Firstly, safeguarding victims from further harm as a result of the proceedings
- Secondly, supporting victims so that they can assert themselves in the proceedings (Böttcher 2012, 122).[136]

---

website (www.polizei-beratung.de), general information –how a crime is prosecuted and tried, victim support organisations, how to record injuries, etc. – is supplemented with detailed information and tips relating to specific offences.

[134] Outside of the police service, Berlin appointed Germany's first state victims' commissioner at the beginning of October 2012 (www.zeit.de/gesellschaft/zeitgeschehen/2012-11/Interview-Opferbeauftrager-Berlin/komplettansicht; viewed 13 December 2012).

[135] 2011 representative survey of 1,138 between 18 and 85.

[136] For Barton, many of the reforms passed by the legislature with the rationale of improved victim protection clearly illustrate the 'victimisation' of German criminal policy (2012, 127).Those reforms mainly related to the law of criminal procedure, but "the legislature [also] repeatedly went into action" in substantive criminal law and in related policy areas. See the list in Barton 2012, 127 ff.Weigand notes that effectively

These goals have been served by several victim-related reforms of the German Code of Criminal Procedure since 1986. Key such reforms include the 1986 Victim Protection Act (Opferschutzgesetz), the 1998 Witness Protection Act (Zeugenschutzgesetz), the first Victim Law Reform Act (Opferrechtsreformgesetz) in 2004 and the second such act in 2009. At the time of writing, the German Bundestag has just (13 March 2013) approved a bill to strengthen the rights of victims of sexual abuse (Gesetz zur Stärkung der Rechte von Opfern sexuellen Missbrauchs/StORMG).[137]

Indeed, after such a long time where victims stood in the shadows, relegated to a "residual procedural role,"[138] all of a sudden "it all went very quickly" (Böttcher 2012, 123). A striking feature has been "the serial nature of the legislation: Even before one victim protection act is implemented in practice, work is generally already underway on the next. One could almost speak of a cascade of victim protection acts" (Barton 2012, 130). However, "no clear systematic approach can really be made out behind these piecemeal changes" (Weigend 2010 a, 55).

Looking at this victim protection legislation, it is hard to dispel the impression of a positive feedback loop between policymaking and the media[139] – or with victim lobbies so influential (Barton 2012, 130)[140], between policymaking and lobbying. This mechanism was most recently seen in action in the debate surrounding child sexual abuse in institutions and the family. In 2010, victims spoke out on events which in most cases lay decades in the past and which were by no means fresh news. Right back in the 1970s, the women's refuge and child protection movement had already brought attention to child sexual abuse, including in institutions. But "now the issue was on the table" (Bergmann 2012, 36). The German government set up a roundtable, whose deliberations and proposals brought forth the government draft of the above-mentioned bill to strengthen the rights of victims of sexual abuse (StORMG). Anyone who thought the second victim law reform act in 2009 had taken victim protection in criminal proceedings as far as it could go had failed to anticipate the "wave of outrage about child sexual abuse." It is consequently to be expected that the current government draft will soon become law (Schöch 2012, 247).[141]

---

safeguarding victims from harm as a result of criminal proceedings requires effort and expense, but does not alter procedure. In contrast, moves to give victims greater participation and perhaps even a say in criminal proceedings would have a more far-reaching impact.

[137] Barton 2012, 128 with information on the substance of the act; see also Schöch 2012; Kölbel 2012.

[138] Thus Kilchling 2002, cited in Böttcher 2012, 123.

[139] On the policymaking-media feedback loop, see Steffen 2008, 233 f.

[140] Barton rates the way that the interim report of the roundtable on sexual abuse was turned at once into a ministry draft bill as "an example of the close links between lobbying and politics" (2012, 130).

[141] The government draft bill as amended by the Committee on Legal Affairs was approved by the Bundestag on 14 March 2013. The Federal Ministry of Justice has fulfilled a remit issued in the final report of the roundtable and published guidelines for the involvement of law enforcement agencies (Leitlinien zur Einschaltung der Strafverfolgungsbehörden) in November 2012 (www.bmj.de). There has been no success so far, however, in setting up a support fund for people inflicted with sexual

Criticisms of the German victim protection legislation not only relate to the lack of an identifiable "systematic approach" coupled with a connectedness to current events and the activities of victim lobbies: The very approach was controversial from the outset. Criminologists and criminal defence lawyers hold the opinion that victims should not be subjects of criminal proceedings with rights of their own, because criminal procedure is only about convicting and sentencing the offender. By this view, any strengthening of victim rights is a threat to the establishment of the truth and the effectiveness of criminal defence (Schöch 2012, 246).[142]

Hassemer's critique is likewise fundamental: "Offenders' and victims' rights to respect and attention are now set one against the other. Their apportionment has turned into a zero sum game: What is given to the victim must be taken away from the offender, what was formerly given to the offender is now taken from the latter in its entirety and allocated to the victim ... Victim orientation in this climate is an orientation away from offenders" (2002, 62 f).

Whatever the case may be, victim protection has evidently not yet gone as far is can go. This is not only assured by demands from victim lobbies,[143] but also by Europe. Victim protection is also an issue for the European Union. Following on from the 2001 Council Framework Decision on the standing of victims in criminal proceedings, from which Germany took up a number of ideas for its 2004 and 2009 victim law reform acts, there is now (dating from 25 October 2012) Directive 2012/29/EU of the European Parliament and of the Council of 25 October 2012 establishing minimum standards on the rights, support and protection of victims of crime, and replacing Council Framework Decision 2001/220/JHA. The directive is binding on member states as to the results to be achieved – "Provision of information and support," "Participation in criminal proceedings" and "Protection of victims and recognition of victims with specific protection needs" – and legislation to comply with it must be brought into force by 16 November 2015. It is therefore thought likely that it will provide legislative impetus for Germany (Böttcher 2012, 125).[144]

---

violence in childhood. "Three years ago, politics were full of shock and outrage. Grand promises were made ... But once the roundtable had brought out its final report, interest quickly tailed off" (www.dradio. de/dlf/sendungen/kommentar/2017234/; viewed 24 February 2013).

[142] For Schöch himself, the charge that victim protection legislation has brought a paradigm shift or obstructs the rational treatment of conflict in criminal procedure is unwarranted. Experience so far has shown that the practice of criminal procedure by and large succeeds "in striking the necessary practical balance between the conflicting interests of the accused and the victim" (2012, 248).

[143] WEISSER RING, for example, has drawn up a "long wish list"; see Böttcher 2012, 125.

[144] On victims' rights in the light of European law, see Bock 2012.
   For Weigend it is an 'open question' whether restrictions to victims' active participation rights – for example, German law allows only victims of specific types of offence to join proceedings as a civil claimant – are compatible with the EU directives (2012, 45).

3.4
The problem of secondary victimisation

An express aim of Germany's victim protection acts is to shield victims from harm in investigation and criminal proceedings – i.e. to prevent secondary victimisation (see above). Whether they succeed at this is impossible to say, since as for other aims of the same legislation, as far as is known no **evaluation** of any kind has been done to date.

There is not even firm knowledge about whether and to what extent secondary victimisation occurs in investigation and criminal proceedings in the first place.[145] At least there is scarcely any empirical proof that conducting a trial against an offender generally inflicts unacceptable distress (even if only subjectively) on the victim – "with one single but important exception: In the domain of sexual offences, the dictum 'the process is the punishment' appears to hold true, with the 'punishment' not infrequently befalling the victim of the crime" (Weigend 1989, 385 f).[146] It is well known that many victims of sexual offences say they would "never again bring charges."[147] Where victims are asked to evaluate criminal proceedings, "retrospective surveys of adult witnesses underscore how the experience of distress depends on the type of offence: The prosecution procedure appears to place a burden on victims of sexual offences in particular" (Volbert 2012 b, 201).

According to Volbert (2012 a, 149 ff; 2012 b, 198), most studies relate to this victim group, and most of all to underage victims of sexual offences. In light of recent research findings, Volbert also confirms Weigend's conclusion – already close to 25 years old – that empirical evidence on secondary victimisation is largely lacking,[148] and points to many weaknesses in the debate surrounding alleged or actual cases of ill-judged responses[149] by criminal prosecution agencies:

---

[145] According to Kölbel, it is unsurprising that the legal policy debate surrounding the "risk of secondary victimisation" does without any empirical frame of reference, as "suitable" findings simply do not yet exist. Overall, the current state of research yields no more than very weak evidence for the prevalence of secondary victimisation. This is not to say the phenomenon of secondary victimisation does not exist, but it does mean legal policy considerations and assumptions relating to it so far lack a reliable systematic and empirical basis. Fears that victims are affected by criminal proceedings are at best supported by individual observations (2012, 224).
On fundamental criticisms of criminological victimology and in particular the lack of (prospective long-term) studies on the psychosocial effects of victimisation, see Greve et al. 2012.

[146] On the victims of rape and sexual coercion and calls for professional treatment of such victims, see Steffen 2012. On the credibility issue see Kreuzer 2012.

[147] Even an "old-school jurist beyond suspicion of female emancipatory leanings" such as the former Berlin chief prosecutor Hansjürgen Karge would "advise a daughter ... in case of doubt from reporting a rape" (Steffen 2012, 155).

[148] Internationally, too, according to Volbert, there are few studies on the question of any secondary victimisation and their findings do not readily transfer across national boundaries.

[149] Applying Schneider's definition of secondary victimisation as the "compounding of primary victimisation by ill-judged responses from the victim's family, friends and acquaintances and from instances of formal social control" (cited in Volbert 2012 a, 150).

- Volbert finds little agreement on what type of harm is meant and argues that a distinction must be made between temporary burdens and long-term harm.

- Passing distress, according to Volbert, does not automatically have long-term effects. Giving testimony, for example, can be highly burdensome at the time, but in the long term it can help enhance self-efficacy and regain control, thus reducing the harm caused by the offence.

- Volbert identifies one of the major difficulties as being how to distinguish symptoms caused by the crime (or other stress factors) from those triggered by court proceedings.

The findings suggest that the factors listed in the following can have an adverse impact in terms of distress during criminal proceedings or the subsequent appraisal of such proceedings (Volbert 2012 a, 155; 2012 b, 206):[150]

- Lack of information about the trial
- Lack of involvement in the trial
- Length of the trial
- Not knowing quite how questioning will take place
- Poor handling by the judge
- Encounter with the accused
- Repeated confrontational questioning
- Unwanted trial outcome

While the changes made in Germany so far indeed target a number of potential stress factors (e.g. the use of video testimony to avoid repeat questioning), "… whether the adopted measures have led to an actual reduction in the strain on victims has been subject to scarcely any evaluation so far. In some instances it is even unclear how far measures have been implemented" (2012 a, 155; 2012 b, 203).[151] Findings are also inconsistent regarding the effects of witness/victim support during court proceedings: Such support evidently improves people's knowledge about court procedure and conditions but does not always lead to less anxiety when giving testimony in main hearings (2012 a, 160).

---

[150] According to the survey of women by Müller/Schröttle (2004, 201 f), respondents were far less happy with court proceedings than with police responses (see above). Encountering the offender in court caused the greatest distress, followed by psychological effects, insufficiently severe sentences or acquittals, and the feeling of being wronged yet again. Other problems resulted from lawyers, judges and prosecutors holding victims directly or indirectly responsible for the crime or believing the accused more readily than the victim. The duration of trials was another problem: "As these findings on court intervention make clear, further action would be helpful in particular in the area of protecting victims in the context of court proceedings."

[151] This not only applies to the frequency of use and the impact of video testimony, but also to other areas such as widening the scope for the victim to **join criminal proceedings as a civil claimant**: How joining the prosecution as a civil claimant impacts the victim's condition is so far unstudied (Volbert 2012 b, 204).

Additionally, Volbert points out, a distinction must be made between potential stress factors that can nonetheless change, such as trial duration, lack of information, or poor handling by those involved, and factors inherent to a trial, such as the need to give a detailed presentation of the crime or critical appraisal of testimony given by parties to the proceedings: The latter set of stress factors are ultimately part and parcel of a fair, impartial trial under the rule of law (Volbert 2012 b, 206).

Volbert concludes in summary: "The opening question of how to explain the discrepancy between the large number of reforms and the virtually unabated lamentations about victims coming under severe strain cannot be answered conclusively, there being hardly any studies on how specific ways of doing things affect victims' emotional constitution … If the aim is to reduce the distress to victims as effectively as possible, then without doubt it would be desirable for greater account to be given to empirical findings on the strain induced by criminal proceedings and means of countering that strain" (2012 a, 160).

Furthermore, it would be desirable "for all involved to consider that certain distress to victims is unavoidable in proceedings under the rule of law, and that precisely because this is the case, it is expedient to change stress factors not necessary to the conduct of a fair trial" (Volbert 2012 b, 210).

3.5
Criminal justice and victims' wishes: Irreconcilable opposites?

It is striking how often German law has been changed in recent years to improve victim rights and safeguards, the fundamental debate and doubts invoking the rule of law that those changes have triggered – and how little empirical knowledge there actually is about the implementation and impact of the changes made, and about whether they match victims' needs and wishes.[152]

Yet those wishes do not appear to be so very big or hard to meet, and least of all do they appear to require major changes to the law of criminal procedure – if indeed any were ever needed. Weigend, for example, points to the empirical finding that "most victims are less interested in having an active part in the proceedings than in three relatively simple things: Being kept informed about the course of the trial, being compensated for their loss or injury, and being treated respectfully as witnesses. Some victims would also like to be heard as part of the main hearings and to be able to say

---

[152] As early as 1995, Kilchling thought it "time to ask what the very lively professional debate has brought in terms of tangible improvements in Germany for the individual victim, in whose name and interests so many purport to speak and act … Because the rediscovery of the victim holds just as little promise of automatic progress as the fact of the problem having been so substantially and extensively described" (1995, 3).
Further, "The basic aim of a victim-oriented reform of procedural law has to be to enhance victim autonomy … As it is not possible to generalise about victim interests … the task at hand is to make available a choice of – where appropriate very varied – options for participation" (1995, 704).

how they think and feel. In a criminal justice system based on the rule of law and the needs of citizens, all this should really be a matter of course" (2010 a, 55).

In particular, victims' **need for information** is evidently severely neglected.[153] This is true of advance information about what awaits them in criminal proceedings, and it is especially true of information about the course of the proceedings: In all studies, lack of information about the course of proceedings was faulted most of all. Because of this, many victims feel that they are passed over and given too little notice, and this is seen to impact negatively on the perceived fairness of the proceedings (Volbert 2012 a, 153; 2012 b, 201).[154]

This information need among victims would be easy to meet – like the other victim interests just mentioned – without any call for new victim rights or powers.

But even if these fairly modest wishes that victims have of the criminal justice system were to be met, it would only benefit a small fraction of crime victims. That is the fraction who come into any contact at all with parts of the criminal justice system and make it as far as criminal proceedings:

- As seen above, most victims – especially victims of violent crime – do not report crimes and do not come into any contact with the police and/or the judiciary.

- When a crime is reported and registered, the police will mostly investigate but by no means will this lead to criminal proceedings.

- This is because most investigations are dropped by the prosecution service: Of the 4.6 million investigation cases against known suspects handled by German prosecution services in 2010, only **11.9 percent led to the bringing of criminal charges**; a further 11.6 percent led to an application for a penal order (Strafbefehl) (Heinz 2012, 53).[155]

---

[153] As far back as 1989, Weigend noted: "Of all complaints about the justice system, the most frequent among crime victims is this: That after reporting the crime to the police and maybe the police collecting initial evidence, nothing more is heard, except perhaps many months later when a court summons to appear as a witness comes through the letterbox" (1989, 405).

[154] A 2011 study by Victim Support in the UK found that victims expect most of all from the criminal justice system to be kept informed and regularly updated about the progress of their case – and the information must be understandable, comprehensive and accurate. This need still goes unmet too often, yet is crucial to victims' satisfaction with the criminal justice system (Left in the dark: Why victims of crime need to be kept informed; www.victimsupport.org.uk).

[155] These figures relate to all investigation proceedings. In the everyday reality of legal procedure, the German prosecution services are said to give the impression of being there to drop cases more than to prosecute them (Heinz 2012, 52).
See also Jehle 2009, 19: In 2006, out of 4.8 million cases handled with a total of 5.8 million investigated individuals, 11.5 percent ended with the bringing of criminal charges (560,427 cases with 661,913 individuals charged); 11.9 percent with an application for a penal order (Strafbefehl); 4.9 percent of cases were dropped subject to conditions; 21.9 percent were dropped unconditionally; 26.5 percent were dropped under section 170 (2) of the German Code of Criminal Procedure; 0.2 percent were dropped on account of diminished responsibility; and 23.3% were closed otherwise.
In relation to **rape**, of the 262 rapes and attempted rapes recorded in the Bavarian Police Crime Statistics

Only a fraction of victims thus have the 'pleasure' of their case coming to trial – though that is not to say proceedings should not be made victim-friendly. However, "What many victims want most is emotional and direct personal support in the crisis precipitated by the crime. The agencies of the criminal justice system, because their dealings with victims are mostly of an official nature, are not generally suited to satisfying the basic need for human warmth" (Weigend 1989, 403).

For all victims, including the few who come into contact with the courts, emotional encouragement, help, social support, acknowledgement that they have been wronged, and recognition must primarily come from outside the criminal justice system – from their immediate social environment and from victim support organisations.

4
Victim support organisations and victims' wishes

When victims speak about what they have experienced – and no means all do – then the first and most important people they turn to are close family and friends (see section 2). That is often enough to stabilise a victim and restore a sense of safety and security.

Otherwise,[156] victims can seek help not only from "new professions who specifically dedicate themselves to crime victims", such as providers of psychotherapeutic treatment and lawyers specialised in representing victims' interests (Barton/Kölbel 2012, 13 f), but most of all from victim support organisations.

4.1
Victim support organisations

Victim support organisations are a reflection of the increased victim orientation in society – and the 'renaissance of the crime victim' came somewhat earlier for them than the 'discovery' of the victim by the criminal justice system. Social movements such as the child welfare and women's refuge movements had a large part in this, both by setting up counselling and support services from the mid-1970s onwards and

---

in 2000, in 58 percent of cases the case was dropped under section 170 (2) of the German Criminal Code, mostly (38 percent) because it was one person's word against the other; criminal charges were brought in a little more than one-third of cases (36 percent).

According to the analysis by Seith et al. (2009), of some 8,118 rapes registered in Germany in 2006, criminal charges were brought in 17 percent of cases and a sentence was imposed in 13 percent of cases. That victims have no means of contesting the **dropping of cases on discretionary grounds** under section 153 and 153a of the German Code of Criminal Procedure, and in most cases need not even be informed, was already criticised by Kilchling (1995, 701). See also the changes advocated in this regard by WEISSER RING (Böttcher 2012, 125)

On the problems resulting from the (increasing) use of plea deals, see Niemz 2011.

[156] Baurmann/Schädler note that such people do not provide victims with as much support as they want, meaning that victims fail to find the support and stabilisation they need. Victims, especially of violent crime, therefore desire state assistance far more frequently than they desire private support: "In our study, ... a majority spoke out on favour of professional and institutionalised victim support," although only about half of the surveyed victims of violence had more specific ideas about how they wanted to be helped (1991, 291 ff).

by engaging in advocacy for the interests of 'their' victims in society and politics.[157]

There are now a wide range of publicly and privately organised and financed victim support organisations[158] and Barton/Kölbel speak of a dedicated service market growing up around the needs of victims and the representation of their interests (2012, 13). Victim support, support services and support facilities for crime victims nonetheless remain relatively neglected career areas. It is only in the last few years that victim support has begun to take shape as a profession with a demanding and highly developed occupational profile of its own, although 'victim support worker' is not yet a defined occupation (Steffen 2009, 50, with further references).[159]

Victim support and counselling is consequently mainly a field for volunteer organisations.[160] A prime example is WEISSER RING e.V., the oldest victim support organisation in Germany and the only one to operate nationwide and with an entirely volunteer staff.[161] WEISSER RING has incidentally been a permanent congress partner to the German Congress on Crime Prevention since the beginnings of the Congress.

4.1.1
Example: WEISSER RING

WEISSER RING e.V., a non-profit association for the support of crime victims and the prevention of crime, was founded in Mainz in September 1976. The seventeen founding members presented the association's founding objects to the public in June 1977. The first branch office was opened in Berlin in December 1977. This marked the beginning of victim support work in practice.

---

[157] After initial focus on physical and sexual violence against children, violence against women became an issue of social work, intervention and prevention from the mid-1970s. The first women's refuges were opened in 1976, the first 'Notrufe' professional counselling services for women rape victims in 1977 and the first 'Wildwasser' professional counselling service for sexually abused girls in 1986 (Helfferich et al. 2012, 8).
Görgen notes the links between victimology and social movements and says it would be desirable "for victimology to continue in its function of giving and picking up social impetus."

[158] For victims of violence against women alone, there are 400 women's refuges, 612 professional counselling service points and 130 intervention service points (Helfferich et al. 2012), and there are counselling services for victims of right-wing violence in almost all German Länder – to mention only a few victim groups. See also the figures in the OpferFibel guide for crime victims published by the Federal Ministry of Justice.

[159] The Alice Salomon University of Applied Sciences in Berlin, for example, offers a one-year part-time certification course leading to a qualification as professional counsellor for victim support. Institut für Opferschutz im Strafverfahren e.V. offers a training course in psychosocial support advocacy for victims in criminal proceedings (www.rwh-institut.de).
In the area of counselling victims of hate crimes and extreme right-wing violence, a modular training course in professional counselling for victims of extreme right-wing violence has been offered since 2011 by the Crime Prevention Council of Lower Saxony (LPR) in cooperation with proVal-Institut, Arbeitstelle Rechtsextremismus und Gewalt (ARUG), and Lidice-Haus Bremen.

[160] "Various voluntary victim support organisations come in here, the most prominent in Germany being Weisser Ring. The huge potential of this organisation is not only seen in the voluntary commitment of numerous helpers, but also in its impressive total income of some €15 million a year" (Barton/Kölbel 2012, 13).

[161] Only the national office in Mainz and the Länder offices have fulltime staff.

Today, over 3,000 unpaid helpers look after crime victims, their families and surviving dependants at some 420 branches across the country. The organisation's funding objects not only include direct tangible and intangible support for crime victims, but lobbying[162] to advocate victims' interests and crime prevention.

"People who have to put up with psychological and physical harm and in many cases financial loss as a result of crime and violence must not be left alone with their often diverse problems. They deserve the same attentiveness and support as has always been accorded to the suspect, the accused and the sentenced offender."[163]

10,702 victims' cases were handled in 2011 and help for victims provided in 18,139 cases with an outlay of €4.7 million.[164] By far the majority of those helped were victims of violent or contact crime: sexual offences 31 percent, bodily injury 21 percent, domestic violence 11 percent, robbery 7 percent, homicide 5 percent, and deprivation of liberty 1 percent; additionally stalking and telephone harassment 4 percent, theft 10 percent and other crimes 8 percent (Jahresbericht 2011/2012, 7).

WEISSER RING offers both compassion and practical assistance:

- Help and support after a crime
- Accompaniment in dealings with police, prosecution services and courts
- Arrangement of assistance from other organisations
- Vouchers for initial consultations with a lawyer/psychotrauma specialist and for a forensic examination, at the victim's free choice
- Payment of lawyers' fees, primarily to assert victims' rights in criminal proceedings and under the Victim Compensation Act

---

[162] Especially in the early days of its activities, this lobbying aspect of WEISSER RING's activities attracted some criticism for its law-and-order tendencies (see, e.g., Weigend 1989, footnote 210).
Böttcher notes the high regard accorded to WEISSER RING, writing: "We must make use of this high regard in the interests of victims of crime and we must maintain it with blameless, committed work in our core task of victim support and with equally committed, soundly based public relations and lobbying in which outrage at prevailing circumstances or specific incidents is professionally presented" (2007, 25).

[163] From the foreword by Roswitha Müller-Piepenkötter , national Chairperson of WEISSER RING, in the association's annual report 2011/2012.

[164] This help for victims is an important supplement to the state compensation available to victims of violent crime on application since the 1976 Victim Compensation Act (Opferentschädigungsgesetz/OEG); prior filing of criminal charges is not required. Processing is the responsibility of Länder pension offices. The fact that entitlement has to be demonstrated, documented and verified causes delays: "The victim in acute distress from a crime will draw little consolation from the prospect even of substantial compensation in a year's time" (Kiefl/Lamnek 1986, 317). Apart from that, few victims apply: In 2010, there were applications for 10.8 percent of all cases of violent crime, and by no means all applications are granted (see the data on this on the WEISSER RING website, "Staatliche Opferentschädigung in Deutschland im Jahr 2010" – "State compensation for victims in Germany, 2010" – www.weisser-ring.de; and Villmow/ Savinsky 2013). Reform of the Victim Compensation Act is needed, and not just in the view of WEISSER RING, but such reform must not lead to cuts in victim compensation (see also the documentation of the 21st Victim Forum, 2010: Moderne Opferentschädigung. Betrachtungen aus interdisziplinärer Perspektive. Baden-Baden 2012).

- Financial support in a crisis precipitated by a crime
- National help line for victims.

WEISSER RING does not provide legal advice or therapy. Alongside personal, human support, a key element is arranging medical, psychological, legal and other professional assistance. In this regard, the victim support workers act in a guiding capacity (Sielaff 2010, 215).

Victim support workers are thoroughly trained before they start. Mandatory basic training[165] and an equally mandatory first advanced course are supplemented with numerous further training modules.[166] Initial and further training has been externally evaluated. To reduce the burden on staff, WEISSER RING provides case supervision, peer counselling and team supervision.[167]

Implemented in this way, the delivery of victim support through a volunteer-based service makes sense and is an appropriate approach. Indeed, as in many other areas, it is not just necessary: It plays a vital role in upholding democratic society. This holds all the more as it is not a case of the state 'retreating' from its social responsibilities in the area of victim support and 'transferring' them to the civil sphere – it is not about volunteering and unpaid work being exploited.[168]

WEISSER RING also takes a notable part in professional congresses. A two-day victims' forum (Opferforum) is held each year. Topics vary; the 24th Victims' Forum in 2013 is themed "The Victim Perspective in Crime Prevention." WEISSER RING has also initiated and funded numerous academic studies, most recently a study on plea bargaining and victims' interests in proceedings joined by victims as civil claimants (Niemz 2011).[169]

Finally, WEISSER RING has inspired similar organisations across Europe and is also a (founding) member of Victim Support Europe, an alliance of now 21 organisations from 18 countries. Over and above its work with non-governmental organisations,

---

[165] Staff can only work independently with victims once they have completed the basic training course and worked alongside a mentor on at least three cases.

[166] The organisation is currently considering the introduction of certificate courses compiled and provided in collaboration with a tertiary social work college or a university teaching faculty.

[167] This addresses legitimate reservations about the work of WEISSER RING, as raised for example by Baurmann/Schädler: "In the sensitive field of victim support – especially when it comes to severely traumatised victims – it is irresponsible for counselling to be provided through laypeople lacking initial and further training and lacking (team) supervision" (1991, 301).

[168] A number of the German Länder have victim support trusts, and witness support is generally provided as a state (court) service. On civil engagement, see also Steffen 2009.

[169] The Mainzer Schriften zur Situation von Kriminalitätsopfern publication series "provides a platform for all forms of academic research into the situation of crime victims from a legal, medical and social perspective." Volume 1 in 1989 focused on risk allocation between citizens and the state, Volume 50 in 2012 on victims' fears after a crime.

WEISSER RING has long communicated directly with EU representatives for targeted advocacy of victim interests.

4.2
The limits of victim support

A victim's help and support needs can be met in a day, but it can also take years. WEISSER RING aims in its work "to motivate victims to use available support facilities and rebuild their lives as quickly as possible after the traumatic event."[170]

The aims of other victim support organisations will be similar. If they succeed in attaining them, then they can help alleviate at least one **problem inherent in helping victims** of crime underscored by Reemtsma: "Anyone who has become the victim of a crime wants to return to normal life as soon as possible and not be constantly reminded of the experience ... any act of support for someone who has been victim to a crime ... [also] labels that person a victim ... it is in the victim's interest both to be recognised as a victim and not to be regarded as a victim ... Any aid must basically have this dual nature: Acknowledging that status to help surmount it ...Because to be a victim is to be passive. To accept help is also to be passive. Help for victims that does not aim at the same time to extend the victim's own activity radius is problematic and mostly counterproductive ... Help for victims is only helpful if it helps them move beyond the state of needing help ... Not every injury can be healed. Accepting this fact is part of minimising suffering ... There is always a certain amount of help, but it is finite. An inherent feature of finite help is that it makes its limits plain. Help for victims always means – not least – making plain where one cannot help. This is required knowledge for all support workers, because anyone who is ignorant of it does more harm than good" (2006, 18, 17).

4.3
Perspectives of victim support: The Parallel Justice framework

Although the criminal justice system is inherently unable to serve the interests of victims – for one thing only a very small percentage of victims come into contact with the agencies of formal social control, and for another criminal proceedings are and remain offender-oriented and the role of the victim as a witness always places a burden on the victim – the increased orientation towards victims in society has indeed advanced the cause of victim assistance and support in various ways.

---

[170] In line with this, the WEISSER RING Victims' Forum and annual campaign in 2012 had the slogan "Sei stark – Hol Dir Hilfe" ("Be Strong: Get Help"), appealing to victims of crime and violence not to be passive, but to report the crime and seek support so as to put the difficult situation behind them or make it more bearable as soon as possible (2012 a, 32).

Yet there is always scope for improvement. One interesting approach in this regard is the Parallel Justice framework[171], which has been proposed by Susan Herman[172] as a framework for work involving victims in the USA[173] and which has already been adopted in a number of localities.

The Parallel Justice framework presented in the following on the basis of publications by Susan Herman is rooted in the conviction that society has an obligation to exercise justice for victims. Parallel Justice is not an alternative to criminal proceedings, but provides an additional, often contemporaneous set of responses geared to victims.

Parallel Justice aims to create a new framework for responding to crime: Two separate, parallel paths to justice – one for victims, and one for offenders:

- Whenever a crime is reported, society responds with efforts to identify, prosecute, sentence and ultimately reintegrate the offender.

- Criminal proceedings offer the offender, so to speak, a forum: If a trial is fair, if the punishment fits the crime and if the trial outcome is in the interests of society, then justice has been done.

- For **victims** of crime there is no comparable response on the part of the community, no forum, and no obligation to do justice for the victim as for the offender.

- There should therefore be a separate societal response for victims, geared to acknowledging that they have been wronged, to ensuring their safety, to helping them cope with the trauma of victimisation, and to restoring their sense of being in control of their lives.

- Those responses do not depend on whether the offender is ever identified or sentenced. The wrong done to the victim is acknowledged come what may, and is addressed separately from criminal proceedings – because the societal obligation to provide justice for victims of crime goes beyond due process.

---

[171] Susan Herman: Parallel Justice for Victims of Crime. 2010; www.paralleljustice.org.

[172] **Susan Herman** is an internationally regarded advocate for victims of crime. She was Executive Director of the National Center for Victims of Crime from 1997 to 2004. Prior to that she worked to promote the cause of victims in various ways, for example in the support of abused women in New York City and as consultant to New York Police. She is now Associate Professor in the Department of Criminal Justice at Pace University in New York.

[173] In the USA, as in other countries with an adversarial legal system, victim participation in criminal proceedings is inherently harder to implement than under an inquisitorial system on the continental European model. In an adversarial system, the victim is mostly the prime witness for the prosecution. This role entails considerable psychological stress and is also hard to reconcile with a simultaneous role as civil claimant. According to Weigend, this may explain why much lip service is paid in English-speaking countries to victim rights in line with the political wish for victim-friendly procedure, while in fact victims in such countries have comparatively little influence and comparatively few safeguards against harm as a result of criminal proceedings.
On the other hand, the USA has well-developed – in some cases non-governmental – practical support provision for crime victims, including support during criminal proceedings (Weigend 2012, 33).

Criminal proceedings are in any case unsuited to providing justice for victims. Only few victims make it to court; the proceedings themselves 'use' victims as witnesses and attend neither to their security nor their wellbeing. Improvements have indeed been made but they are still not enough: Criminal proceedings remain offender-focused.

For the agencies comprising the criminal justice system – the police, prosecution services, courts and penal institutions – the new vision of justice for victims of crime as well as for offenders means that they must respond more effectively than before to victims and their safety and give greater priority to preventing further victimisation. Social and healthcare services, too, should realign their practices so as to help victims rebuild their lives. Every part of civil society can make a key contribution to Parallel Justice.

Parallel Justice calls for a targeted, communal response that is fair, just and tailored to the needs of each victim. Such a response not only helps crime victims but delivers major benefits for society as a whole: Given the links between victimisation and alcohol abuse, drug abuse, depression, suicide, teenage pregnancy, poor school and education outcomes, difficulties at work, repeat victimisation and delinquency, justice for victims can not only have a positive impact on such negative factors but can also help reduce crime.

Parallel Justice decouples the pursuit of justice for victims from the administration of justice for offenders. Justice for victims is an end in itself and no longer an occasional byproduct of a system focused elsewhere (i.e., on the offender). In this way, justice can be attained by two separate pathways with scope for interaction and linkage between the two.

When it comes to communal **implementation** of Parallel Justice, there is no formula recommending a specific approach for policy and practice. Instead, the framework is based on principles that can help guide communities in implementation Herman 2010, 131 ff):

- Building strong public understanding of victims' needs
- Creating broad-based support for reform
- Basing the argument for reform on solid research (crime analysis; victim surveys on victimisation experiences, needs, etc.)
- Conducting an inventory of current help and support for victims
- On this basis, a Parallel Justice task force develops priorities and communicates the idea through forums, workshops, the media, holders of office and other opinion leaders.

"We must meet our obligation to victims, not just because we are a compassionate society, but because helping victims rebuild their lives is an essential component of justice" (Herman 2010, 140).

Appraisal:

An approach such as Parallel Justice is likely to improve the position for victims more than has already been achieved by victim support and victim protection. In the Parallel Justice framework, victims no longer define themselves through the victim but as someone who has been wronged and who is entitled in their own right to social support and restitution.

The framework calls for the victim's perspective to be brought into all areas of society and hence for integration, cooperation and coordination. It is reminiscent in its formulation and implementation of the idea of Community Crime Prevention, except that in this instance the focus of efforts to establish the appropriate cross-cutting task forces is not on crime as a whole but on the victims of crime.

Instead of setting up new task forces for Parallel Justice, thought should be given to using the existing Community Crime Prevention task forces in Germany as a locus for implementing the Parallel Justice framework.

5
More prevention, fewer victims

No matter how efficient and effective the criminal justice, victim protection and victim support systems, it is always better to stop crimes and consequently victimisation from happening in the first place. No criminal justice system, however victim-oriented, and no victim support system, however well-established and capable, can hope to make good, let alone undo, the physical and material harm to victims and the often severe psychological impacts of a crime.

Hence the best way to protect victims is to prevent crime: No crime means no victim and no harm done. People want to live in safety and to be shielded from crime. Nobody wants to become the victim of a crime – and certainly not a second or a third time (Sielaff 2010, 216).[174]

Victim-oriented crime prevention is concerned on the one hand with the implications of findings on and problems relating to the effects of victimisation.

---

[174] Herman notes in this connection the lack of readiness to become involved on behalf of victims and that this could have to do with a fear of being confronted with the same sort of thing ('What did she do to deserve it') or with thinking it may be unpleasant for victims to speak about what has happened (2010, 117). Anders Barton 2012, 117: "Victimhood is associated in the victim society with prestige, recognition, attention, rights and privileges ... Slightly exaggerating, the victim society can even be said to be a society in which 'everyone wants to be a victim.'"

- Avoiding or alleviating the psychological, physical and material harm
- Preventing or reducing fear of crime with its potential impacts on behaviour and wellbeing
- Preventing or reducing revictimisation by providing protection and support for victims
- Avoiding the 'cycle of violence'
- Taking into account victims' wishes for social support, information and counselling, for confirmation that they have been wronged, for retribution and restitution.

On the other hand, **victim-oriented crime prevention** is concerned quite conventionally with preventing and reducing victimisation. In this victim-oriented form of crime prevention – as with other forms, such as offender-oriented crime prevention – it is useful to draw a distinction between universal, selective and indicated prevention (Steffen 2011, 103). After all, victimisation and delinquency, victim and offender, represent two faces of the same coin – the two faces of crime – and successful offender-oriented crime prevention is always also successful in preventing victimisation. While 'victim-oriented crime prevention' places the emphasis on the victim, it does not mean the kind of prevention that has to be or can be put into practice by victims themselves, but crime prevention in the usual comprehensive sense taking in victims, offenders and situations.

5.1
Victim-oriented prevention as universal, selective and indicated prevention

Universal prevention
Universal prevention targets the population and/or communities as a whole with generally beneficial programmes and measures. Rather than focusing on specific grounds for suspicion, the aim is to apply consistent social, labour, youth, family, business, transport and education policies in such a way that crime and victimisation do not arise in the first place.

Because of its very unspecific – as the name says, universal – scope, universal prevention should not be referred to and thought of as a form of crime prevention. While factors such as socialisation, upbringing and individual and social circumstances doubtless have a strong influence on crime trends, no direct link can be shown between such global factors and crime. The definitions of crime and prevention should also be prevented from becoming watered down. Crime is therefore not the right frame of reference for universal prevention strategies, and falls short of their full significance.

In any case, if everyone is a potential victim,[175] the outcome could be crime policy that plays on the public's fear of crime. Fear of crime is governed by laws of its own and thus "supports and feeds the demand for stringent policy, even if the extraneous factors that might justify this greater stringency have long ceased to exist" (Hassemer/ Reemtsma 2002, 109).[176]

Strategies, measures and projects should therefore only be considered part of crime prevention if preventing or reducing crime and victimisation is their direct or indirect aim. Such strategies, measures and projects come under the headings of selective or indicative crime prevention (Steffen 2011, 102).[177]

Selective prevention

Selective prevention targets specific subgroups, individuals and situations with heightened risk factors and hence greater risk of victimisation and delinquency ('potential victims and potential offenders') and situations where there is a risk of crime ('opportunities for crime').

Selective crime prevention is directly or indirectly geared to preventing or reducing crime or improving safety and people's sense of safety.

Measures include help and support for people with specific problems, information,[178] and education for potential victims.

Indicated prevention

Indicated prevention targets victims and offenders with the aim of preventing repeat victimisation or delinquency. Victim protection and victim support come under indicated prevention and aim to prevent revictimisation and secondary victimisation. Resocialisation measures are indicated prevention measures for offenders.

---

[175] According to Kilchling's findings, if personal experience, indirect victimisation in the close social environment and witnessed victimisation are aggregated over a lifelong perspective, then victimisation is "almost a ubiquitous phenomenon", but the many victimisation-related experiences differ considerably in intensity and directness (1995, 622 f).

[176] To cite a recent example, a commission was appointed in late January 2013 to review the entire "security architecture and security legislation in Germany after 11 September 2001," but according to a report in Die Welt, a national newspaper, on 30 January 2013, the Federal Ministry of the Interior had "no interest in a 'critical general review.'"

[177] Dissenting, Kahl (2012, 26) calls for the action radius of crime prevention not to be further delimited, but to be widened and its limits removed both in practice and hence also conceptually.

[178] A case in point is the German **Police Crime Prevention Programme**, which followed these aims from the outset. A police crime prevention education campaign was launched in Bavaria as early as 1964, using the media to disseminate tips on how to avoid burglary, theft and other crimes. The idea was then taken up by the Criminal Police Prevention Programme (KPVP), which included all German Länder from 1970. A slogan was adopted, 'Die Kriminalpolizei rät' ('The police advise'). From 1997, in a reorientation and restructuring of police crime prevention, the tasks were taken over by the Programm Polizeiliche Kriminalprävention der Länder und des Bundes (ProPK – Federal/Länder Police Crime Prevention Programme).

Indicated prevention also includes programmes and measures for crime hotspots.

5.2
Problems of victim-oriented prevention

Aside from the problem mentioned above about victims being instrumentalised for legislative ends,[179] victim-oriented prevention has two main problem areas: The fact that crime prevention cannot be separated from fear of crime, and the demand that victims should not be allotted any or all of the blame for their victimisation.

Crime prevention must avoid raising fears

When the German Police Crime Prevention Programme, for example, gives recommendations and advice on how to protect against crime with the slogan "Wir wollen, dass Sie sicher leben" ("We want you to live safely"), or urges people to intervene and help victims of crime in campaigns like "Aktion-Tu-was" ("Do something!"), it is impossible to avoid appealing to people's fear of becoming victims of crime themselves.

This may not be too much of a problem when it comes to potential victims.[180] For people who have already become the victim of a crime it can amplify post-victimisation fears. There is no way out of this dilemma. At best, an attempt can be made to alleviate fears by providing recommendations and where appropriate help that are as specific as possible and relate to the individual's own case – preferably in personal consultation with victim support and victim counselling workers.

Victims have no part of the blame for their victimisation

Victim-oriented crime prevention always runs the risk of apportioning victims part or even all of the blame for their victimisation, or of them taking part of the blame upon themselves.[181]

It is not just burglary and theft victims who tend to be given part of the blame ("Why didn't you lock the door?", "Why did you leave the window open?"), but most of all victims of violent and contact offences. For people who know the victim, ascribing the victim some of the blame helps combat their own fears: "I don't act like that, so it won't happen to me."

The idea of the victim being partly responsible and to blame for a crime was also prev-

---

[179] Kölbel concludes in his analysis that there is so far no evidence that victims are 'instrumentalised' to make criminal law more punitive: "This is of course a preliminary impression and requires scrutiny. Ultimately, the choice between the instrumentalisation hypothesis and the conventional reading of the ongoing proliferation of victim rights in criminal procedure as a welfare state project can only be made through closer analysis of how the legislation came about" (2012, 228).

[180] Schwind notes the phenomenon of 'forting up', the booming security industry and people retreating into their own four walls out of fear of crime (2011, § 16, at 13a; § 20, at 14).

[181] This has been studied and shown in particular for victims of sexual offences; see Steffen 2012 a.

alent in the early days of victimology: "The beginning of the ... history of victimology was marked not by the thought that the victim of crime warranted special care, but by the consideration that the offence was to be understood not solely as an emanation of the personality of the offender but as the outcome of an interaction between offender and victim ... [it was] believed that an important approach for explaining how crime came about while enabling a de-demonisation of the offender had been found in the idea that the victim was co-responsible for 'their' offender" (Weigend 1989, 299 f).[182]

Whatever the victim's conduct, whether 'careless', 'provocative' or 'reckless', provided it is within the scope of what is socially appropriate and allowed by law, it must not be held up in reproach against the victim and it must most certainly not lead to legal consequences: "As ... there is no legal duty of self-protection, disregard of precautions, however much the precautions are recommended by the police, can do nothing to change the status of the affected party as a 'legitimate' victim warranting protection" (Weigend 1989, 395).[183]

That applies without restriction to this day – even if it is not always easy to put it into practice in victim-oriented crime prevention.

---

[182] This notion of victims being partly to blame not only prevailed in the early days of victimology but still causes problems today, as highlighted by Görgen, who notes that it is often hard to make people understand the distinction between analysing the victim's role in how a crime came about and being perceived as pointing the finger at the victim (2012, 92).

[183] On victim precipitation, see Weigend 1989, 396 ff.

References

Baier, Dirk et al. (2009): Jugendliche in Deutschland als Opfer und Täter von Gewalt. Kriminologisches Forschungsinstitut Niedersachsen e.V. Forschungsbericht Nr. 107. Hannover.

Barton, Stephan (2012): Strafrechtspflege und Kriminalpolitik in der viktimären Gesellschaft. Effekte, Ambivalenzen und Paradoxien. In Barton/Kölbel (Eds.), p. 111-137.

Barton, Stephan/Kölbel, Ralf (2012) (Eds.): Ambivalenzen der Opferzuwendung des Strafrechts. Zwischenbilanz nach einem Vierteljahrhundert opferorientierter Strafrechtspolitik in Deutschland. Baden-Baden.

Baurmann, Michael C. (2000): Opferbedürfnisse, Mitschuldgefühl und Strafbedürfnis sowie die Erwartungen von Kriminalitätsopfern an Politik, Justiz und Polizei. DPolBl H. 2/2000, p. 2-5.

Baurmann, Michael C./Schädler, Wolfram (1991): Das Opfer nach der Straftat – seine Erwartungen und Perspektiven. Bundeskriminalamt (Eds.). BKA – Forschungsreihe Band 22. Wiesbaden.

Bergmann, Christine (2012): Ängste von Opfern sexuellen Missbrauchs. In WEISSER RING (2012 b) (Eds.), p. 36-49.

Bieneck, Steffen/Pfeiffer, Christian (2012): Viktimisierungserfahrungen im Justizvollzug. KFN Forschungsbericht Nr. 119. Hannover.

Bock, Stefanie (2012): Opferrechte im Lichte europäischer Vorgaben. In Barton/Kölbel (Eds.), p. 67-88.

Böhm, Klaus Michael (2012): Mehr Begutachtung im Strafverfahren: mehr Opferschutz? Kriminalpolitische Perspektiven. In Pollähne/Rode (Eds.), p. 129-147.

Böttcher, Reinhard (2012): Perspektiven für den Opferschutz im Strafverfahren. NK Neue Kriminalpolitik 4/2012, p. 122-125.

Böttcher, Reinhard (2012 a): Bedeutung der Medienöffentlichkeit für die Opfer. In WEISSER RING e.V., p. 187-199.

Böttcher, Reinhard (2007): Rechtspolitische Forderungen des WEISSEN RINGS – Bilanz und Ausblick. In WEISSER RING (Eds.), p. 15-26.

Bundeskriminalamt (2012) (Eds.): Polizeiliche Kriminalstatistik 2011. Bundesrepublik Deutschland. 59. Ausgabe. Wiesbaden.

Bundesministerium der Justiz (2012): OpferFibel. Rechte von Verletzten und Geschädigten im Strafverfahren. 3. Auflage. Berlin.

Bundesministerium des Innern/Bundesministerium der Justiz (2006) (Eds.): Zweiter Periodischer Sicherheitsbericht. Berlin.

Deegener, Günther (1996): Psychische Folgeschäden nach Wohnungseinbruch. Erfahrungen von Opfern nach Einbruchsdiebstahl und Raubüberfall. WEISSER RING (Eds.): Mainzer Schriften zur Situation von Kriminalitätsopfern. Band 15. Mainz.

Directive 2012/29/EU of the European Parliament and of the Council of 25 October 2012 establishing minimum standards on the rights, support and protection of victims of crime, and replacing Council Framework Decision 2001/220/ JHA.

Dudeck, Manuela (2012): Psychische Folgeschäden bei Delinquenzopfern. Generalisierbares Wissen und individueller Nachweis. In Pollähne/Rode (Eds.), p. 121-127.

Ellrich, Karoline et al. (2011): Gewalt gegen Polizeibeamte. KFN Forschungsbericht Nr. 3. Hannover,

Elsner, Erich/Steffen, Wiebke (2005): Vergewaltigung und sexuelle Nötigung in Bayern. München.

Feldmann-Hahn, Felix (2011): Opferbefragungen in Deutschland. Bestandsaufnahme und Bewertung. Holzkirchen/Obb.

Frederking, Gisela (2007): Informiertheit über Opferrechte aus der Sicht des Opferanwalts. In WEISSER RING (Eds.), p. 33-35.

Gelbert, Claudia/Walter, Michael (2013): Probleme des Opferschutzes gegenüber dem inhaftierten Täter. NstZ 2/2013, p. 75-83.

Görgen, Thomas (2012): Zum Stand der internationalen viktimologischen Forschung. In Barton/Kölbel (Eds.), p. 89-109.

Görgen, Thomas et al. (2010): Sicher leben im Alter? Ergebnisse einer Studie und Konzept eines Aktionsprogramms zur Förderung der Sicherheit älterer Menschen. Kriminalistik 11/2010, S. 644-651.

Görgen, Thomas/Rauchert, Kathrin/Fisch, Sarah (2011): Langfristige Folgen sexuellen Missbrauchs Minderjähriger. Published online: 20.9.2011 (DOI 10.1007/ s11757-011-0129-0) Springer-Verlag.

Greve, Werner et al. (2012): Bewältigung krimineller Opfererfahrungen: Entwicklungsfolgen und Entwicklungsregulation. In Barton/Kölbel (Eds.), p. 263-288.

Hartwig, Sabine (2012): Beitrag im Rahmen des 22. Mainzer Opferforums. In WEISSER RING (2012 b) (Eds.), p. 54-58.

Hassemer, Winfried/Reemtsma, Jan Philipp (2002): Verbrechensopfer: Gesetz und Gerechtigkeit. München.

Haverkamp, Rita (2012): Gefühlte Sicherheiten und Sicherheitsgefährdungen – Barometer Sicherheit in Deutschland (BaSiD). Internetdokumentation des Deutschen Präventionstages. Hannover (www.praeventionstag.de/Dokumentation.cms/2047).

Heinz, Wolfgang (2012): Das strafrechtliche Sanktionensystem und die Sanktionierungspraxis in Deutschland 1882 – 2010. KIS – Konstanzer Inventar Sanktionsforschung. Stand: Berichtsjahr 2010; Version: 1/2012 (www.ki.uni-konstanz.de/kis).

Heinz, Wolfgang (2006): Zum Stand der Dunkelfeldforschung in Deutschland. In Obergfell-Fuchs, Joachim/Brandenstein, Martin (Eds.): Nationale und internationale Entwicklungen in der Kriminologie. Festschrift für Helmut Kury zum 65. Geburtstag. Frankfurt am Main, p. 241-263.

Helfferich, Cornelia et al. (2012): Bestandsaufnahme zur Situation der Frauenhäuser, der Frauenberatungsstellen und anderer Unterstützungsangebote für gewaltbetroffene Frauen und deren Kinder. Gutachten im Auftrag des Bundesministeriums für Familie, Senioren, Frauen und Jugend. Berlin.

Herman, Susan (2010): Parallel Justice For Victims Of Crime. Washington, DC.

Hilgendorf, Eric/Rengier, Rudolf (2012) (Eds.): Festschrift für Wolfgang Heinz zum 70. Geburtstag. Baden-Baden.

Jehle, Jörg-Martin (2009): Strafrechtspflege in Deutschland. Fakten und Zahlen. Hrsg. vom Bundesministerium der Justiz. 5. Auflage 2009. Mönchengladbach.

Kahl, Wolfgang (2012): Eine gute Sozialpolitik ist die beste Kriminalpolitik. forum kriminalprävention 2/2012, p. 26-27.

Kerner, Hans-Jürgen et al. (2012): Täter-Opfer-Ausgleich in Deutschland. Auswertung der bundesweiten Täter-Opfer-Ausgleichs-Statistik für den Jahrgang 2010. Herausgegeben vom Bundesministerium der Justiz. Berlin.

Kiefl, Walter/Lamnek, Siegfried (1986): Soziologie des Opfers. Theorie, Methoden und Empirie der Viktimologie. München.

Kiefl, Walter/Sieger, Monica (2008): Kenntnisse und Meinungen über Opfer von Gewaltverbrechen. Kriminalistik 1/2008, p. 40-44.

Kilchling, Michael (1995): Opferinteressen und Strafverfolgung. Max-Planck-Institut für ausländisches und internationales Strafrecht. Ed. iuscrim. Freiburg i. Br.

Kirchhoff, Gerd Ferdinand (1990): Opferhilfe in internationaler Betrachtung. Entwicklung und Bestandsaufnahme. In Schädler et al. (Eds.), p. 22-48.

Kölbel, Ralf (2012): Kriminalpolitische Instrumentalisierung der „Gefahr sekundärer Viktimisierung"? In Barton/Kölbel (Eds.), p. 213-232.

Kreuzer, Arthur (2012): Aussage gegen Aussage – Zum Dilemma von Täter- und Opferschutz bei Beziehungsdelikten. In Kerner, Hans-Jürgen/Marks, Erich (Eds.): Internetdokumentation des Deutschen Präventionstages. Hannover 2012 (www.praeventionstag.de/Dokumentation.cm/2004).

Kreuzer, Arthur (2010): Prävention von Gewalt gegen Senioren. BewHi 1/2010, p. 88-105.

Kühnrich, Bernd/Kania, Harald (2005): Attitudes Towards Punishment in the European Union: Results from the 2005 European Crime Survey (ECSS) with Focus on Germany. ECSS Project: Research Report MPI (30/12/2005).

Kunz, Karl-Ludwig (2011 a): Kriminologie. 6. Auflage. Bern e.a.

Kunz, Karl-Ludwig (2011 b): Opferschutz und Verteidigungsrechte im Kontext von Strafrechtstheorie und symbolischer Rechtspolitik. Sociology in Switzerland. Online Publications (socio.ch/cri/t_kunz1.htm; last update: 18 October 2011; viewed: 11 January 2013)

Ladenburger, Petra (2012): Strukturelle und praktische Defizite der institutionalisierten Opferhilfe in Deutschland. In Barton/Kölbel (Eds.), p. 289-299.

Maercker, Andreas (2006): Opfererfahrungen im Kontext: Soziale Bedingungen für psychische Spätfolgen. In WEISSER RING (Eds.), p. 49-58.

Müller, Ursula/Schröttle, Monika (2004): Lebenssituation, Sicherheit und Gesundheit von Frauen in Deutschland. Eine repräsentative Untersuchung zu Gewalt gegen Frauen in Deutschland. Gutachten im Auftrag des Bundesministeriums für Familie, Senioren, Frauen und Jugend. Berlin 2004.

Niemz, Susanne (2011): Urteilsabsprachen und Opferinteressen – in Verfahren mit Nebenklagebeteiligung. Mainzer Schriften zur Situation von Kriminalitätsopfern Bd. 49. Baden-Baden.

Pollähne, Helmut (2012): „Opfer" im Blickpunkt –„Täter" im toten Winkel? In Pollähne/Rode (Eds.), p. 5-19.

Pollähne, Helmut/Rode, Irmgard (2012) (Eds.): Opfer im Blickpunkt – Angeklagte im Abseits? Probleme und Chancen zunehmender Orientierung auf die Verletzten in Prozess, Therapie und Vollzug. Berlin.

PSB: Periodischer Sicherheitsbericht; see Bundesministerium des Innern/Bundesministerium der Justiz (2006).

Reemtsma, Jan Philipp (2006): Was sind eigentlich Opferinteressen? Überarbeitetes Manuskript einer Ansprache anlässlich des 25-jährigen Jubiläums des WEISSEN RINGS in Hamburg. die neue polizei 03/2006, p. 16-18.

Reemtsma, Jan Philipp (1999): Das Recht des Opfers auf die Bestrafung des Täters – als Problem. München.

Richter, Harald (1997): Opfer krimineller Gewalttaten. Individuelle Folgen und ihre Verarbeitung. WEISSER RING (Eds.): Mainzer Schriften zur Situation von Kriminalitätsopfern. Band 17. Mainz.

Rössner, Dieter (1990): Historische Aspekte des Opferschutzes und opferorientierter Sanktionen. In Schädler et al. (Eds.), p. 7-27.

Sautner, Lyane (2010): Opferinteressen und Strafrechtstheorien. Zugleich ein Beitrag zum restaurativen Umgang mit Straftaten. Viktimologie und Opferrechte (VOR). Schriftenreihe der Weisser Ring Forschungsgesellschaft. Band 6. Innsbruck e.a.

Schädler, Wolfram (2012): Opferschutz in der deutschen straf- und prozessrechtlichen Gesetzgebung und dessen Umsetzung in die Judikatur. In Barton/Kölbel (Eds.), p. 51-65.

Schädler, Wolfram et al. (1990): Hilfe für Kriminalitätsopfer als internationale Bewegung. Ein Vergleich mit den Niederlanden und den USA. Beiträge aus einer Tagung der Evangelischen Akademie Arnoldshain. Bonn: Godesberg.

Schneider, Hans-Joachim (2010): Das Verbrechensopfer gestern und heute. Neue Erkenntnisse der kriminologischen Verbrechensopferforschung. Kriminalistik 11/2010, p. 627-635.

Schöch, Heinz (2012): Opferperspektive und Jugendstrafrecht. ZJJ 3/2012, p. 246-

255.

Schöch, Heinz (2003): Das Opfer im Strafprozess. In Egg, R./Minthe, E. (Eds.): Opfer von Straftaten. Kriminologie und Praxis. Band 40. Wiesbaden, p. 19-36.

Schwind, Hans-Dieter (2011): Kriminologie. Eine praxisorientierte Einführung mit Beispielen. 21., neubearbeitete und erweiterte Auflage. Heidelberg e.a.

Seidler, Günter H. (2006): Ergebnisse der Heidelberger Gewaltopferstudie. In WEISSER RING (Eds.), p. 61-68.

Seith, Corinna et al. (2009): Unterschiedliche Systeme, ähnliche Resultate? Strafverfolgung von Vergewaltigung in elf europäischen Ländern. Länderbericht Deutschland (www.cwasu.org).

Sessar, Klaus (2012): Kriminalitätswirklichkeit im Licht des Dunkelfeldes. In Hilgendorf/Rengier (Eds.), p. 262-274.

Sielaff, Wolfgang (2010): Kriminalitätsopfer – Situation, Problematik, Hilfe. Kriminalistik 4/2010, p. 212-217.

Standler, Lena et al. (2012): Repräsentativbefragung Sexueller Missbrauch 2011. KFN – Kriminologisches Forschungsinstitut Niedersachsen e.V. Forschungsbericht Nr. 118. Hannover.

Steffen, Wiebke (2012 a): Polizeiliches Verhalten bei Opfern von Sexualstraftaten am Beispiel der Opfer von Vergewaltigungen und sexuellen Nötigungen. In Barton/Kölbel (Eds.), p. 141-158.

Steffen, Wiebke (2012 b): Sicherheit als Grundbedürfnis der Menschen und staatliche Aufgabe. Gutachten zum 17. Deutschen Präventionstag am 16. und 17 . April 2012 in München (www.praeventionstag.de/nano.cms/17-DPT/ Seite/3).

Steffen, Wiebke (2011): Moderne Gesellschaften und Kriminalität. Der Beitrag der Kriminalprävention zu Integration und Solidarität. Gutachten zum 14. Deutschen Präventionstag. In Marks, E./Steffen, W. (Eds.): Solidarität leben – Vielfalt sichern. Ausgewählte Beiträge des 14. Deutschen Präventionstages 2009. Godesberg.

Steffen, Wiebke (2009): Bürgerschaftliches Engagement in der Kriminalprävention. Gutachten zum 13. Deutschen Präventionstag. In Marks, E./Steffen. W. (Eds.): Engagierte Bürger – sichere Gesellschaft. Ausgewählte Beiträge des 13. Deutschen Präventionstages 2008. Godesberg.

Steffen, Wiebke (2008): Jugendkriminalität und ihre Verhinderung zwischen Wahrnehmung und empirischen Befunden. Gutachten zum 12. Deutschen Präventionstag. In Marks, E./Steffen, W. (Eds.): Starke Jugend – starke Zukunft. Ausgewählte Beiträge des 12. Deutschen Präventionstages 2007. Godesberg.

Steffen, Wiebke (1995): Veränderungen in der polizeilichen Aufgabenwahrnehmung – Gemeinwesenorientierung als moderne Zielperspektive? In 50 Jahre polizeiliche Bildungsarbeit in Münster. Polizei-Führungsakademie Nr. 3/4 1995, p. 107-122.

Steffen, Wiebke (1993): Kriminalitätsanalyse I: Dunkelfeldforschung und Kriminologische Regionalanalysen. Lehr- und Studienbriefe Kriminologie Nr. 4. Hilden.

Steffen, Wiebke (1982): Inhalte und Ergebnisse polizeilicher Ermittlungen. München.

Steffen, Wiebke (1976): Analyse polizeilicher Ermittlungstätigkeit aus der Sicht des späteren Strafverfahrens. BKA-Forschungsreihe Bd. 4. Wiesbaden.

Stock, Jürgen (2012): Stand und Perspektiven der Dunkelfeldforschung in Deutschland und international. In Hilgendorf/Rengier (Eds.), p. 317-331.

Stöckel, Heinz (2006): Opferschutz und Opferhilfe (zu) lange vergessen? die neue polizei 03/2006, p. 3-5.

Treibel, Angelika et al. (2008): Alltagsvorstellungen über Gewaltopfer in Abhängigkeit von Delikt und Geschlecht – eine internetbasierte Studie. MschrKrim. 91. Jahrgang – Heft 6 – 2008, p. 458-470.

van Dijk, Jan (2012): The International Crime Victims Survey: Latest Results And Prospects. Criminology in Europe. 2012/3, p. 24-33.

van Dijk et al. (2007): The Burden of Crime in the EU. A Comparative Analysis of the European Crime and Safety Survey (EU ICS). Brussels.

van Hüllen, Helgard (2006): Opferschutz im europäischen Kontext. die neue polizei 03/2006, p. 12-15.

Villmow, Bernhard/Savinsky, Alescha Lara (2013): Staatliche Opferentschädigung nach der Jahrtausendwende – statistische Daten, methodische Probleme und einige Anmerkungen zur gegenwärtigen Praxis des OEG (Published in Festschrift für Jürgen Wolter. Berlin 2013).

Volbert, Renate (2012 a): Sekundäre Viktimisierung: Alte Klagen – neue Erkenntnisse? In Pollähne/Rode (Eds.), p. 149-163.

Volbert, Renate (2012 b): Geschädigte im Strafverfahren: Positive Effekte oder sekundäre Viktimisierung? In Barton/Kölbel (Eds.), p. 197-212.

Voß, Stephan (2003): „Du Opfer ..." Berliner Forum Gewaltprävention. Nr. 12, p. 56-59

Voß, Hans-Georg W./Hoffmann, Jens/Wondrak, Isabel (2006): Stalking in Deutschland. Aus Sicht der Betroffenen und Verfolger. WEISSER RING (Eds.): Mainzer Schriften zur Situation von Kriminalitätsopfern. Band 40. Baden-Baden.

Waller, Irvin (2011): Rights for Victims of Crime. Lanham e.a.

Weigend, Thomas (2012): Internationale Entwicklungen bei der Stellung des Verletzten im Strafverfahren. In Barton/Kölbel (Eds.), p. 29-50.

Weigend, Thomas (2010 a): „Die Strafe für das Opfer"? – Zur Renaissance des Genugtuungsgedankens im Straf- und Strafverfahrensrecht. RW – Heft 1 2010, p. 39-57.

Weigend, Thomas (2010 b): Das Opfer als Prozesspartei. Bemerkungen zum 2. Opferrechtsreformgesetz 2009. In Dölling, Dieter et al. (2010) (Eds.): Verbrechen – Strafe – Resozialisierung. Festschrift für Heinz Schöch zum 70.

Geburtstag. Berlin. p. 947-961.

Weigend, Thomas (1989): Deliktsopfer und Strafverfahren. Berlin.

WEISSER RING e.V. (2012 a) (Eds.): Jahresbericht 2011/2012. Finanzbericht 2011. Mainz.

WEISSER RING e.V. (2012 b) (Eds.): Ängste des Opfers nach der Straftat. Dokumentation des 22. Mainzer Opferforums 2011. Mainzer Schriftenreihe zur Situation von Kriminalitätsopfern. Band 50. Baden-Baden.

WEISSER RING e.V. (2007) (Eds.): Opferschutz unbekannt? Dokumentation des 17. Mainzer Opferforums 2006. Mainzer Schriftenreihe zur Situation von Kriminalitätsopfern. Band 44. Baden-Baden.

WEISSER RING e.V. (2006) (Eds.): Opfer bleibt Opfer? Dokumentation des 16. Opferforums 2004 Berlin. Mainz.

Ziegleder, Diana/Kudlacek, Dominic/Fischer, Thomas (2011): Die Wahrnehmung und Definition von Sicherheit durch die Bevölkerung. Erkenntnisse und Konsequenzen aus der kriminologisch-sozialwissenschaftlichen Forschung. Forschungsforum Öffentliche Sicherheit. Schriftenreihe Sicherheit Nr. 5. Berlin.

The German Congress on Crime Prevention and Congress Partners

Bielefeld Declaration of the 18th German Congress on Crime Prevention

Bielefeld, 22 and 23 April 2013

"More Prevention, Fewer Victims"

The 18th German Congress on Crime Prevention elected as its principal topic the victims of crime. This choice was based on a number of convictions and considerations:

Today's visibly increased orientation towards the victim – in society, research, legal policy and legislation, in policing, criminal justice and crime prevention – seems in many minds to be natural or even imperative. In actual fact, however, this increased victim orientation is the outcome of a fairly recent trend. Lasting change in the understanding of victimisation only took hold in Germany towards the end of the 1970s, linked with the conviction that change was also needed at all levels in how crimes and their consequences for victims and others are dealt with. In a turn of phrase used from an early stage, the changes involved are aptly characterised as the 'rediscovery' of the victim.

Some 25 years after the inception of these changes, the time appears right for a review of the current status, problems and perspectives of victim orientation: What has since changed for victims in society and in the other areas mentioned? What problems recognised and named back then have been resolved or at least made less prevalent or severe? Are there new problems that need to be addressed? What perspectives currently have priority for a positive way forward? What do we now know for certain about victimisation and about the needs and wishes of victims and how best to address them? How can it be persuasively communicated to practitioners, policymakers, academics and the public that the best way to protect victims is to prevent crime?

In the light of the foregoing, and notably supported by the considerations and findings presented in the report by Dr. Wiebke Steffen, "Victim orientation in society, research, criminal justice and crime prevention: Status, problems and perspectives", the German Congress on Crime Prevention and its congress partners – the German Federal Ministry of Family Affairs, Senior Citizens, Women and Youth (BMFSFJ), the German Association for Social Work, Criminal Law and Criminal Policy (DBH), the State of North Rhine-Westphalia, the German Police Crime Prevention Programme (Pro PK), the City of Bielefeld, the German Forum for Crime Prevention (DFK), and the WEISSER RING victim support organisation – hereby publish this **Bielefeld Declaration**.

The state of empirical knowledge on victimisation and victim needs is unsatisfactory

Even after a quarter of a century of increased victim orientation in society, research, criminal justice and crime prevention, the state of empirical knowledge on the victims of crimes and on their needs remains far from satisfactory. In particular, there is a lack of recent findings.

The *German Congress on Crime Prevention* urges:

- That victim-oriented crime statistics record more information on victims and victim characteristics than they include so far.

- To shine light on unreported victimisation, that representative victim surveys be conducted on a regular and also nationwide basis, and that additional research be carried out with a qualitative focus to gain more knowledge about the consequences of victimisation and the needs and wishes of victims.

Especially considering demands for greater victim autonomy, it is essential to know what victims' interests are and for the criminal justice and victim assistance systems to take that knowledge into account.

It is unproven whether victim orientation in criminal justice has done much for victims of crime

Victims' rights in criminal proceedings have been steadily enhanced since Germany's first Victim Protection Act (Opferschutzgesetz) of 1986. The status of victims has additionally advanced in practice with psychosocial measures provided by witness and victim support services. There is also broad ongoing debate about how criminal proceedings may place a burden on victims. Complaints nonetheless continue almost unabated that too little allowance is made for victim needs in criminal proceedings and – under the heading of secondary victimisation – proceedings are unreasonably traumatic for victims.

The lack of empirical knowledge means that this discrepancy cannot currently be explained. There is no data to show if Germany's victim protection acts have attained their express aim of protecting victims from adverse impacts in investigations and criminal proceedings; in some instances it is even unclear how far measures have been implemented. There is not even firm knowledge about the degree to which secondary victimisation arises in investigation and criminal proceedings in the first place and what the victims of crime actually want or need with regard to such proceedings.

The *German Congress on Crime Prevention* urges:

- That Germany's crime prevention acts be evaluated, notably with regard to the extent to which measures – such as video testimony – are actually put into practice, and to what extent and with what aims victims make use of their rights to participate in proceedings;

- That both quantitative and qualitative criminological and victimological research be carried out to identify the needs and wishes of victims with regard to criminal proceedings and what burdens such proceedings place on victims.

Evidence-based crime policy requires sufficiently reliable underlying data, and compiling such data is a matter of urgency.

In a criminal justice system based on the rule of law and the needs of citizens, the *German Congress on Crime Prevention* considers that it should be a matter of course for victims' wishes to be met in terms of information (in particular about the progress of proceedings), compensation and redress, acknowledgement of the wrong done to them, and respectful treatment.

The information obligations for judicial authorities introduced in recent reforms of the German Criminal Code must be fully complied with across the board and should be evaluated to identify the need for any improvements and additions.

Precisely because certain burdens on victims are unavoidable in proceedings based on the rule of law, the *German Congress on Crime Prevention* calls for requirements to be retained or introduced only if they are absolutely necessary to the conduct of a fair trial.

The *German Congress on Crime Prevention* further calls in this connection for Directive 2012/29/EU of the European Parliament and of the Council of 25 October 2012 establishing minimum standards on the rights, support and protection of victims of crime to be evaluated in light of the German legal situation and transposed as soon as possible into German law.

Social support, help and recognition for victims must primarily come from outside the criminal justice system

The criminal justice system is inherently unable to serve the interests of crime victims. Firstly, it is and remains offender-oriented; secondly, the role of the victim as a witness always places burdens on the victim; and thirdly, only a very small percentage of victims make it into court because reporting rates are low and most criminal investigation are dropped by the prosecution service. Only about 12 percent of criminal investigations involving known suspects or accuseds lead charges being brought. It also appears that victims' wishes in terms of punitiveness and redress are of comparatively minor importance. Instead, victims are far more strongly interested in acknowledgement of the wrong done to them and of their not being under any obligation to accept the offender's behaviour.

For all victims, including the few who come into contact with the courts, emotional encouragement, social support (including acknowledgement that they have been wronged), recognition and help must primarily come from outside the criminal justice system – from their immediate social environment and from victim support organisations.

The *German Congress on Crime Prevention* expressly recognises the services of victim support organisations for victims of crime: Care and support after a crime, arranging medical, psychological and legal help, making allowance for the fact that not all victims are the same – all of these things are decisive in helping victims find their way back as far as possible to their lives before the traumatic event.

The *German Congress on Crime Prevention* nonetheless considers that more needs to be done, notably for two specific groups of victims: Firstly, victims of non-violent crime – such as burglary – deserve greater attention than they receive so far. Secondly, with regard to violent crime, it is frequently overlooked that not just the perpetrators, but also the victims of violent crime are often adolescent males or young adult males. Not infrequently, victims share this failure to perceive themselves as such, reflecting the stereotype that men cannot be 'victims'. The outcome is that this group is served only poorly if at all by victim support organisations. Change is needed here, and not just to ensure equal support for all. It is also important to look at the problem of victim-offender role swapping, i.e. the risk, both for the individual and for society, of victims turning into offenders.

The problems of male victimhood in violent crime must be given greater attention in the public and academic discourse. In particular, qualitative victimological research is needed to find out how violent assaults against men 'work', what behaviours men perceive as violence – and how such behaviours can be prevented.

It should also be investigated whether victim support can or perhaps even should be improved using the Parallel Justice framework. Parallel Justice does not call the criminal justice system into question, but provides an additional, often simultaneous, cross-disciplinary, inter-agency response focusing on the victim and rooted in the conviction that help for victims in rebuilding their lives is a key part of justice. It would be possible to implement this framework through the local crime prevention units in place in many towns, cities and districts across Germany.

The best way to protect victims is to prevent crime

No matter how efficient and effective the criminal justice, victim protection and victim support systems, it is always better to stop crime and consequently victimisation from happening in the first place. No criminal justice system, however victim-oriented, and no victim support system, however well-established and capable, can hope to make good, let alone undo, the physical and material harm to victims and the often severe psychological consequences of crime. The best way to protect victims is therefore to prevent crime.

The *German Congress on Crime Prevention* calls for tried and tested crime prevention efforts to be continued and for those efforts to be appraised in particular with regard to the available empirical evidence on avoiding revictimisation and secondary victimisation, while at the same time being careful to avoid raising (unnecessary) fears and strictly to avoid allocating victims any part of the blame.

With regard to what crime prevention means, what is required of it, what it can achieve and what has already been accomplished, the 18th German Congress on Crime Prevention refers to the proceedings of the 12th, 13th, 14th, 15th, 16th and 17th German Congresses on Crime Prevention and to the demands and appeals set out in the respective declarations.

Bielefeld, 23 April 2013

Program of the 7th Annual International Forum

Monday, 22. April 2013

11:00 - 12:30 – City Hall: "Großer Saal"
Opening Plenum of the German Congress on Crime Prevention
(German with interpretation into English)
- **Welcome by the Executive Director of the German Congress on Crime Prevention**
  Erich Marks, German Congress on Crime Prevention
- **Victims must not be forgotten**
  Ralf Jäger, Minister of the Interior and Municipality of the State of North Rhine-Westphalia
- **Prevention in Bielefeld**
  Pit Clausen, Lord Mayor of the City of Bielefeld
- **Remarks on the Correlation between Criminology, Victimology and Crime Prevention**
  Professor Dr. Hans-Jürgen Kerner, President of the German Foundation for Crime Prevention
  and Assistance of Criminal Offenders
- **Remarks about the main topic of the congress**
  Dr. Wiebke Steffen, Author of the Report for the Congress
- **The Future of Victim Assistance**
  Roswitha Müller-Piepenkötter, Federal Chairwoman for the National Victims Right Organization
  "White Ring"
- **More Prevention - A National Task**
  Professor Gerd Neubeck, Head of Concern Security at the "Deutsche Bahn" (German Railways)
- **Prevention, Sport and Voluntary Work**
  Sebastian Rode, Professional Soccer Player (Eintracht Frankfurt) and Ambassador of the Crime
  Prevention Council of the State of Hesse
- **Current developments of the International Crime Victimization Survey**
  Professor Dr. Jan van Dijk, Tilburg University, The Netherlands
- **Evidence-based Crime Prevention: State of Affairs and Future Challenges**
  Professor Dr. Andreas Beelmann, University of Jena

12:30 - 14:00
Luncheon for International Guests

14:00 - 15:00 – Hotel Bielefelder Hof: "Kaminzimmer"
Situational crime prevention works; or why burglary rates dropped less steeply in Germany
than in The Netherlands
Prof. Dr. Jan van Dijk, Tilburg University, The Netherlands

15:30 - 16:30 – Hotel Bielefelder Hof: "Kaminzimmer"
Restoring Societies. Norway after the atrocities
Prof. Dr. Nils Christie, University of Oslo, Norway

17:00 - 18:00 – Hotel Bielefelder Hof: "Kaminzimmer"
The development of the Swedish model of Crime Prevention in the last two decades and its
future challenges
Dr. Erik Wennerström, Director-General Swedish Council for Crime Prevention

AIF-Chairs: Dr. Marc Coester (German Congress on Crime Prevention)
              Dr. Burkhard Hasenpusch (Crime Prevention Council Lower Saxony)

18:15 - 20:00 – City Hall
Evening Reception of the German Congress on Crime Prevention

Tuesday, 23. April 2013

09:00 - 10:00 – Hotel Bielefelder Hof: "Kaminzimmer"
"Security, Democracy and Cities" - a new manifesto of European cities on urban security
Elizabeth Johnston, Executive Director, European Forum for Urban Security, France

10:30 - 11:30 – Hotel Bielefelder Hof: "Kaminzimmer"
GIZ's systemic approaches to violence prevention
Rubeena Esmail, Program Coordinator, and Terence Smith, Advisor, Deutsche Gesellschaft für Internationale Zusammenarbeit (GIZ) GmbH, South Africa

11:30 - 12:30 - Catering Area City Hall - Opportunity for Lunch

12:30 - 13:00 – Hotel Bielefelder Hof: "Kaminzimmer"
The Crime Prevention Maturity Model: Embedding security within urban design & planning
Dr. Caroline L. Davey and Andrew B. Wootton, Co-Directors of the Design Against Crime Solution Centre, University of Salford, United Kingdom

13:00 - 13:30 – Hotel Bielefelder Hof: "Kaminzimmer"
A Study on Comprehensive Plan to Protect Children and Youths from Sexual Violence and Support Victims
Dr. Ok-Kyung Yoon, professor at Kyonggi University and Dr. Eugene Lee, senior research fellow at National Youth Policy Institute, Seoul, South Korea

14:00 - 15:00 – Hotel Bielefelder Hof: "Kaminzimmer"
European Crime Prevention Network (EUCPN): Crime prevention activities on EU, national and local level
Belinda Wijckmans, Research Officer, European Crime Prevention Network, Belgium

AIF-Chairs: Dr. Marc Coester (German Congress on Crime Prevention)
Dr. Burkhard Hasenpusch (Crime Prevention Council Lower Saxony)

15:00 - 16:00 - City Hall "Großer Saal"
Closing Plenum of the German Congress on Crime Prevention
(German with interpretation into English)

- **Closing Remarks**
  Prof. Dr. Hans-Jürgen Kerner, Congress President
- **The "Bielefeld Declaration" from the German Congress on Crime Prevention**
  Dr. Wiebke Steffen, Author of the Report for the Congress
- **"Parallel Justice" – Why we need the Strengthening of the Victims in Law and Society**
  Professor Dr. Christian Pfeiffer, Director of the Criminological Research Institute of Lower Saxony
- **Outlook and closing address**
  Erich Marks, Executive Director of the German Congress on Crime Prevention

Authors

Cecilia Andersson
UN Habitat, Kenia

Prof. Dr. Nils Christie
University of Oslo, Norway

Dr. Marc Coester
Crime Prevention Council of Lower Saxony (CPC), Germany

Dr. Caroline L. Davey
University of Salford, United Kingdom

Dr. Noël Klima
European Crime Prevention Network (EUCPN), Belgium

Erich Marks
German Congress on Crime Prevention, Hannover, Germany

Prof. Dr. Christian Pfeiffer
Kriminologisches Forschungsinstitut Niedersachsen (KFN) e. V., Germany

Dr. Wiebke Steffen
German Congress on Crime Prevention, Hannover/Heiligenberg, Germany

Prof. Dr. Dr. Jan van Dijk
Tilburg University, Netherlands

Belinda Wijckmans
European Crime Prevention Network (EUCPN), Belgium

Andrew B. Wootton
University of Salford, United Kingdom

www.ingramcontent.com/pod-product-compliance
Lightning Source LLC
Chambersburg PA
CBHW061736270326
41928CB00011B/2252